REDIASPORIZATION

REDIASPORIZATION
African-Guyanese Kwe-Kwe

By Gillian Richards-Greaves

University Press of Mississippi / Jackson

The University Press of Mississippi is the scholarly publishing agency of
the Mississippi Institutions of Higher Learning: Alcorn State University,
Delta State University, Jackson State University, Mississippi State University,
Mississippi University for Women, Mississippi Valley State University,
University of Mississippi, and University of Southern Mississippi.

www.upress.state.ms.us

The University Press of Mississippi is a member
of the Association of University Presses.

First printing 2020
∞

Library of Congress Control Number: 2020020399

Hardback: 978-1-4968-3115-6
Trade Paperback: 978-1-4968-3116-3
Epub Single: 978-1-4968-3117-0
Epub Institutional: 978-1-4968-3118-7
PDF Single: 978-1-4968-3119-4
PDF Institutional: 978-1-4968-3120-0

British Library Cataloging-in-Publication Data available

Contents

Contents

Acknowledgments

Rediasporization: African-Guyanese Kweh-Kweh is the culmination of more than a decade of ethnographic research that I started in 2005. Throughout this journey, I was supported by my family and colleagues. I also received financial support in the form of professional development funding, which allowed me to travel to conferences, where I presented my ideas and received critique, feedback, and questions that helped make the writing process productive.

The research and writing process was long and arduous but my husband, Chris, and my sons, David and Josiah, were patient and supportive, particularly during my sixteen-month ethnographic research stay in Guyana, South America. They also often read my work and provided feedback and the emotional support I needed throughout the process. My mother Waveney Richards, nieces and nephews, cousins (especially Hazel Harris), friends, and seven siblings also provided moral support that sustained me, even though we live in different parts of the world. I am especially grateful for the continued support I received from members of my church families in Guyana and New York City, including Lucille Marks, Claire and Compton Roberts, Kenneth and Caroline Saul, Allison Wren, Michael and Jackie Clarke, Alexander and Lynette Hodge, Wendell and Sharmine Blair, Steven Locke and Beverly Crawford-Locke, Tyrone and Feliz Jackson, and Fitzpatrick and Yvette Dublin.

The research for this monograph would not have been possible without the support of the Guyanese people in New York City, Guyana, and even the state of Georgia. Many individuals opened their homes and provided information through formal and informal interviews, making it possible for me to learn much more about Guyanese culture than the *kweh-kweh* ritual I set out to study. From the time I expressed interest in studying *kweh-kweh*, Dr. Vibert Cambridge, the president of the Guyana Cultural Association (GCA) in New York City, assisted me in networking with former and current *kweh-kweh* practitioners in Guyana and enabled me to attend, record, and collect data at every Come to My Kwe-Kwe celebration since its inception in 2005. Dr. Rose October-Edun, members of the Guyana Folk Festival Committee, the Kwe-Kwe Ensemble, and musicians like Akoyaw Rudder, Winston "Jeggae" Hoppie, and Hilton Hemerding also played crucial roles in helping me obtain the data I needed to complete this monograph. They made the research process enjoyable.

My research journey and writing were also supported by my former professors and colleagues, with whom I discussed my work and from whom I received advice. Drs. Barbara Hampton, Daniel B. Reed, Anya Peterson Royce, Daniel Suslak, Marvin Sterling, Ruth Stone, Mellonee Burnim, and Richard "Rick" Wilk offered invaluable insight and feedback at different phases throughout this process.

A few of my colleagues also played integral roles in the research and completion of this project. Drs. Austin Okigbo and Mintzi Martinez Rivera were two of the first individuals with whom I discussed the concept of *rediasporization* in great detail. They listened to my ideas, read my work, and offered suggestions for developing my arguments beyond the seminal stages. My countrywoman and friend Dr. Pauline Baird was a catalyst and supportive big sister throughout the process. Her advice was particularly crucial because it was deeply rooted in her in-depth knowledge of Guyanese history and culture. At Coastal Carolina University, my colleague Dr. Emma Howes eagerly read my work, provided valuable feedback, and asked copious probing questions that helped me sharpen my focus and arguments. My colleague Dr. Richard Aidoo also read some of my chapters, listened to my ideas, and provided feedback from an Africanist perspective.

Abstract

Come to My Kwe-Kwe is a reenactment of a uniquely African-Guyanese prewedding ritual called *kweh-kweh*, sometimes referred to as *karkalay, mayan, kweh-keh,* and *pele.* Since the fall of 2005, African-Guyanese in New York City have celebrated Come to My Kwe-Kwe (more recently, Kwe-Kwe Nite) on the Friday evening before Labor Day. This book draws on more than a decade of ethnographic research data to examine the role of Come to My Kwe-Kwe in the processes of African-Guyanese *rediasporization,* that is, the creation of a newer diaspora from an existing one. To do so, this work also interrogates the factors that affect African-Guyanese perceptions of their racial and gendered selves, and how these perceptions in turn impact their engagement with African-influenced cultural performances like the Come to My Kwe-Kwe ritual. It shows how the malleability of Come to My Kwe-Kwe allows African-Guyanese to negotiate, highlight, conceal, and even reject complex, shifting, overlapping, and contextual identities, particularly those influenced by race, class, and religion. Ultimately, this work demonstrates how Come to My Kwe-Kwe performances in the United States facilitate African-Guyanese transformation from an imagined community to a tangible community that does the same things with each other, at the same time, and in the same physical space.

PROLOGUE

The Processes of *Diasporization* and *Rediasporization*

Physical Separation

The first stage in the process of *diasporization* is the physical separation or *physical fracture* of a group from a geographic space of residence, particularly one in which they have resided for several generations and regard as "home" (Clifford 1994; Gilroy 1993; Lesser 2003; Okpewho 2009). Ethnic groups become separated from their homelands for diverse reasons, including enslavement (Gomez 2007; Klein 2010), war (Sonneborn 2006; Alajaji 2015; Ibrahim 2016), and other negative or "push" factors. In other instances, the pursuit of economic advancement (Munasinghe 2006; Sinn 2012), religious freedom (Morse 1912; Milbrandt 2017), and other "pull" factors entice or compel people to migrate from their homelands (Morier-Genoud and Cahen 2012). The reasons for separation also affect the composition of the displaced group in their new homeland (Okpewho 2009), as well as the type and degree of interaction they have with other ethnic groups with whom they share space (Kasinitz 1992; Foner 1998; Gonzalez and McCommon 1989). Robin Cohen (1997) has argued that the diverse reasons for separation also create different types of diasporas, including "victim diasporas," "labour diasporas," "trade diasporas," "imperial diasporas," and "cultural diasporas." This book emphasizes not just the cause for separation from an ancestral African homeland but also the internal processes that work actively and collectively to shape a group's cohesion and identity. These are the processes of *diasporization*, which, over subsequent generations, might be repeated severally as significant numbers of the displaced group relocate to even newer homelands while deliberately and inadvertently maintaining connections, broadly construed, with former homelands (Butler 2000, 127). The redoing of the diasporic process with multiple homelands actively in focus is what constitutes *rediasporization*.

Memory

The second stage of *diasporization* is remembering, which entails *emotional/psychological fractures* (Bastide 1978; Yelvington 2001, 240; McGavin 2017, 130). At this stage, it is imperative that members of the displaced group draw on what they already know to create a sense of normalcy. Displacement creates emotional and psychological fractures because the things, practices, and people that the displaced group regards as mundane and normal are no longer present, and "neither the sending or [sic] receiving country serves any longer as a stable source of social belonging" (Tsuda 2003, 122). This is particularly important for members of groups who have been forcibly displaced. In their new space, they begin to identify or emphasize commonalities between their present state and former homeland in order to reconstitute norms. In this stage also, they draw heavily on the senses to materialize memories and reconstruct experiences of the past. More specifically, memories of the physicality or geography of former homelands, memories of languages, and memories of rituals and other cultural enactments form the foundation of the new life the displaced will create (Shelemay 1998; Sutton 2001; Ray 2004). However, even though they may remember, they must convey those memories in tangible ways to others in the group, particularly the young, through songs, stories, food, and other cultural enactments (Slobin 1994; Hall 2005).

As time progresses and subsequent generations emerge, the displaced group gradually becomes "placed" in their new geographic space. This "placing" involves some remembering and some forgetting of practices from previous homelands, particularly by older generations. Sometimes, the forgetting is simply a feature of displacement and distance, but sometimes it is also a mental purge of survival (Tsuda 2003, 135). To survive in the new homeland, the displaced must learn new things and, in the process, discard older, more distant realities that have become mentally burdensome or otherwise irrelevant. In some instances, also, the memory purge is not deliberate, or even a purge, but a gradual decay of thoughts and recollections, which lie dormant or become extinct as the need, desire, or ability to conjure them wane, or the people themselves die.

Cultural Mixing

The third stage of *diasporization* is "cultural mixing," which necessitates *cultural fractures*. Even when memories remain, they must coexist in the minds and realities of the displaced in tandem with more recent experiences and memories that might be more crucial for survival. Often, the newer experiences include "transnational and trans-ethnic mixing" (Anthias 1998b, 565–66) that uniquely colors the cultural values and interpretations and reshapes the everyday lives of those who are "placed"—a diaspora (see also Brah 1996).

As much as diasporas draw on elements of the past—particularly former homelands—to inform their sense of group identity, their experiences with other ethnic groups uniquely shape what they subsequently become. Through the process of *acculturation*, whereby ethnic groups experience cultural changes due to sustained, long-term contact with each other (Kottak 2015, 34; Redfield, Linton, and Herskovits 1936), a diaspora learns new languages, adopts new foods, and undergoes other metamorphoses. In the process, the diaspora retains some of the cultural elements of the past but

becomes significantly different from people still residing in previous homeland(s). The diaspora, and its cultural expressions, can
therefore be said to have become *creolized*—a new entity in a new
place, created from older, more distinct elements from other places.

Even though uniquely different from residents of former
homelands, diasporas are diasporas because they, in tangible and
symbolic ways, identify with those homelands (Yelvington 2001,
229). Moreover, in many instances, they draw on cultural practices
and ideals of former homelands to articulate diasporic identities that
distinguish them from other ethnic groups. Their interpretations of
"tradition" are often innovative, reflecting both cultural continuity
and change.

Rediasporization

Rediasporization encompasses all the processes of *diasporization*
previously discussed but also entails the refracturing of a community, which complicates and compounds their experiences (Takyi
2002). The displaced primary diaspora must simultaneously connect to multiple former homelands, though not with equal fervency,
often privileging one homeland over another depending on the context. In the secondary diaspora (and later diasporas), memories of
the first homeland ("root") are distant and sometimes nonexistent,
depending on how much time has passed. Thus, the secondary or
more recent homeland—the "route" to the current homeland or
hostland—which shaped experiences in the more recent homeland,
is privileged with respect to memories (Clifford 1997; Anthias 1998b,
568). The first or primary homeland, however, often continues to be
the standard of authenticity by which diasporas evaluate cultural
expressions. In many instances, diasporas tend to overlook the cultural changes taking place in the primary or previous homelands,
which may put the authenticity of their cultural practices into question. Diasporas also overlook the fact that, in many instances, they
have retained older and thus more "authentic" iterations of cultural
practices, because they have had to remember the past in order to

diminish the cultural and psychological fracture that results from displacement and "homeland-lessness" (Tsuda 2003, 122), and distinguish themselves from other ethnic groups (Jackson and Cothran 2003). According to Paul Zeleza, "The relations between the old and new diasporas can be characterized by antagonism, ambivalence, acceptance, adaptation, and assimilation" (2009, 45). Nevertheless, the *rediasporized* community must exist in multiple realms of belonging and dis-belonging, while at the same time navigating connections to multiple homelands (Mori 2003; Levy and Weingrod 2005; Burns 2009, 127–45; Wrazen 2012, 146–60). As Kim Butler argues, "conceptualizations of diaspora must be able to accommodate the reality of multiple identities and phases of diasporization of time" (2000, 127).

REDIASPORIZATION

Introduction: "Who Karkalay?"
From Wedding-Based *Kweh-Kweh* to Cultural Reenactment

Introduction

Since the fall of 2005, African-Guyanese in New York City have celebrated a ritual called Come to My Kwe-Kwe (more recently, Kwe-Kwe Nite) on the Friday evening before Labor Day. Come to My Kwe-Kwe is a reenactment of a uniquely African-Guyanese prewedding ritual called *kweh-kweh*, also known as *karkalay, mayan, kweh-keh*, and *pele* (fig. 1.1).[1] A typical traditional (wedding-based) *kweh-kweh* has approximately ten ritual segments, which include the pouring of libation to welcome or appease the ancestors; a procession from the groom's residence to the bride's residence or central *kweh-kweh* venue; the hiding of the bride; and the negotiation of the bride price.[2] Each ritual segment is executed with singing and dancing, which enable participants to chide, praise, and tease the bride and groom and their respective "nations" (relatives, friends, and representatives) on conjugal matters such as sex, domestication, submissiveness, and hard work.[3] Come to My Kwe-Kwe replicates the overarching segments of the wedding-based *kweh-kweh*, which I will discuss in greater detail later, but a couple (male and female)

3

is chosen from the audience to act as the bride and groom, and props simulate the boundaries of the traditional *kweh-kweh* performance space, such as a gate and the bride's home. However, unlike traditional *kweh-kweh*, which focuses exclusively on the nations of the bride and groom, Come to My Kwe-Kwe engages the larger Guyanese community, albeit for an entry fee.

When the Folk Festival Committee of the Guyana Cultural Association (GCA) in New York City first sponsored Come to My Kwe-Kwe in 2005, they envisioned it as a one-time event that would contribute to the year's theme, "Celebrating Guyanese Dance." However, at the end of the event, the overwhelmingly positive feedback from the audience inspired the GCA to make Come to My Kwe-Kwe a fixture of the annual Folk Festival (fig. 1.2). Thus, every year on the Friday before Labor Day, Guyanese from all over the world convene in Brooklyn to celebrate the accidental tradition of Come to My Kwe-Kwe and to connect or reconnect with other Guyanese. Consequently, Come to My Kwe-Kwe has increasingly become a symbol of African-Guyaneseness, which participants manipulate to facilitate group solidarity and to distinguish themselves from other ethnic groups.

This book examines the role of Come to My Kwe-Kwe in the construction of a secondary African-Guyanese diaspora (*rediasporization*) in New York City by exploring how African-Guyanese in the United States draw on the ritual to articulate their tricultural (African-Guyanese-American) identities. This work also interrogates the factors that affect African-Guyanese perceptions of their racial and gendered selves, and how these perceptions in turn impact their engagement with African-influenced cultural performances like Come to My Kwe-Kwe. By drawing on longitudinal research data, this work demonstrates how the malleability of Come to My Kwe-Kwe allows African-Guyanese to negotiate, highlight, conceal, and even reject complex, shifting, overlapping, and contextual identities. Ultimately, this work demonstrates how Come to My Kwe-Kwe performances in the United States facilitate African-Guyanese transformation from an imagined community to a tangible community

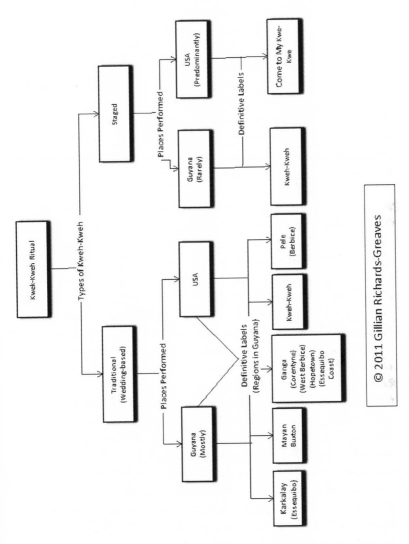

Figure 1.1: Deconstructing traditional *kweh-kweh*.

© 2011 Gillian Richards-Greaves

that does the same things with each other, at the same time, and in the same physical space.

Ethnographic Data

As a young girl growing up in Guyana, I only observed the *kweh-kweh* ritual from a distance because it was considered "grown folk business" (adult matters) and African (pagan, ungodly, *taboo*). However, I became interested in *kweh-kweh* as a research topic in 2002 while gathering data to write an end-of-term paper on the ritual. Due to the paucity of literature on *kweh-kweh*, I decided to interview older African-Guyanese who were knowledgeable about the ritual. However, instead of gaining a wealth of information from them, I was met with resounding silence, shunning, and statements such as "we don't do that thing anymore," "*kweh-kweh* is vulgar," and "*kweh-kweh* is dead." Only a few individuals I spoke with at the time regarded *kweh-kweh* as an important facet of African-Guyanese culture and identity, but some argued that the ritual was dead or dying. What I found particularly interesting about their responses, however, was the fact that each time there was an impending wedding these very individuals actively celebrated *kweh-kweh*. For example, "Patsy," a deaconess in a local church in Brooklyn, refused to discuss *kweh-kweh* with me because she perceived it as pagan and vulgar. However, months later, in an unguarded moment, this church mother informed me that she was getting ready to throw (sponsor) a *kweh-kweh* in her daughter's honor. Annoyed and confused, I said, "I thought you didn't celebrate *kweh-kweh*!" Patsy responded almost apologetically: "Girl, you can't have a wedding without a *kweh-kweh*, but not everybody would understand." During subsequent discussions with other African-Guyanese I discovered that, like Patsy, they held views on *kweh-kweh* that were contradictory to their actual engagement with the ritual. Their inconsistent behavior piqued my interest and inspired me to conduct further research on the ritual.

Although I am a native Guyanese, gaining research access to African-Guyanese communities in Guyana and New York City was

Guyana Folk Festival WE 2015 Season
BRIDGIN'

FOLK FEET IN THE STREET
(Street Festival)
(GCA in collaboration with Brooklyn Arts Council)
SATURDAY, JULY 25, 2015 - 2 - 6 p.m.
2806 Newkirk Ave. (E28 - E29 Sts.)
Brooklyn, NY 11226   FREE ADMISSION

CARIBBEAN HERITAGE
SUMMER WORKSHOP
JULY 6 - AUGUST 13 2015
AGES: 5-13 YEARS
St. Stephen's Church Auditorium
2806 Newkirk Ave. (E28 - E29 Sts.) Brooklyn, NY 11226

GCA AWARDS
WEDNESDAY, SEPTEMBER 2, 2015
Brooklyn Borough Hall
209 Joralemon Street, Brooklyn, NY 11226
6.00 p.m.   BY INVITATION ONLY

WHO ARE WE?
GCA developing partnerships in the global Guyanese community to make Guyana's collective history accessible to Guyanese at home and in the diaspora.

COMING SOON
GUYANA ARTS & CULTURAL CENTER
BROOKLYN, NEW YORK

FOR DETAILS
CONTACT THE GCA SECRETARIAT
800-774-5762
VISIT OUR WEBSITE www.guyfolkfest.org

KWE KWE NITE
FRIDAY, SEPTEMBER 4, 2015 -8 P.M.
St. Stephen's Church Auditorium
2806 Newkirk Ave. (E28 - E29 Sts.) Brooklyn, NY 11226
ADMISSION: $20.00

LITERARY HANG
SATURDAY, SEPTEMBER 5, 2015
1.00 P.M.
St. John's Episcopal Church Auditorium
139 St. John's Place, Brooklyn, NY 11226

FOLK FESTIVAL FAMILY DAY
SUNDAY, SEPTEMBER 6, 2015
Old Boys High School Grounds
736 Rutland Road & Troy Avenue, Brooklyn, NY 11203
12 NOON - 7 P.M.   SHOWTIME 4 P.M.
ADMISSION: ADULTS $10. (Seniors, Kids under 16) - FREE

SYMPOSIUM
SATURDAY, NOVEMBER 7, 2015
Venue to be announced

Figure 1.2: Guyana Folk Festival flyer, 2015.

a slow, painstaking process because I occupy a liminal state of existence in each community. I am both Guyanese and American. To Guyanese in Guyana, I am a "foreigner"; to older, more seasoned *kweh-kweh* performers, I am young, and thus a novice; to older Guyanese women I am too mannish to be considered a proper woman; to Africanist Guyanese who embrace *kweh-kweh*, I am a Christian and therefore a potential threat to the ritual; and to many Guyanese I am an academic voyeur, lurking with cameras and the pen, waiting to capture their most awkward, intimate moments to publicize them to strangers. My "halfie" status, to cite Lila Abu-Lughod (1993), rendered me simultaneously "insider" and "outsider" to the Guyanese community. Nevertheless, with the help of some well-placed and respectable contacts in the community, I was able to successfully execute my research.

I later conducted multisited, transnational, and comparative dissertation research on *kweh-kweh* performance in New York City (2005–2008) and Guyana (2008–2010), where I examined the role of traditional *kweh-kweh* and its reenactment in Come to My Kwe-Kwe in African-Guyanese identity negotiations. I also started preliminary investigations into the processes of *rediasporization* in New York City. In addition to archival research, I conducted more than sixty interviews with current and former participants of traditional *kweh-kweh* and Come to My Kwe-Kwe. I also attended several rituals, where I participated in *kweh-kweh* music, dance, and verbal art as well as the daily activities pertinent to the execution of the ritual. By using diverse research methods, I was able to compare what people said about *kweh-kweh* and Come to My Kwe-Kwe with what they actually did and, in the process, gained a better understanding of the role of the ritual in the larger community.

Since its inception in 2005, Come to My Kwe-Kwe has quickly eclipsed the traditional wedding-based *kweh-kweh* in performance frequency and significance in the African-Guyanese community in New York City. In fact, Come to My Kwe-Kwe has become such a significant symbol of African-Guyaneseness that it has influenced the rise of similar expressions in Guyana and in other urban areas in the United States such as Atlanta. Each year when African-Guyanese from all over the world convene in Brooklyn to celebrate Come to My Kwe-Kwe, they refine ritual performances and through food, music, dance, and other cultural expressions reaffirm and display multifaceted Guyanese identities.

In the fall of 2013, I embarked on a new longitudinal research project (fall 2013–fall 2018) that exclusively examined the role of Come to My Kwe-Kwe in the African-Guyanese community in the United States. By drawing on research data I obtained through participant observation, archival research, and interviews, I was able to examine the ways that African-Guyanese in the United States perform Come to My Kwe-Kwe to negotiate African-Guyanese-American identities during the process of creating a new, secondary African diaspora (*rediasporization*).

Overview of the Traditional (Wedding-Based) *Kweh-Kweh*

Traditional *kweh-kweh* emerged among African slaves in Guyana and historically functioned as a medium for matrimonial instruction for soon-to-be-married couples. Although African-Guyanese argue that *kweh-kweh* is their African heritage, there is no known African ritual by the name of *kweh-kweh*; however, as an entity, *kweh-kweh* is strikingly similar to indigenous African marriage ceremonies such as the "black (indigenous) wedding" among the Yoruba; Ìgba Nkwü, a wine-carrying ceremony practiced by the Igbo of Nigeria (Smith 2001, 129–51); and the Zambian Kitchen Party, a women-only celebration that resembles a synthesis of a bridal shower, a *kweh-kweh* ritual, and a bachelorette party. Also, individual *kweh-kweh* ritual practices—such as the procession from the groom's residence to the bride's home or *kweh-kweh* venue (Bassir 1954; Ottenberg 1988), the negotiation of the bride price (Ogbu 1978; Mbiti 1999, 137; Ikwuagwu 2007, 88), and the pouring of libation (Ikwuagwu 2007, 43)—mirror indigenous African marriage rituals. However, the most striking similarities between indigenous African marriage rituals and *kweh-kweh* unfold during music performance, particularly in the connectedness of music and dance: pervasive call-and-response singing (Pitts 1989, 137–49; Weaver 1991, 53–61; Hinson 2000, 163–88); the use of percussive timbres in singing (Hurston 1981; Burnim 1985a; Burnim 1988); the use of percussive instruments such as drums, and found sounds (Borde 1973, 45; Johnson 1998, 64; Dudley 2002, 18); the expression of social commentary through music (Epstein 2015, 36); and the counterclockwise movement of the ritual dance (Rosenbaum 1998; Henderson 2009). For diverse reasons, *kweh-kweh* continues to be practiced by African-Guyanese in Guyana and abroad, and it generally unfolds in two overarching stages: (1) a preparatory stage, and (2) the *kweh-kweh* proper.

The preparatory stage of *kweh-kweh* can last anywhere from a few days to several weeks, depending on the financial capabilities of the families involved, the expected size of the *kweh-kweh*, the locations of the residences of relatives, and other factors. This stage is crucial to the successful execution of *kweh-kweh* because it is the period during which every member of the community has an opportunity to be directly or indirectly involved with various aspects of the ritual. For example, men often erect the canvas or tarpaulin tent in the yard for the *kweh-kweh* ritual, cut palm branches for the procession, slaughter animals for meat, or assist with procuring copious quantities of alcohol and foodstuffs such as rice, sugar, and ground provisions (plantain, cassava, and other tubers); women generally control the preparation of large quantities of food; while youngsters provide assistance with cleaning, food preparation, and various aspects of ritual preparations. However, young children are generally excluded from the actual *kweh-kweh* proper, as the ritual content is overwhelmingly risqué in nature.

A typical *kweh-kweh* begins around ten in the evening and often lasts until dawn. The ritual may take place in a house (ideally with wooden floors), a "bottom house," or a tent in the yard built specifically for the ritual. *Kweh-kweh* is led by a captain, tutor, or raconteur who is generally male and assumed to be an expert in *kweh-kweh* music and Guyanese culture.[4] The ritual begins with a procession, followed by the meeting of the nations at the bride's gate, the hiding of the bride, and the negotiation of the bride price. Each ritual segment of *kweh-kweh* constitutes a physical or symbolic obstacle that the groom and his nation must overcome before gaining access to the bride (table 1.1). After the successful completion of all obstacle courses, the *kweh-kweh* celebration takes on a more communal tone, as the nations of the bride and groom move closer to becoming one unified nation. After the nations agree upon a bride price, the third major obstacle, they continue the ritual with communal singing and the choreographed *kweh-kweh* ritual dance, which is executed in a circle called a *ganda* (GHAN-dah). In addition to the wedding-based *kweh-kweh* dance, the bride and groom are also expected to "show yuh science," or demonstrate sexual prowess.[5]

In New York City, the traditional wedding-based *kweh-kweh* is celebrated in similar ways as in Guyana. However, in instances when the bride's and groom's nations are from different regions of Guyana, there may be slight variations in performance practices or major disagreements regarding the nature or sequence of ritual segments. Constraints surrounding the availability or suitability of perfor-mance spaces in New York City also provide impediments to the smooth execution of *kweh-kweh*. When space is an issue, performers often improvise. I have observed several instances in which families drove to the central *kweh-kweh* venue, and then started their proces-sion a few houses or blocks away from the actual site. Although the wedding-based *kweh-kweh* in New York City ushers in a wedding, these improvisations that participants must enact lend a degree of dramatization to the ritual.

African-Guyanese hold disparate views on the role of *kweh-kweh* in their community, and these views affect their involvement with the ritual. Some Guyanese regard *kweh-kweh* as defunct or contrary to their moral and religious values and thus may refuse to openly participate in the ritual, or they may reject it altogether. However, an increasing number of African-Guyanese embrace *kweh-kweh* as a crucial symbol of their identity and work tirelessly to promote the ritual and educate younger generations about its virtues. Moreover, at the onset of a wedding, African-Guyanese of diverse socioeconomic backgrounds and religious persuasions fabricate ways to celebrate *kweh-kweh*, because many still regard the ritual as an indispensable precursor to a successful wedding. Although *kweh-kweh* celebrations began to dissipate by the early 1980s, my research has shown that there has been an upsurge in ritual performances since 1992, when the predominantly East Indian People's Progressive Party (PPP) ended the thirty-year political reign of the mostly African People's National Congress in Guyana. There has also been an intensification of *kweh-kweh* performances among expatriate Guyanese who are actively constructing African-Guyanese-oriented ethnic identities and communities in new homelands. The renewed interest in the wedding-based *kweh-kweh* has given rise to staged reenactments of the ritual, such as Come to My Kwe-Kwe in New York City and similar expressions in Atlanta.

Reinventing Tradition: Come to My Kwe-Kwe

Unlike the traditional *kweh-kweh*, Come to My Kwe-Kwe is a public event that takes place in public spaces such as banquet halls, gymnasiums, and auditoriums where Guyanese as well as non-Guyanese are welcomed. However, these public venues also constitute public-private spaces in that they conceal the event from the view of the public and delineate the constitution of the audience in various ways.

Come to My Kwe-Kwe also differs from the wedding-based *kweh-kweh* in the composition of its audience. While the presence of children is frowned upon at wedding-based *kweh-kweh*, Come to My Kwe-Kwe features individuals of diverse age groups, including children and young adults who are first- and second-generation Americans of Guyanese heritage. In this atmosphere, children sometimes participate in the singing and dancing as a way of learning Guyanese heritage—even though their presence at the event is generally discouraged. However, Come to My Kwe-Kwe is, to an extent, exclusionary in that the audience is restricted to individuals who are able or willing to pay the entry fee for the event. Thus, the audience at Come to My Kwe-Kwe is basically a body of paying customers who are also interested in celebrating *kweh-kweh* for the evening.

Table 1.1. Overarching Ritual Segments in Wedding-Based Kweh-Kweh

Ritual Segments	Ritual Performances	Musical Examples
(1) Procession to the home of the bride or groom	Walking, singing, waving (palm) tree branches or "bunch of roses."	"Coming Down with a Bunch of Roses"
Obstacle #1: Physical (2) Meeting at the gate or door	Through song, the groom's nation requests permission to enter the bride's premises. Pouring libation.	"Open the Door Let the Man Come In"
3) Nations of the bride and groom meet and greet each other in song	Singing, hugging, and other forms of greeting. (Pouring libation.)	"Goodnight, Ay"; "Nation"
Obstacle #2: Physical (4) Hiding of the bride; searching for the bride	The groom and his nation search for the bride, who has been hidden somewhere on the premises prior to the opening of the door or gate.	"Search Am Go Find Am"
Obstacle #3: Symbolic (5) Buying of the bride (exchange of bride price)	After the bride is found, she is covered with a white sheet and made to sit in a chair. The bride's and groom's nations then engage in the symbolic exchange of bride price in the form of money, alcohol, or other goods. At the conclusion of the bride-price exchange, the groom's nation celebrates by hoisting the bride in her chair and dancing her around.	"Ah Who Go Stan' Am?"
(6) Science dance	The bride and groom *wine* (gyrate) alone and with/on each other to demonstrate sexual prowess.	"Show Me Yuh Science"
(7) Saying goodbye	Cleaning up; singing; dancing; greeting; making final wedding arrangements.	"Gyal Yuh Glorious Maanin' Come"; "Here Aunty Bess Ah Hallah"; "Las' Wan"

Another key difference between Come to My Kwe-Kwe and the wedding-based *kweh-kweh* is the nature of the performance practices. At wedding-based *kweh-kweh* rituals, performances are generally executed with coded language, which is then interpreted by the *kweh-kweh* community based on their knowledge of Guyanese history and culture. However, at Come to My Kwe-Kwe, with its diverse audience, very little is left to the imagination. Each ritual segment is explained before it is executed, and often performances are unmasked and made overt in order to convey the intended message. An example of this is the red circular patch that is sewn onto the white sheet that covers the bride. The red patch symbolizes the bleeding that results from the tearing of the hymen during the bride's first sexual encounter. In wedding-based *kweh-kweh*, however, there is no red circular patch on the sheet, as it is assumed that the *kweh-kweh* community is familiar with the implication of the white sheet and Guyanese values regarding sex. Also, in the American context, the red dot and other explicit performances represent African-Guyanese rejection of what many regard as unnecessary and backward approaches to sex. In America, many African-Guyanese not only have learned the importance of openly discussing sexual matters but do so in ways that are unambiguous. By unveiling *kweh-kweh* performances in the context of Come to My Kwe-Kwe, African-Guyanese-Americans accommodate participants who are unfamiliar with implicit Guyanese cultural values associated with those performances.

The Come to My Kwe-Kwe celebration is led by a core group of performers, collectively referred to as the Kwe-Kwe Ensemble.[6] This ensemble often includes drummer Akoyaw Rudder, keyboardist Hilton Hemerding, and dancers Verna Walcott-White and Dr. Rose October-Edun, among others. This uniformly attired group of singers, musicians, and dancers also serve in various capacities in the GCA and on the Guyana Folk Festival Committee. Many are also former members of the Guyana National School of Dance (GNSD), which was founded in 1977 by Haitian American choreographer and dancer Lavinia Williams. When in Guyana, members of the GNSD have performed a variety of ethnic dances including

African dances, ballet, Indian dances, and reenactments of *kweh-kweh*. These performances were executed before local, national, and international audiences, and they required a great deal of dramatic improvisation to keep audiences engaged (Rose October-Edun, interview, February 26, 2011; Akoyaw Rudder, interview, November 23, 2005). Members of the Kwe-Kwe Ensemble have worked and traveled together for decades and have a unique understanding of each other's performance styles. More importantly, these members have performed many reenactments of the *kweh-kweh* ritual all over Guyana, including at the Guyana National Cultural Centre. At Come to My Kwe-Kwe, these former members of the GNSD, now in the Kwe-Kwe Ensemble, transcribe their entertainment-focused performances of *kweh-kweh* to accommodate American audiences.

During Come to My Kwe-Kwe, the ensemble leads the procession at the beginning of the ritual, and throughout the evening they provide instruction to attendees and encourage audience participation. Every year, the number of performers in the ensemble increases, since the members invite other drummers and musicians from the community to perform with them. In this amplified and vibrant setting, the ensemble provides entertainment for other participants and crucial support to the *kweh-kweh* captain(s) leading the event.

Under the leadership of the Come to My Kwe-Kwe captain and members of the Kwe-Kwe Ensemble, participants reenact the ritual segments of the traditional wedding-based *kweh-kweh* for the entertainment and edification of the audience. While Come to My Kwe-Kwe replicates the overarching segments of traditional *kweh-kweh*, the captain and the Kwe-Kwe Ensemble often improvise many of the performances to make them accessible and exciting to an increasingly diverse group of attendees who might have competing engagements on Come to My Kwe-Kwe night. This point was succinctly articulated during an interview with October-Edun, secretary of Guyana Folk Festival Committee and dancer, who stated:

> So people are coming, already dressed for their parties and they don't wanna sweat. And we are asking them to get involved. . . . We need to make it enticing to the crowd coming, not losing the

original fabric of what *kweh-kweh* is about, because *kweh-kweh* is about the night before [the wedding]. (February 26, 2011)

Migration, Transnationalism, and *Rediasporization*

Migration across national boundaries and the subsequent development of transnational communities have been widely discussed in academia (Glick Schiller, Basch, and Blanc 1995; Foner 1998; Mintz 1998; Portes and Rumbaut 1996). As James Clifford noted: "[A]t different times in their history, societies may wax and wane in diasporism, depending on changing possibilities—obstacles, openings, antagonisms, and connections—in their host countries and transnationally" (1994, 6). However, scholarly literature has tended to focus disproportionately on "victim diasporas" (Cohen 1997, 11). Scholarship that addresses other types of diasporas overwhelmingly focuses on the disruptions between primary diasporas and their original homelands (Needham 1975; Gilroy 1987; Safran 1991; Tölölyan 1991; Shepperson 1993), and the strategies that ethnic groups implement to maintain solidarity with homelands, police ethnic boundaries (Cohen 1997; Kliger 1988; Foner 1998; Green and Scher 2007), or integrate into the dominant society of their new homelands (Gonzalez and McCommon 1989; Kasinitz 1992; Waters 1994; Foner, Rumbaut, and Gold 2000; Stavans [1995] 2001). Studies on diaspora particularly address the ways that ritual, particularly *rites of passage* associated with life-cycle events (van Gennep 1960), are heightened and traditionalized, as ethnic groups seek to construct diasporic identities and ensure cultural survival (Summit 2000).

Scholarship on diaspora is rooted in the assumption that a diaspora is automatically created once an ethnic group is displaced from its primary homeland and takes up residence in a new homeland. I argue that relocation to the same geographic region does not complete the process of *diasporization*, as there must be a process of gelling that enables the transplanted group to transform themselves from an "imagined community," to cite Benedict Anderson ([1983]

1991), to a tangible community. I argue, therefore, that becoming a diaspora is a bipartite process that includes (1) removal from an original homeland and (2) regrounding in a new homeland.

The imagined African-Guyanese community in the United States systematically engages in the same acts—reading Guyanese newspapers, cooking and eating Guyanese food, celebrating individual *kweh-kweh* rituals—but they do so in fragmented ways, disconnected from the larger African-Guyanese community. The real or tangible community is formed when individuals, families, and the larger African-Guyanese-American community consistently and systematically come together as a unit to participate in these various cultural acts. Their ritualistic coming together helps to unify them and facilitates the creation of a new and different African-Guyanese community in the United States. Since the African-Guyanese already constitute a primary African diaspora, which underwent the processes of uprooting (from Africa) and regrounding and crystallizing (in Guyana), their experiences in the United States move them toward becoming a secondary diaspora. Thus, I regard the collective process of African-Guyanese uprooting (migration) from Guyana and regrounding (gelling) in the United States as *rediasporization* (Boyarin and Boyarin 2002; Clifford 1994; Falzon 2004; Sundquist 2005).

While the regrounding is crucial to the gelling of the African-Guyanese-American community, it also facilitates a type of cultural sanctification through which the community consistently separates itself from other ethnic groups among whom they reside and bonds with their fellow African-Guyanese in America. Fredrik Barth asserts: "Entailed in ethnic boundary maintenance are also situations of social contact between persons of different cultures: ethnic groups only persist as significant units if they imply marked difference in behavior, i.e. persistent cultural differences" (1969, 15–16). Thus, the visible displays of African-Guyanese culture in the United States, by means of *kweh-kweh* and Come to My Kwe-Kwe, emphasize the boundaries that define the African-Guyanese community and facilitate the processes of regrounding. Through the repeated coming together of the African-Guyanese community to celebrate the *kweh-kweh* ritual, but more specifically Come to My Kwe-Kwe,

African-Guyanese assert a secondary diasporic identity and expedite the process of *rediasporization* in the United States.

Rediasporization is a process that stems from an existence of "otherness" in a dominant society. For African-Guyanese, this "otherness" facilitates a *triple consciousness*, which prevents them from fully embracing American culture. Triple consciousness is rooted in the assumption that there is a single consciousness that stems from a people's sense of wholeness or oneness with their racial (black) and national selves. My discussion of triple consciousness builds on W. E. B. Du Bois's concept of "double consciousness," in which he describes African-Americans as existing in a state of twoness, whereby they are both "American" and "Negro"—two diametrically opposed ideals ([1903] 2009). According to Du Bois, the sense of twoness that African-Americans feel is compounded by the fact that their existence is examined through the lens of a white standard.

For African diasporic groups who are members of the "victim diaspora" that was created as a result of slavery, the sense of twoness is common to their existence. For African-Guyanese who endured slavery under the British, the sense of twoness (African and Guyanese) was negotiated in diverse ways. Some attempted to mask their blackness through a strict adherence to Christianity or a rejection of Africanized cultural practices, while others openly embraced their dual existence through Faithism, Santería, and other African-centered syncretic religious practices. The twoness that African-Guyanese in Guyana experience becomes a threeness (African and Guyanese and American) when they migrate to the United States. As Takeyuki Tsuda succinctly stated:

> By its very nature, transnational displacement can produce conditions of liminality and social alienation among migrants, who are geographically separated from their country of origin but remain socially marginalized in the host society. Such liminal social detachment can be highly problematic, ultimately producing a disorienting state of "homeland-lessness" abroad, where neither the sending or [sic] receiving country serves any longer as a stable source of social belonging. (2003, 122)

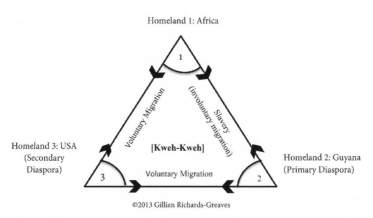

Figure 1.3: *Rediasporization* Explored

African-Guyanese's liminal state of existence, which is caused by triple consciousness, compels them to construct a reality that is *tri-cultural*—of three distinct culture groups (Turner 1969). My use of *triculturalism* draws on Hope Landrine and Elizabeth Klonoff's discussion of biculturalism. According to Landrine and Klonoff: "Some members of minority groups are highly traditional, some bicultural, and others are highly acculturated. Still others are *marginal*, and either reject (or never acquired) the beliefs and practices of their own culture or of the dominant culture, as well" (1996, 2). Based on Landrine and Klonoff's model of cultural identity, minority individuals fall within two extremes of a continuum: those who cling to the practices of their own culture, and those who are acculturated and have adapted "cultural traditions, values, beliefs, and practices" of the dominant "White" society (1996, 1). In the middle of that continuum are bicultural individuals who "retain the beliefs and practices of their own culture (their culture of origin) but also have assimilated the beliefs and practices of the dominant White society and so participate in two very different cultural traditions simultaneously" (1996, 1–2). Based on this model, then, African-Guyanese fall into the "marginal" category, as they do not fit this cultural schema. I argue that minority groups do not necessarily advance on a continuum from "highly traditional" to "acculturated" but that they add culture groups and, over time, learn how to skillfully navigate the demands of each group (Royce 2011, 4–5). Thus, African-Guyanese-Americans do not remain traditional or become acculturated but embrace triculturalism. This work looks at the ways that Come to My Kwe-Kwe allows African-Guyanese-Americans to navigate the shifting compositions of their communities and articulate unique self-perceptions.

Interrogating the "African Diaspora"

The term "African diaspora" has been historically used to refer to darker-skinned peoples of African descent who, for diverse reasons, now reside outside of the continent of Africa (Herskovits 1930; Gilroy 1993; Gomez 2007; Okpewho and Nzegwu 2009; Rahier, Hintzen, and Smith 2010). While in my work I adhere to the established parameters of the "African diaspora," in my discussions about African-Guyanese and the larger African diaspora, and for the purposes of accuracy and transparency, it is imperative that I also acknowledge that there are nonblack peoples (phenotypically speaking), such as white South Africans, who were born on the continent of Africa and claim African descent. Nonblack Africans are technically part of the African diaspora, but because they are overwhelmingly descendants of colonizers and more recent immigrants from Europe and Asia, they are generally excluded from the category "African diaspora." Moreover, before deconstructing the African diaspora, it is also crucial that I reexamine the nature of the "African" who gave rise to the category "African diaspora." Based on my interrogations, I have placed Africans into two overarching categories: (1) the original or historical "black" Africans who are dark skinned and who are regarded as the original inhabitants of the continent; and (2) the "other" Africans who are voluntarily or involuntarily excluded from the category "African" and thus from the "African diaspora."

Historical "Black" African Diasporas

Historical African diasporas fall into two predominant categories, which are determined by the conditions under which these groups emigrated from Africa.[7] The first group resulted from involuntary migrations of peoples of African descent during the African slave trade.[8] Robin Cohen (1997, 11) refers to this segment of the African diaspora as a "victim diaspora," but for clarity and specificity, I prefer to use the term "Enslavement African Diaspora." Thus, the Enslavement African Diaspora is composed of African-Americans, Afro-Caribbean peoples (West Indians), Afro-Europeans, Afro-Latinos, and other groups whose ancestors were enslaved.

The second group of historical African diasporas emerged largely because of voluntary migration and is a more recent phenomenon than the Enslavement African Diaspora. Included in this diaspora are voluntary migrants from Africa who come directly from Ghana, Nigeria, and other parts of the continent. Also included in this group are African refugees, political asylum seekers, and others who migrated from the continent due to negative push factors that compelled them to leave. Isidore Okpewho and Nkiru Nzegwu collectively categorize these groups as "new diaspora Africans" (2009, 5). Even though it can be argued that the more recent migration of African immigrants who are refugees and political asylum seekers is involuntary because negative factors forced them to leave, I do not include them in the first group of the historical Enslavement African Diaspora because they are not descendants of the enslaved Africans. Moreover, for all intents and purposes, they also possessed some degree of agency in their leave of the continent. The second group of historical African diasporas also includes peoples who emigrated from other regions of the world such as the Caribbean, Europe, and Latin America. It is important to note that while some groups, such as West Indians (Afro-Caribbean migrants) and Afro-Latinos, can be collectively categorized as "cultural diasporas" (Cohen 1997) because they migrate to the United States and other parts of the world voluntarily, they are also part of the Enslavement African Diaspora because they (their ancestors) were also enslaved and brought from Africa.

The Primary African Diaspora in Guyana

The African diaspora in Guyana accounts for about 38 percent of the country's population of less than one million persons, and is largely the result of forced migration during the Atlantic slave trade. While African-Guyanese collectively self-identify as "black people" (of African descent), they originated from diverse African ethnicities (nations) such as Igbo, Yoruba, and Akan (Schuler 1980, 71; Costa 1994, 75; Warner-Lewis 2003, 115). Over time, and due in large part to the brutal and destructive nature of slavery and subsequent oppressive tactics of enslavers, the cultural differences between different African ethnic groups began to dissipate, as Africans in Guyana capitalized on their commonalities as a means of survival. African-Guyanese are still a diverse group of people, but their differences today are overwhelmingly influenced by class, religion, and their perceptions of race, particularly blackness. The divisions among African-Guyanese are particularly striking when they address African-influenced cultural and religious expressions, such as *comfa* (Gibson 2001), *obeah* (Costa 1994, 76; Browne 2011), *'nansi 'tory*, and *kweh-kweh* (Gibson 1996).[9] Thus, for example, some African-Guyanese self-identify as "only African" and some as "only Guyanese" (without a prefix), while others opt for more hybrid *dougla* identities that conceal or distinguish them from their African heritage.

Regardless of how African-Guyanese in Guyana choose to racially self-identify, they are uniquely aware of the fact that they are different from East Indians, Amerindians, and other Guyanese ethnics. Moreover, recent political and cultural developments in Guyana have caused African-Guyanese to realize that the criteria they utilize to embrace their Africanness, create hybrid identities, or distinguish themselves from blackness are the same that ethnic "others" use to classify them. Thus, as African-Guyanese in Guyana struggle to gain political power and economic capital, they are compelled to acknowledge that, regardless of their financial capabilities, religious affiliations, or social class, they *are* competing against their fellow Guyanese as "black people." While this racialized sociopolitical struggle inspires some African-Guyanese to revisit or embrace African cultural traditions, others regard it as a compelling reason to further distance themselves from their African "pagan" past, which constitutes an impediment to progress. Nevertheless, as race continues to be a determining and divisive factor on Guyana's political, social, and economic landscapes, more African-Guyanese are forced to acknowledge the blackness that binds them to an original homeland (Africa) and the experiences that render them uniquely Guyanese.

The Secondary African-Guyanese Diaspora in New York City

When African-Guyanese migrate to New York City, they become members of a Guyanese diaspora that includes Amerindians, Chinese, East Indians, and other Guyanese ethnics. However, they also become part of the larger African diaspora, which is composed of three overarching groups: African-Americans, Afro-Caribbeans (West Indians), and historical "black" Africans (Jackson and Cothran 2003; Humphries 2009, 271).[10] African-Guyanese-Americans share unique bonds with each segment (ethnic group) of the larger African diaspora. With African-Americans and Afro-Caribbean peoples, they share an involuntary migrant (slave) past, but, like historical "black" Africans and Afro-Caribbeans, they also share a voluntary diaspora status in the United States (Mars 2009, 483–99). Moreover, while a common origin (Africa), race (blackness), and discriminatory experiences unify members of the African diaspora in the United States, each group seeks to highlight ethnic differences and strengthen bonds that make them culturally unique and viable. Msia Clark argues that "when African immigration to America increased in the 1980s, there had not been a serious need for blacks in America to reevaluate their identities" (2009, 257). It is the need to carve out unique identities that drives African-Guyanese-Americans to temporarily and symbolically suspend membership in the larger Guyanese, Caribbean, and African diasporic communities to formulate and solidify a diaspora of their own. As Clark observed, "Blacks from the Caribbean seem to see no contradiction in embracing both their racial and ethnic identities (2009, 266). However, this begs the question: how is membership in the African-Guyanese-American diaspora determined?

A more in-depth examination of the African-Guyanese-American diaspora reveals that it is an extremely diverse group in which membership is largely determined by four principal factors: migration, reproduction, marriage, and association (fig. 1.4). Group 1 of the African-Guyanese diaspora is the *migrated diaspora*, which is composed of individuals who were born in Guyana and later migrated to the United States.[11] Group 2, the *procreated or reproduced diaspora*, is composed of the children of one or both Guyanese parents and other individuals of Guyanese ancestry. Group 3 is the *affinal diaspora*, which encompasses non-Guyanese individuals who, because of marriage to a Guyanese national, completely or contextually self-identify as Guyanese. In Group 4 are *strangers* and *visitors*. These individuals are not Guyanese or their consanguineal or affinal kin, but, for diverse reasons, they are committed to the Guyanese community and actively participate in various cultural expressions within the Guyanese community, particularly those involving music, dance, food, and folklore. While the African-Guyanese diaspora in the United States is diverse, it is their sense of a common origin in Africa, a shared or adopted homeland (Guyana), and a need to remain culturally viable that compel them to articulate unique and useful identities to reform and solidify a new community in the United States.

Chapter Outline

Each chapter below examines how intersections of gender, race, religion, and migration, among other factors, shape the ways in which African-Guyanese-Americans simultaneously create and sever bonds with three homelands—Africa, Guyana, and the United States—to negotiate unique tricultural identities and facilitate the creation and gelling of a secondary diaspora (*rediasporization*). Each chapter also investigates the ways that issues of authenticity often shape behaviors and performance practices at Come to My Kwe-Kwe rituals, as African-Guyanese-Americans work to accommodate the changing composition of their community. While this work focuses on African-Guyanese in New York City, I will systematically reference the performance practices of traditional *kweh-kweh* in Guyana to demonstrate the changes

Dissecting the Secondary African Guyanese Diaspora in the United States

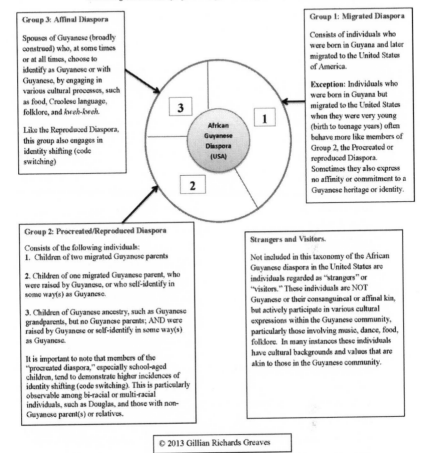

Group 3: Affinal Diaspora

Spouses of Guyanese (broadly construed) who, at some times or at all times, choose to identify as Guyanese or with Guyanese, by engaging in various cultural processes, such as food, Creolese language, folklore, and *kweh-kweh*.

Like the Reproduced Diaspora, this group also engages in identity shifting (code switching)

Group 1: Migrated Diaspora

Consists of individuals who were born in Guyana and later migrated to the United States of America.

Exception: Individuals who were born in Guyana but migrated to the United States when they were very young (birth to teenage years) often behave more like members of Group 2, the Procreated or reproduced Diaspora. Sometimes they also express no affinity or commitment to a Guyanese heritage or identity.

3 **1** African Guyanese Diaspora (USA) **2**

Group 2: Procreated/Reproduced Diaspora

Consists of the following individuals:
1. Children of two migrated Guyanese parents

2. Children of one migrated Guyanese parent, who were raised by Guyanese, or who self-identify in some way(s) as Guyanese.

3. Children of Guyanese ancestry, such as Guyanese grandparents, but no Guyanese parents; AND were raised by Guyanese or self-identify in some way(s) as Guyanese.

It is important to note that members of the "procreated diaspora," especially school-aged children, tend to demonstrate higher incidences of identity shifting (code switching). This is particularly observable among bi-racial or multi-racial individuals, such as Douglas, and those with non-Guyanese parent(s) or relatives.

Strangers and Visitors.

Not included in this taxonomy of the African Guyanese diaspora in the United States are individuals regarded as "strangers" or "visitors." These individuals are NOT Guyanese or their consanguineal or affinal kin, but actively participate in various cultural expressions within the Guyanese community, particularly those involving music, dance, food, folklore. In many instances these individuals have cultural backgrounds and values that are akin to those in the Guyanese community.

Figure 1.4: The subgroups of the African-Guyanese diaspora in the United States.

taking place in the reenacted ritual and the dialectical influences that are taking place between the two communities.

Chapter 2, "'Where's the Cookup Rice?' Extracting the 'African' and Reconstructing 'Home' through Food," explores the integral role that food plays in creating tangible and imagined African-Guyanese communities in New York City. This chapter articulates the ways that African-Guyanese-Americans draw on the plethora of cuisines they collectively regard as "Guyanese food" to celebrate their Guyaneseness, while simultaneously extracting the African-influenced foods on the menu to highlight racial identities that distinguish them from other Guyanese and American ethnicities. By examining the menu at Come to My Kwe-Kwe, I demonstrate the ways in which African-Guyanese-Americans maintain "traditional" (African and Guyanese) foodways that bind them to past experiences, geographies, and people, known and unknown. The menu also indexes the changes that African-Guyanese-Americans are compelled to make to accommodate modifications to traditional *kweh-kweh*, their personal schedules, tastes, health concerns, and other aspects of their changing, heterogeneous community, while also seeking to maintain notions of gastronomic authenticity.

In chapter 3, "Wipin', Winin', and Wukkin': Constructing, Contesting, and Displaying Gender Values," I examine gendered values in the Guyanese community and the ways that these values are articulated in *kweh-kweh* through singing, dancing, and other ritual performances. I specifically investigate what it means to be a "proper woman," a "real man," and other ideals in the African-Guyanese community. I also examine how factors surrounding migration, including changing views on women's roles in society, influence women's engagement with ritual and their reevaluation of gendered roles in the Guyanese community in New York City. More importantly, I discuss the ways that *kweh-kweh* performers innovate or reject ritual practices to celebrate, challenge, or conceal established gender ideals in a transnational Guyanese community.

Chapter 4, "'Beat de Drum and de Spirit Gon Get Up': Music, Dance, and Authenticity in *Rediasporization*," scrutinizes the most crucial and visible performances in Come to My Kwe-Kwe—music and dance. Here, I examine singing (including repertoire, form, textual content, and language use), musicians, instruments (including "found sounds"), and ritual dance to delineate the boundaries and intersections of African-Guyanese music aesthetics and systems of meaning-making. An examination of music performance in this transnational space affords a unique opportunity to reveal ways that performers use music to comment on who they perceive themselves to be and construct a new diaspora in the United States. It is in this chapter also that issues of authenticity particularly come to the fore, as musicians, singers, and other performers manipulate musical practices to accommodate non-Guyanese and a new African-Guyanese community.

Chapter 5, "'Borrow a Day from God': Navigating the Boundaries of Race and Religion in *Rediasporization*," examines *rediasporization* as religious enactments. I discuss the limits and intersections of salvation, sanctification, and ritual innovation that result when a changing community draws on a reinvention of tradition to carve out transnational identities. I delve into the ways that Africanists (those who embrace African cultural practices) and Christians conceptualize salvation and apply its relevant principles to their daily lives. I specifically examine how their views of salvation and sanctification affect their perceptions of blackness, and how these perceptions influence their engagement with *kweh-kweh*. The chapter also examines the ways that migration complicates religious perspectives and African-Guyanese identities, forcing African-Guyanese to reevaluate initial stances and engage *kweh-kweh*. Ultimately, this chapter demonstrates the role of agency in African-Guyanese's persistent modifications of themselves, their religious beliefs, and *kweh-kweh* ritual in their identity negotiations in the United States.

In chapter 6, "Wholly Fractured, Wholly Whole: Innovating 'Traditions' and Reconstructing Self in Come to My Kwe-Kwe Rituals," I situate Come to My Kwe-Kwe as a point of return, as "home." Moreover, I examine this reenactment of the wedding-based ("traditional") *kweh-kweh* as the new "tradition" with increasing validation of authenticity by African-Guyanese who seek to fit in and to stand out, to highlight individual and collective fractures, and to feel whole.

2

"Where's the Cookup Rice?"
Extracting the "African" and Reconstructing "Home" through Food

You can't plant plantain and reap cassava

GUYANESE PROVERB

During intermission at the 2015 Come to My Kwe-Kwe, attendees filed out of the main hall and made their way up the stairs to the back room where food vendors had set up their wares. An assortment of Guyanese foods was displayed in large foil pans, heated by small cans of methanol fuel. As attendees passed by the tables, they purchased chicken feet souse, curried channa (chickpeas), black pudding (blood sausage), pholourie (an East Indian delicacy), and other Guyanese foods. This was the first time that my Guyanese-born friend, whom I'll refer to as Patricia, attended the event. Although she was familiar with traditional kweh-kweh, she had not attended one in a while and thus viewed Come to My Kwe-Kwe as a welcomed reprise. We purchased an assortment of foods and sat down to eat. With each bite, she provided an unsolicited critique of the food, such as "umhm, this good," "this ain't sayin' nothin'," and so on. After a few minutes had elapsed, Patricia became visibly agitated and exclaimed, "But, where's the cookup rice? Kweh-kweh gotta have cookup!" There was no cookup

Figure 2.1: Pigeon peas and red beans cookup rice with chicken feet, pumpkin, and other veggies, prepared by Waveney Richards (the author's mom). Photo by Gillian Richards-Greaves (first published in 2012).

rice on the menu that night. She "sucked her teeth" (an oral expression of displeasure) and continued eating.

Introduction

Culture is said to be instrumental because it takes our natural biological urges and teaches us how to express them in unique ways (Kottak 2014, 25). Hunger is one such biological urge that is addressed differently from one society to the next. What we eat, how we eat, where we eat, and with whom we eat are all influenced by the societal values with which we were raised; as Anne Murcott notes, "what and how people eat or drink may usefully be understood in terms of a system whose coherence is afforded by the social and cultural organisation with which it is associated" (1983, 1). Moreover, while food assuages hunger and nourishes the body (Harris-Shapiro 2006, 78), it also has a voice that communicates powerful messages—both overt and subliminal—about the ways members of a group perceive themselves, as well as how others view them (Douglas 1971; Mintz 1989, 4; Counihan 1999; Wilk 1999). Anne Bower argues that food is "an excellent locus for the study of group dynamics—how different populations exclude, include, reject, accept and otherwise influence each other" (2007, 8).

In the Guyanese community, food is a crucial tool in the process of *enculturation*. Through food, identities and social values surrounding race, class, gender, religion, nationality, and more are produced, articulated, and consumed (Douglas 1971; Counihan 1999). Claude Fischler argues: "Food is central to our sense of identity. The way any given human group eats helps to assert its diversity [and] hierarchy . . . and at the same time, both its oneness and the otherness of whoever eats differently" (1988, 275). Food is a powerful symbol of identity partly because it is "associated with nearly every dimension of human social and cultural life" (Gabaccia 1998, 8) and thus serves as a "universal medium that illuminates a wide range of other cultural practices" (Watson and Caldwell 2005, 1–11). From the time they are very young, Guyanese children are taught how to plant crops, to negotiate the best prices for produce in the marketplace, to prepare meals, and to evaluate the authenticity of the meals they consume. Gastronomic socialization in the Guyanese community generally begins in the home and is further perpetuated in academic and religious institutions. In each sphere of society, the intrinsic values of the Guyanese community are instilled and perpetuated through preparation and consumption of a diverse body of cuisines collectively referred to as "Guyanese food" (Richards-Greaves 2013).

Guyanese foods—both crops and cuisines—reflect the ethnic diversity of the Guyanese people, as well as Guyana's long and complex history of creolization, which gave rise to newer, more hybrid cuisines. For instance, the culinary influence of Amerindian peoples is demonstrated through foods like *pepperpot*, Guyana's national dish. Pepperpot is made with cassareep (a by-product of the cassava root), meats, peppers, and spices and is served with bread, rice, or cassava bread, the preference of many Amerindians (Richards-Greaves 2013, 84). African-influenced foods include *fufu*, a starchy staple made from boiled and pounded tubers like cassava, plantains, and yams; *cookup rice*, a one-pot meal made with rice, peas or beans, coconut milk, meats, and vegetables; and *metemgee* (also called *metegee* or *metem*), another one-pot meal, made with tubers and boiled in coconut milk with meats, dumplings, and spices. Nevertheless, many Guyanese cuisines are of East Indian origin and include foods like curries; *roti* (often pronounced "rootee" by Guyanese), a type of flatbread; *dahl* (a type of lentil soup); and *channa* (chickpeas meal) (Richards-Greaves 2013, 87–89). Even though the Chinese population in Guyana is minuscule, their culinary influence is significant and includes *chow mein* (a type of noodle), fried rice, and a wide range of soups. Europeans have also left a mark on Guyana's culinary landscape through foods such as black pudding (blood sausage) and *souse*, a dish made with meats like chicken feet and cow's jowls (often called "cow face" by Guyanese), ears, and feet, which are boiled until they become a lightly pickled, spicy aspic. Although one can relatively easily identify the geographic and cultural origins of individual Guyanese foods, cuisines like "cassava lick-down" and "rice flour bakes" are more recent creations that emerged from food scarcity during Guyana's economic downturn in the 1980s, Guyanese outmigration, and other cultural factors (Richards-Greaves 2013, 79).

This chapter examines how African-Guyanese of the secondary diaspora in the United States police the boundaries of Guyanese food at Come to My Kwe-Kwe to "remember," to articulate blackness, and to facilitate *rediasporization*. This chapter further reveals the delicate balance often established between the desires of the attendees-customers and the financial goals of vendors who provide Come to My Kwe-Kwe meals. Although diverse types of foods are sold at Come to My Kwe-Kwe, attendees who were raised in Guyana, who are accustomed to eating Guyanese food, or who are familiar with traditional *kweh-kweh* often come expecting to consume specific cuisines. The cuisines often requested by attendees are those viewed as "real Guyanese food," particularly those associated with rural Guyana, and foods regarded as African in origin or function. However, an examination of the cuisines at Come to My Kwe-Kwe demonstrates some of the changes to Guyanese food that result from migration and the disruptions or innovations it facilitates, as well as the changing needs of the African-Guyanese community. Thus, this chapter demonstrates how Guyanese food sold at Come to My Kwe-Kwe functions to simultaneously diminish the symbolic distance between diasporas and homelands and establish new distances through cost, cuisines, and creativity.

Food and Social Values in the Guyanese Community

Food is a crucial and powerful symbol of identity in the Guyanese community because it encompasses, intersects with, and articulates many of the core values of the society in manners that are unique and distinct from other cultural expressions. In her 1988 monograph *Food, Gender, and Poverty in the Ecuadorian Andes*, Mary Weismantel argues: "It is because they are ordinarily immersed in everyday practice in a material way that foods, abstracted as symbols from this material process, can condense in themselves a wealth of ideological meanings" (1988, 7–8). Through food, gender, race, class, religion, and nationhood, to cite a few societal values in the Guyanese community, are deliberately and unintentionally articulated (Marks 2015; Richards-Greaves 2012; 2013; 2015). Since this chapter focuses on Come to My Kwe-Kwe, a reenactment of the traditional African-Guyanese *kweh-kweh* ritual, greater emphasis will be placed on the intersections of food and gender, race, nationhood, and religion. Religion is particularly foundational to this discussion because it underscores and informs most Guyanese values.[1] For instance, while Guyanese cuisines generally have identifiable racial or ethnic roots, these roots intersect with entrenched religious values. Thus, for instance, pepperpot, Guyana's national dish, is of Amerindian origin and is usually prepared with several types of meats (Richards-Greaves 2012, 143). However, Muslim Guyanese and

Seventh-Day Adventists avoid cooking or eating pork, Hindus avoid beef, Catholics and other Christians avoid meats during the Lenten season, and Rastafarians generally reject the consumption of meat altogether. This is not to diminish the role of class—and people's subsequent ability to afford certain food items—but to emphasize the role of religion as a powerful force that often overshadows other influences on the Guyanese foodscape.

Food is one of the principal ways that Guyanese teach, reinforce, and display gender values. While both boys and girls are taught to cook when they are very young, the onus of cooking is generally on women, as cooking validates one's womanhood. Food is a "powerful voice, especially for women, who are often heavily involved with food acquisition, preparation, provisioning, and cleanup" (Counihan 2004, 1). When a young woman can cook well, her mother is often celebrated for instilling proper "home training" in her child. Conversely, a woman who cannot cook or who cooks poorly, particularly one who is married, often becomes a source of ridicule for her mother (DeVault 1997, 184). The ability to cook diverse meals and to do so competently can set a young woman apart from her peers and render her more desirable for marriage or as "marriage material." In fact, during courtship, young women often cook several meals for their intended husbands to demonstrate their readiness to run a home and, more importantly, to serve their husbands. The idea of service to one's husband is a deep-rooted cultural value not just in the Guyanese community, but one that is often underscored in biblical scriptures and other religious texts that advise women to be subservient to their husbands (Ephesians 5:22–23, NIV). Thus, it is not surprising that food is often cited as a source of discord in many Guyanese homes, including domestic abuse (DeVault 1997, 180), or as a remedy for unfaithful husbands (Ellis 1983, 164–71). From this perspective, then, food is regarded as a source of power, which women can wield to control men. However, while the food power women wield may lie in their ability to cook delicious meals, some women have been accused of combining food and magico-religious practices like obeah to control or overpower men (Behar 1989, 180). Sometimes, also, food is a source of empowerment for women who sell their wares to earn or supplement the household income. Even when women work outside of the home, they are often expected, or feel compelled, to demonstrate their usefulness as women by consistently preparing meals for their family, especially on holidays and holy days. Nevertheless, emigration from Guyana often forces Guyanese to reconstruct gendered spaces to accommodate shifting economic and food resources, domestic responsibilities, and power dynamics in the home. Migration often results in more fluid gendered spaces of cooking in that men increasingly move into the kitchen, so to speak, to prepare meals or to render assistance.

Gender values are also highlighted and reinforced through acts of eating. In the Guyanese community, some meats and raw food items, including certain vegetables and tubers, are regarded as having masculine or feminine qualities or power. Foods like plantains, cassava, and others shaped like the male or female genitalia are often viewed as being imbued with sexual or reproductive powers. Thus, by eating meals made with these raw foods, individuals symbolically consume the powers embodied in those foods. For instance, from a male perspective, foods believed to "strengthen a man's back" or enhance his virility are often coveted. Porridges; "ground food" (foods made with ground provisions or tubers) such as *metemgee*; broth (often pronounced "broff") made with large fish heads; thick soups such as cow-heel soup, with split peas; various types of meats and duff (large dumplings sometimes called "tiger"); custards; sea moss; and *mannish water* are a few of these male-enhancing foods (Richards-Greaves 2013). These same foods are viewed as nourishing to a woman's body, and some, such as the porridges, custards, and thick soups, are often amply consumed after a woman has given birth and needs to "rebuild" her body. Nevertheless, how one eats reflects on the opposite gender partner, who is stereotypically viewed as responsible for providing the economic stability necessary to purchase the food items (in the case of men) or having the skill necessary to prepare appropriate meals.

African Continuities in Guyanese Food and Traditional *Kweh-Kweh* Ritual

As previously mentioned, Guyanese crops and cuisines often serve as symbols of diverse racial heritages or ethnic identities. According to Sidney Mintz, foods "have histories associated with the pasts of those who eat them; the techniques employed to find, process, prepare, serve, and consume the foods are all culturally variable, with histories of their own" (1996, 7). Thus, for instance, African-Guyanese often claim that crops used to prepare hearty (heavy) meals are of African origin, since many embrace the stereotype of the physically strong "black man" (person of African descent) (Richards-Greaves 2012). Black-eyed peas or cow peas (Albala 2007, 3), "ground provisions" (tubers) like yams (Pollitzer 2005, 139), okra (Harris 2003, 12; Hughes 1997, 242), and rice (Stanonis 2015, 93–106) are some of the crops that African-Guyanese regard as African continuities. As such, they frequently use these crops to prepare cuisines that are integral to their daily lives, to the fueling of life-cycle rituals like traditional *kweh-kweh*, and to the libations they offer to their ancestors. Some of their cuisines utilize these "African" food crops in preparation including cookup rice, *fufu*, *metemgee*, and a plethora of one-pot meals (Singleton 1991). African-Guyanese who are familiar with traditional *kweh-kweh* often attend the ritual with their mouths set to eat "African" foods like *conkee*, which is made with cornmeal and wrapped in banana leaves (akin to tamales), and one-pot meals like *metemgee* and cookup rice. Even African-Guyanese-Americans like Patricia who attend Come to My Kwe-Kwe do so with the expectation that the gustatory standards at the event will be like those of traditional *kweh-kweh*. In order to keep these cuisines as part of their diet, however, African-Guyanese, particularly those in the United States, must ensure that they are able to obtain the food crops necessary to prepare them.

Rice, one of the food crops integral to Guyanese meals, is often viewed as being of Asian origin. However, scholars argue that the *Oryza glaberrima* strain, "African rice," was domesticated on the African continent about two to three thousand years ago and is distinct from the *Oryza sativa* strain that was domesticated in Asia (Carney 2001, 38–46; Stanonis 2015, 93–106). Even though the high-yielding *Oryza sativa* eventually replaced *Oryza glaberrima* rice, many African ethnic groups possessed the techniques for rice cultivation long before the advent of slavery (McGowan, Rose, and Granger 2009, 8). It is for this reason that during the Atlantic slave trade, ethnic groups from rice-growing regions of Africa, such as modern-day Sierra Leone and Gambia, were strategically targeted by enslavers who sought to capitalize on their agricultural skills in the New World (McGowan, Rose, and Granger 2009, 8). Africans' skill at rice farming was especially crucial to the economic development of places like the southern United States, particularly the Carolinas (Littlefield 1981; Pollitzer 2005, 196), Guyana, South America (Smith [1962] 1980, 61–66), and the Caribbean at large (Carney 2001, 1). While African-Guyanese may not be aware of the history and intricate details surrounding the domestication of rice, many argue that rice is a part of their African heritage because their enslaved ancestors cultivated rice in Guyana.

Rice is an integral ingredient in cookup rice, one of the most popular one-pot meals served at traditional *kweh-kweh* (see the recipe at the end of this chapter). Made with rice, peas or beans, coconut milk or cream, meats, and vegetables, cookup rice is relatively inexpensive to prepare and thus is often regarded as "po-man" (poor people's) food. Guyanese often refer to cookup rice as "*dougla* pot" as a way of simultaneously indexing the unity and diversity of its ingredients, using a Guyanese racial category. The term *dougla* is derived from the Bhojpuri and Hindi word *doogala*, meaning "two-necks" (Mehta 2004, 543), and it historically referred to a mixed-raced (East Indian and black) person; however, today the term is used to refer to any mixed-raced person who is partially black (Richards-Greaves 2012).[2] Like a *dougla* person, who is said to be "no-nation" (not being of a specific race) or "all-nation" (being of every race), cookup rice is a dish that sometimes occupies a position of ethnic ambiguity on the Guyanese foodscape, even though African-Guyanese often claim it as their heritage. Because cookup rice can be prepared in copious quantities and contains all the important food groups or nutrients, it is often served at key life-cycle events like birthday parties, christenings, *kweh-kweh* rituals, weddings, wakes, and repasts. While cookup rice is prepared throughout the year, Guyanese view the meal as mandatory for the Old Year's Night (New Year's Eve) menu. African-Guyanese are particularly keen on cooking cookup rice with black-eyed peas on Old Year's Night and for life-cycle events like *kweh-kweh*, partly because black-eyed peas are of African origin (Witt 1999; Albala 2007, 117–26; Henderson 2007). Moreover, many individuals of the Enslavement African Diaspora view black-eyed peas as possessing innate, almost spiritual powers that bring wealth and overall good luck, particularly for the New Year (Miller 2013, 120–24). In fact, for the average traditional *kweh-kweh*, African-Guyanese prepare "black-eye cookup," as it often called, and in Guyana they often use a coalpot or wood fire as inexpensive sources of cooking fuel, which they claim make the food taste "sweeter" and more flavorful. While folks attend *kweh-kweh* rituals to celebrate the couple and their nations, to dance, and to drink, they also look forward to nourishing themselves with "African foods" like black-eyed cookup.[3]

Cookup rice is one of the first meals that young Guyanese women learn to cook, and it is often referenced in traditional *kweh-kweh* when older women chide the bride on her domestic abilities by asking questions like, "Girl, yuh know how fuh cook a pot a cookup?" (Girl, can you at least prepare a simple one-pot meal like cookup rice?). At Come to My Kwe-Kwe celebrations, the audience often asks the volunteer bride similar questions but with much less seriousness or urgency. The importance of being able to cook is also referenced in traditional *kweh-kweh* songs like "Pack She Back" (Send Her Back) (example 2.1), in which the lyrics state: "She don't know to cook, she wouldn't read a book, pack she back to she ma." "Pack She Back" not only indexes the importance of being a competent cook but also implies the usefulness of having an education (being able to "read a book") or being inquisitive, particularly when one is culinarily challenged. While this song is sung at *kweh-kweh* rituals, it is also sung by children as part of their play. The performance of this song serves as an example of how music functions in the process of enculturation, and how subliminal gendered values are inadvertently and simultaneously transmitted from one generation to the next through food, music, and play.

Example 2.1: "Pack She Back"

Creolese	English
Pack she back to ma mo,	Send her back to her mother
Pack she back to she ma.	Send her back to her mother
She don't know to cook,	She doesn't know to cook
She wouldn't read a book,	She's uneducated and uninquisitive
Pack she back to she ma.	Send her back to her mother

African-Guyanese also often claim "ground provisions" or tubers—including cassava (*Manihot esculenta* Crantz, Euphorbiaceae), eddo, dasheen (*Colocasia esculenta*), plantains, and yams—as African continuities. However, many of these ground provisions are not indigenous to Africa but were domesticated in other parts of the world and later diffused to Africa. For example, cassava was domesticated in South America and later diffused to other parts of the world (Elias, Rival, and Mckey 2000; Schacht 2013); dasheen is believed to have been domesticated in China and Japan and later spread to other parts of the world (Purseglove 1972); and plantains ("cooking banana") are believed to have originated in Southeast Asia and later dispersed to Africa, the Caribbean, and other parts of the world, where subspecies were further developed (Robinson and Saúco 2010, 1–3). Nevertheless, African-Guyanese often view these starchy staples as heavy and filling, and thus possessing the ability to nourish and strengthen those who consume them. Because many also embrace the stereotype of black people as being physically strong, they are further inclined to believe that ground provisions are indeed uniquely African foods. This sentiment of the physically strong black person is often expressed in sayings like "plantain and duff mek Blackman tuff" (plantain and dumplings make black people physically strong) (Richards-Greaves 2012).

At many traditional *kweh-kweh* rituals, *metemgee*, much like cookup rice, is regarded as integral to the ritual. *Metemgee* ("ground food" or "dry food") is a Guyanese dish that is made with ground provisions (tubers), plantains, meats, vegetables, and fluffy dumplings, all boiled together in coconut milk. Some of the meats used in *metemgee* reflect the influences of slavery and include "leftover ears, tails, feet, fat, ribs, tripe, chicken feet, heads, tongues, and innards" (Covey and Eisnach 2009, 97). *Metemgee* is generally consumed during the day, particularly at lunchtime, when individuals plan to do strenuous work or need energy for a long day. *Metemgee* is also often coveted by men who seek to "strengthen their backs" (increase virility), and by pregnant and breastfeeding women who desire to nourish or rebuild their bodies after giving birth. While *metemgee* is filling and can anchor or "hold" a person for extended periods of time, it is often prepared at *kweh-kweh* rituals because it is perceived to be of African origin. At *kweh-kweh*, *metemgee* provides sustenance for participants throughout the night and into the wee hours of the morning. Some families often forego *metemgee* at their *kweh-kweh* because it is costlier to prepare than cookup rice. *Metemgee* also spoils relatively quickly, so if the meal is not consumed by attendees, the family stands to lose the money they spent on food, the time invested in preparing the food, and the food itself. Even though the term *metemgee* appears to come from an Amerindian language, many African-Guyanese view the presence of coconut milk, tubers like yams (Pollitzer 2005, 139), and some of the vegetables like okra (Harris 2003, 12; Hughes 1997, 242) as evidence of the African origins of this one-pot meal. Many African-Guyanese also point to the fact that the same meal is prepared in the Caribbean and other regions of the world with significant black populations, even though it is referred to by different names, such as "oil down" in Grenada and Trinidad and Tobago, "Sancoche" in Antigua, "rung down" in Belize, and "run down" or "run dun" in Jamaica and Panama (Cleary 1986). Thus, when African-Guyanese attend a traditional *kweh-kweh* to celebrate an impending marriage, they also honor their immediate and distant ancestors by pouring libation (with food and alcohol) and continuing what they perceive to be their gustatory traditions.

At traditional *kweh-kweh* rituals, some African-Guyanese also prepare *fufu*, a quintessentially African meal that survived slavery (Covey and Eisnach 2009, 42). *Fufu* is made with tubers like cassava, plantains, and yams, which are boiled and then pounded in a mortar with a pestle until they attain a solid, rubbery constitution. *Fufu* is paired with diverse types of stews and is eaten with the bare hands (fingers). Not many African-Guyanese still "pound *fufu*" using a mortar and pestle, but an increasing number of individuals in the villages of Guyana, and those who are conscientiously and deliberately returning to their African roots, have reacquired the habit of pounding *fufu*. More recently, African-Guyanese have begun using pounded (powdered) yams and other powdered tubers to prepare their *fufu*. The preparation of *fufu* may signal a cultural reawakening and return to Africanness that is influenced by diverse factors, including the increasing exposure of African-Guyanese to African cultures through travel to other parts of the world, the increased presence of Nigerians and other African nationals in Guyana, a deliberate reeducation on African history, and the preponderance of African movies in Guyana. Although *fufu* is an African continuity, the way it is prepared by African-Guyanese reflects the acculturation and creolization that resulted from their displacement from the African continent and sustained contact with other ethnic groups in Guyana. Even though many African-Guyanese may be unfamiliar with *fufu* because it is not a common meal on the Guyanese daily foodscape, by preparing it during traditional *kweh-kweh*, African-Guyanese are able to articulate racialized identities through food.

The term "*kweh-kweh* foods" also encompasses an assortment of beverages served at the ritual. While store-bought alcoholic and nonalcoholic beverages are staples at most *kweh-kweh*, attendees often quench their thirst throughout the evening with beverages made with sorrel (*Hibiscus sabdariffa*), passion fruit (*Passiflora edulis*), carambola *Averrhoa carambola*; also called starfruit or "five fingers", limes or lemons, and other local fruits. Local beverages are relatively inexpensive to make since they basically require only sugar, water, and fruits, which can be obtained cheaply or for free. While many of the previously mentioned fruits and many others used to make local beverages are cultivated on the African continent today, they are not necessarily indigenous to the continent. For instance, sorrel is believed to be indigenous to West Africa (Cobley 1976) or Asia (Morton 2013), carambola to Malaysia (Lim 2012, 455), and passion fruit to South America (Morton 2013, 320–28). Thus, African-Guyanese preparation of local drinks at *kweh-kweh* seems to focus more on the Guyaneseness of the beverages than on their African origin. Additionally, on the few occasions when African-Guyanese referenced race in discussing local drinks, they emphasized what they regarded as the African and African diasporic practice of "making something from nothing" (Marks 2015, 80), instead of the origin of the fruits used to make the beverages. Thus, many *kweh-kweh* sponsors who are tasked with feeding a large and unspecified number of attendees serve local beverages simply because it is cost effective to do so.

Migration, Memory, and Food at Come to My Kwe-Kwe Rituals

In the United States, African-Guyanese continue to prepare Guyanese foods on a regular basis, for diverse reasons. In order to continue cooking the way they did "back home," Guyanese devise various strategies, including planting kitchen gardens; buying groceries at the open markets; bringing spices and other food items from Guyana; having food items shipped to them from other parts of the world; and sometimes improvising when they are unable to obtain key ingredients for their meals. Uniquely Guyanese foods like cassareep, the brown flavoring sauce used to make pepperpot; homemade pepper sauces; saltfish; and even Guyanese rum, which is used to make black cake (a dark fruitcake eaten at Christmastime or used as wedding cake), are some of the items that Guyanese-Americans often go to great lengths to obtain. Although expatriate Guyanese continue to cook Guyanese foods because they are accustomed to eating them, many also use food to reconstruct a home abroad, create a community, and establish ethnic boundaries that separate them from West Indians and other groups in America.

African-Guyanese-Americans prepare all types of Guyanese foods, but during African-centered rituals they make a concerted effort to prepare foods they regard as "African foods." While African foods are prepared at traditional *kweh-kweh* in the United States, Come to My Kwe-Kwe opens the door, as it were, to the entire village of Guyanese. Moreover, in this new context, food becomes a symbol of Africanness, Guyaneseness, and the diversity of identities reflected in the secondary African-Guyanese diaspora in the United States; as David Sutton notes, "objects can shift levels of identity when experienced in new contexts, becoming a symbol not just of home or local place, but of countries or perhaps regions" (2001, 74). Moreover, unlike traditional *kweh-kweh* in the United States, where the bride's and groom's nations prepare the food, at Come to My Kwe-Kwe the standards of preparation are evaluated not only based on the established reputation of the cook or the village in Guyana from which the cook came but also by the Food and Drug Administration, the US Department of Agriculture, and other organizations in the United States. Each year, the Folk Festival Committee of the Guyana Cultural Association (GCA) chooses the vendor that sells the food at Come to My Kwe-Kwe. Claire Goring, the cultural director of the GCA in New York City and executive director of the Guyana Arts and Cultural Center, explained that vendors are asked to prepare foods similar to those served at traditional *kweh-kweh* in Guyana as well as other cuisines that speak to the theme of the year's Folk Festival (personal communication, November 28, 2018). Throughout the evening, attendees climb the flight of stairs and file past the rows of foil pans and large plastic containers that hold various cuisines, making purchases and offering unsolicited commentary on the dishes, based largely on their past experiences and preferences. At Come to My Kwe-Kwe, food becomes the vehicle by which African-Guyanese reassert their Africanness and Guyaneseness, recall past experiences, and reaffirm the ties that bind them.

Come to My Kwe-Kwe food allows African-Guyanese to engage in gustatory nostalgia (Roy 2002; Manekar 2002; Ray 2004) by symbolically transporting them to specific geographic spaces in Guyana, past experiences, and individuals with whom they shared food and

Figure 2.2: An assortment of "Guyanese foods" sold at the 2018 Come to My Kwe-Kwe: *channa* (top left); fish cakes and fried fish (bottom left); black pudding (blood sausage) (top right); and *pholourie* (bottom right); Brooklyn, 2018.

by helping them recall similar foods they previously consumed (Sutton 2001, 9). Food is one of the ways that displaced members of the secondary African-Guyanese diaspora reconstruct a sense of belonging, of home. Psyche Williams-Forson argues that food is a powerful symbol of communication, because it "conveys messages about where we come from, who we are as individuals, and how we think and feel at any given moment" (2012, 139). Each time they consume cookup rice, *conkee*, chicken feet, *souse*, and other Guyanese foods, they recall previous instances when they ate such foods, and each subsequent consumption; as Mary Douglas notes, food helps to recall other foods (1971, 67). Moreover, because eating is a communal experience at Come to My Kwe-Kwe, eating certain foods also facilitates the recollection of persons with whom the food was consumed in the past (Sutton 2001; Counihan 2002; Counihan 2004). Very often, as African-Guyanese eat the foods purchased at Come to My Kwe-Kwe, they comment on the way specific individuals from their past used to prepare the same cuisines. Mothers, grandmothers, and other women (Holtzman 2006, 176–80) are often referenced during the reminiscence that pervades Come to My Kwe-Kwe, because women were, and still are, the principal cooks in the Guyanese home and at traditional *kweh-kweh* rituals. By consuming Guyanese foods, participants are also symbolically transported to the villages and communities where they would have habitually consumed these foods and formed relationships. Food serves as a catalyst for remembering, even among members of the *affinal* and *procreated* segments of the African-Guyanese diaspora in the United States, who may have never physically experienced Guyana but who live in households where Guyanese foods are often prepared and consumed. Sutton argues that "food's memory power derives in part from synesthesia, which I take to mean the synthesis or crossing of experiences from different sensory registers (i.e., taste, smell, hearing)" (2001, 17). Thus, by consuming "*kweh-kweh* foods" and other Guyanese foods, African-Guyanese-Americans reaffirm group connections by recalling previous experiences and relationships and creating a symbolic link between the past and the present, and even between the living and the dead (Sutton 2001; Mintz 2003).

Another crucial role that food serves for African-Guyanese-Americans is to bind them to each other. Even though the Come to My Kwe-Kwe audience is often diverse, the African roots of the celebration are central and visible. Linder Keller Brown and Kay Mussell argue: "Foodways bind individuals together, define the limits of the group's outreach and identity, distinguish in-group from out-group, serve as a medium of inter-group communication, celebrate cultural cohesion, and provide a context for performance of group rituals" (1984, 5). As participants eat Guyanese foods, they find commonality based on their Africanness, their Guyaneseness, and their "otherness" in the United States. However, many of the foods sold at Come to My Kwe-Kwe are also eaten by other West Indians and people of African descent in New York City. Thus, it becomes imperative that the Guyanese versions of these cuisines be distinct in their taste and appearance to meet the community's perceived notion of authenticity. For instance, many other Caribbean countries prepare a "rice a peas" dish, which some also call "cookup rice"; however, Guyanese often argue that they can tell if the meal was prepared by a Guyanese national or someone else, based on the combination of spices used and the appearance of the meal. Gastronomic authenticity is here viewed from a temporal perspective; it "is roughly synonymous with traditional and is, thus, permeated by history, which determines how a recipe changes over time" (Weiss 2011, 76). Therefore, at Come to My Kwe-Kwe, eating Guyanese foods transcends nourishment, and remembrance and serves as a means of actively policing the ethnic boundaries established through food (Richards-Greaves 2013). Even though several "African" foods are usually served at Come to My Kwe-Kwe, all African-Guyanese-Americans come with their individual expectations based on personal preferences and even the manner in which they were previously exposed to traditional *kweh-kweh*. Thus, some attendees argue that for Come to My Kwe-Kwe to be "real" or authentic, the menu must include cookup rice, *conkee*, *metemgee*, and foods they regard as "African." While some of the foods—like *metemgee*, which is made with coconut milk and spoils easily—are sometimes excluded from the menu because they are not economically viable options for the vendors, they continue to be requested by African-Guyanese who regard authenticity as oldness or connectedness to the past (Hobsbawm 1983; Theodossopoulos 2013, 348). Even though African-influenced foods may be excluded from the menu, however, by requesting them every year, reminiscing about their presence on the traditional *kweh-kweh* menu, and thereby connecting them to authenticity, African-Guyanese-Americans ensure that those foods remain a part of the Come to My Kwe-Kwe menu, albeit symbolically. Come to My Kwe-Kwe allows African-Guyanese-Americans not only to reaffirm the boundaries of Guyaneseness but to reestablish the culinary ethnic boundaries that mark their African heritage and situate them in the United States.

It is important to note that while many African-Guyanese-Americans value or crave Guyanese foods, an increasing number of them have a more complicated relationship with traditional *kweh-kweh* foods. In an analogous manner, Krishnendu Ray observes that Bengali migrants in the United States have also modified their food consumption patterns, particularly breakfasts, due to diverse factors, including "convenience, pressures of time, and changing taste" (2004, 49). For some African-Guyanese, living in the United

States for an extended period has affected their food values, taste, and even their diet. For instance, some African-Guyanese do not consume foods at Come to My Kwe-Kwe because the ritual is held late in the evening and the foods served are heavy, starchy, and sometimes fried. Thus, while they may still enjoy cookup rice, *souse*, or black pudding on a regular basis, they may forego eating these foods late in the evening as a means of embracing healthier eating habits. Some also consume certain foods but reject other cuisines they grew up eating and enjoying. A few attendees at Come to My Kwe-Kwe I spoke with lamented the fact that they grew up eating and enjoying gizzards, liver, and other organ meats as well as animal parts like cows' tongues, feet, stomach, and testicles, but as they got older, they became repulsed by such foods. Thus, some may view *conkee* and white pudding nostalgically but do not purchase or consume it. Many African-Guyanese-Americans also forego certain foods because of dietary choices they have made. For instance, an increasing number of them have begun reducing their meat intake, or have become pescatarians (eating only fish), vegetarians, or vegans. For some, changes to their diet is a way of managing conditions like diabetes and high blood pressure, while for others it is about preventing diseases. Thus, while Come to My Kwe-Kwe allows African-Guyanese-Americans to revisit traditional *kweh-kweh* foods, these cuisines cannot fully accommodate the complex and changing dietary needs of this heterogeneous secondary diaspora.

Conclusion

This chapter has explored the crucial role that food plays in the African-Guyanese community. More importantly, it has attempted to demonstrate how migration and a changing African-Guyanese community affect perceptions, preparation, and consumption of "Guyanese food" at the Come to My Kwe-Kwe ritual in New York City. Encompassed by the term "Guyanese food" are a plethora of cuisines that reflect the diversity of the Guyanese population, processes of acculturation, and New World innovations. Thus, for example, African *fufu*, Amerindian pepperpot, East Indian *pholourie*, Chinese fried rice, and European black pudding are all Guyanese foods. While Guyanese foods generally reflect the racial or ethnic origins of the Guyanese people, they are also used instrumentally to negotiate and articulate a wide range of values and identities including class, gender, religion, and nationality. The identities negotiated through food are often situational in that the meanings attached to food can change based on the context of preparation and consumption. Thus, for example, African-Guyanese may prepare and consume cookup rice at a wake because it is a relatively inexpensive one-pot meal that can feed large numbers of people; however, they may also consume the same cookup rice, made with black-eyed peas, on Old Year's Night because the black-eyed peas symbolize the wealth and overall good luck they hope to achieve in the coming year. Moreover, at African-centered rituals and celebrations, cookup rice may serve as a symbol of African heritage and a means of paying homage to African ancestors.

Come to My Kwe-Kwe is a crucial space where African-Guyanese use food (and local beverages) strategically to say who they are in contradistinction to other Guyanese ethnics. As they prepare a wide range of Guyanese foods and local beverages to feed the revelers, they ensure that *conkee*, cookup rice, *metemgee*, *fufu*, and other foods they regard as "African" are prominent on the menu. In this ritual context, food feeds not only the living but also the dead (Kalčik 1984, 48), who, in African and African-Guyanese belief systems, continue to reside among the living and partake in their daily lives. Some of the African-centered meals served at traditional *kweh-kweh* and Come to My Kwe-Kwe are prepared with crops that were domesticated and cultivated on the African continent such as okra, black-eyed peas, and rice, but many others such as plantains, cassava, and other tubers used to make *metemgee* were domesticated in other parts of the world and then diffused to the African continent. In other instances, "African foods" encompass meals that emerged during slavery, which are made with innards and other parts of animals that were traditionally discarded by enslavers. These New World creations are also categorized as ancestral foods because they have been passed down from one generation to the next for centuries and, like African-American "soul food" (Baraka 1966; Miller 2013), have become staples in the African-Guyanese community. Thus, the criteria for categorizing "African food" at traditional *kweh-kweh* and Come to My Kwe-Kwe seem to transcend the origins of crops and include their use in creating popular cuisines on the African continent and in the African diaspora.

When African-Guyanese migrate to the United States, they, like other Guyanese, continue to cook Guyanese foods, but they must sometimes go to great lengths to obtain the ingredients necessary to prepare such meals. In some instances, Guyanese bring back their ingredients when they travel abroad; or, they may ask friends or relatives in large urban areas in the United States or "back home" to ship ingredients to them. When these measures are not feasible, many improvise by using ingredients that are similar. Sometimes, improvisation is not only about lack of ingredients but also about accommodating the changing lives of African-Guyanese-Americans, many of whom work outside the home and may not have the time or leisure needed to prepare some of the meals. Thus, for instance, substituting canned coconut milk for the milk of grated dried coconuts is one of the ways that African-Guyanese-Americans may enjoy cookup rice while foregoing a lengthy cooking process. Sometimes, the changes to Guyanese foods are also due to a deliberate effort on the part of African-Guyanese-Americans who modify certain cuisines to accommodate their changing tastes, health concerns, and other factors. Thus, for example, African-Guyanese who have become vegetarians forego meat in their foods, while those who are diabetic may limit the types and quantities of foods they eat as well as the time of day they consume them. Such changes to Guyanese food preparation and consumption, whether incidental or deliberate, are further facilitating changes in ritual settings where Guyanese foods and, specifically, African-centered foods are served.

During Come to My Kwe-Kwe, African-Guyanese of the secondary diaspora (*migrated, procreated,* and *affinal*) reaffirm their Africanness and Guyanese heritage, in tandem with American identities, in a public forum that gels them to each other, even as they accommodate and distinguish themselves from the strangers among them. Even though foods at Come to My Kwe-Kwe must be purchased, the menu reflects that of an average traditional *kweh-kweh* as well as the Americanized (fusion) tastes of the secondary African-Guyanese diaspora. As African-Guyanese-Americans survey the diverse cuisines displayed at Come to My Kwe-Kwe, they look for foods that remind them of the traditional *kweh-kweh*, of people, of experiences, of "home." As they consume Guyanese foods, African-Guyanese also identify the "African" foods that help them demarcate Come to My Kwe-Kwe as "we ting." The foods at Come to My Kwe-Kwe are, therefore, not only for nourishment and nostalgia but also for policing the ethnic boundaries of the African-Guyanese community. Thus, the authenticity of Come to My Kwe-Kwe foods is based not only on how closely they resemble foods "back home" but on how the Guyanese foods, even in their improvised forms, serve the diverse secondary African-Guyanese diaspora and their changing needs in United States (Abarca 2004, 9). Sylvia Ferrero observed that Mexican restaurants in the United States were transformed to facilitate community building and renegotiation of ethnic identity by serving foods that signify "home cooking" and thus bind patrons to the homeland (2002, 194–220). In an equivalent manner, African-Guyanese-Americans consume African-centered cuisines with an unmatched gratification and sometimes a sadness that reaffirm the ties that connect them to their fellow African-Guyanese at Come to My Kwe-Kwe as well as those with whom they form an imagined community through food. More importantly, the Guyanese foods at Come to My Kwe-Kwe serve to connect African-Guyanese-Americans to Guyana as well as to a more distant African homeland.

Recipe: Black-Eyed Peas Cookup Rice

Ingredients:
1 small dried coconut (grated)/1 can of coconut milk
1 pint of long-grain parboiled rice
3 lbs. meat (1 lb. pork, 1lb. beef, 1lb. tripe)
1 pint of dried black-eyed peas

1 small onion (finely chopped)

1 plumb tomato (diced)

2 green onions/scallions (finely chopped)

2 cloves of garlic (finely chopped)

Other "fresh" seasonings: thyme, celery (finely chopped/blended)

2 lemons/1 cup of lemon juice

2 bouillon cubes

2 tbsp butter/margarine (optional)

2 tbsp browning/soy sauce (for color)

Other (optional) condiments: all-purpose seasoning, black pepper, cumin, basil, red pepper

Directions:

Wash peas; soak overnight; boil or pressure cook with minimal salt until half-cooked or parboiled.

Wash pork, beef, and tripe using lemon or lemon juice; rinse.

Season meats with chopped/blended fresh seasonings, all-purpose seasoning, black pepper, red pepper, cumin, and basil. Meats can be seasoned and refrigerated overnight.

Sauté onion, tomato, garlic, and a portion of fresh seasonings.

Add seasoned meats and browning or soy sauce to sautéed condiments; stew together until meats are half cooked.

Combine parboiled peas, stewed (half-cooked) meats, coconut milk, bouillon cubes, and butter/margarine. Bring to a boil for about 15 minutes, then add condiments/seasonings to taste.

Cover pot, lower heat, and let cook for about 30 minutes or until rice is soft.

Serve with fried yellow plantains, fried fish, salad, and/or achar.

3

Wipin', Winin', and Wukkin'
Constructing, Contesting, and Displaying Gender Values

It tek face powder fuh get de man, but baking powder fuh
keep de man
GUYANESE PROVERB

Teeth and tongue must bite
GUYANESE PROVERB

*After a fifteen-minute intermission, dancer Dr. Rose October-Edun
entered the performance space and called out to the young woman
who would serve as the bride for the evening's second reenactment of
kweh-kweh. The performers quickly gathered together and executed
the meeting at the gate, followed by the buying of the bride. Shortly
thereafter, the young woman left the ganda (performance circle), and
Rose called out to her to return. Once the bride was in the circle, Rose
shouted, "We gaffa wipe up" (We have to wipe the floors). Rose left the
circle and quickly returned with an aluminum pail and a white "floor
cloth" (rag used to wipe the floor). She looked at the young woman,
dropped the cloth on the floor, and said, "Come, show me wuh yuh
could do. Wipe!" Almost instinctively, the young woman put her right*

Figure 3.1: Acting bride no. 2 is ordered to wipe the floors to demonstrate domestication. She uses a bucket and "floor cloth," traditionally used in many Guyanese households. Come to My Kwe-Kwe, Brooklyn, August 29, 2014. Photo by Gillian Richards-Greaves.

foot on the rag and began wiping the floor with her foot. The crowd erupted in laughter as Rose expressed disappointment and instructed the bride to "go down pun yuh knees!" (get on your knees). But before the bride had a chance to follow orders, Rose got down on her hands and knees and demonstrated how she wanted the bride to wipe the floor. She then ordered the bride to "wipe, wipe!" As the bride got down on her hands and knees and started wiping the floor, the drummers began to beat the drums. Rose then ordered the bride to "squeeze that cloth in the bucket now! You gaffa know how fuh squeeze" (You have to know how to squeeze). At one point, the bride began gyrating on her hands and knees and wiping the floor, inspiring laughter and applause from the audience. The interaction between the bride and the community of attendees continued throughout much of the evening as she was called upon to demonstrate various attributes of a "proper" Guyanese woman.

Introduction

Every society has established gender values, which are reinforced by gender roles and the gender stereotypes associated with them (Friedl

1975, 6; Ortner and Whitehead 1981, 6–9; Bourque and Warren 1987, Lorber 2003, 55). As Judith Butler argued: "The very injunction to be given gender takes place through discursive routes: to be a good mother, to be a heterosexually desirable object, to be a fit worker, in sum, to signify a multiplicity of guarantees in response to a variety of different demands all at once" (1990, 145). In the Guyanese community, there are established gendered behaviors that men and women are expected to exhibit to be regarded as appropriately socialized and, ultimately, "marriage material." There are three overarching gendered categories in the Guyanese community—male, female, and homosexual—but only heterosexual men and women are deemed marriageable. Consequently, only heterosexual marriages currently have traditional *kweh-kweh* and Come to My Kwe-Kwe rituals associated with them. In addition to being heterosexual, however, one must also demonstrate that he is a "real" man or that she is a "good" or "proper" woman before being deemed marriageable by the larger Guyanese community. Within each Guyanese ethnic group, overarching Guyanese gender values are further shaped, interpreted, and articulated in unique ways and for diverse functions.

Among African-Guyanese, gender values are shaped by historical and cultural factors such as slavery, plantation and village living, interethnic contact, religion, and migration (Jones 1985; White 1985; Collins 2009). Although slavery was in many ways destructive to African cultures, African-Guyanese have retained many cultural values and have transmitted them from one generation to the next through processes of enculturation. Over the course of centuries and multiple infusions of newer African slaves, interactions with other ethnic groups in Guyana, and exposure to multiple religions, African-Guyanese carved out gendered values that were grounded in the African homeland, yet often influenced by or shrouded in the values of other ethnic groups and religions. Thus, in the primary African diaspora in Guyana, many of the gendered values that existed on the African continent continued to thrive among the slave population. These African-centered values are often highlighted in traditional *kweh-kweh* songs and dances but are uniquely reinterpreted, contested, or sometimes discarded altogether in Come to My Kwe-Kwe celebrations in the United States.

Thus, while Come to My Kwe-Kwe is a time for jollification and reedu-cation of the African-Guyanese community, as it also serves a space for the negotiation of Guyanese gender values.

This chapter examines *rediasporization* as a gendered process. It interrogates the ways that African-Guyanese-Americans articulate, construct, and reject Guyanese gendered values through music, dance, and other ritual performances at Come to My Kwe-Kwe celebrations. While gendering is a multilayered process, this chapter specifically focuses on the ways that notions of "real man" and "good" or "proper woman" are negotiated and displayed in Come to My Kwe-Kwe rituals through performances that address domestication,[1] economic provi-dence, and sexuality broadly construed.[2] I argue that the characteristic innovative performances at Come to My Kwe-Kwe, which include elaborate dramatizations and improvisations of traditional ritual con-tent, highlight overt and subtle differences between the gender values of the primary African diaspora in Guyana and those of the second-ary, *rediasporized* diaspora in the United States. I further contend that close examinations of the connections between gendered values in precolonial Africa and preemancipation Guyana will reveal persis-tent underlying themes and structures of African-Guyanese systems of gendering as well as the complicated process of *rediasporization*.

Gendered Ideals in the African-Guyanese Community

In the African-Guyanese community, gender is an ascribed role one is given at birth as well as an achieved identity, established through sanctioned behaviors and performances. In this gender system, which is composed of three overarching categories (male, female, and homosexual), men are regarded as the first sex and overwhelmingly occupy the highest political and socioeconomic strata of society.[3] Women, on the other hand, are regarded as the second or weaker sex and are viewed as inherently subservient to men. Homosexuals and other genders are generally viewed as outli-ers and social misfits who exist outside of the parameters of what constitutes "normal." Gender normalcy is, however, accomplished not only by one's adherence to the male-female dichotomy but also through the attainment of the goal of "real" man or "good" or "proper" woman. While there are observable differences in the ways that African-Guyanese in the primary diaspora in Guyana and secondary diaspora in the United States express themselves as gendered beings, some deep-rooted gender values continue to be pervasive and observable in traditional *kweh-kweh* and Come to My Kwe-Kwe.

The Economics of "Real" Men

One of the principal gender roles that African-Guyanese men are expected to fill is that of provider or wage earner. Thus, a real man acquires and maintains employment, particularly before he takes a wife or starts a family. From the time they are very young, boys are often admonished by parents and clergy to work to become industrious men. Parental and pastoral (religious) advice is often reinforced with scripture, such as, "If a man will not work, he shall not eat" (2 Thessalonians 3:10, NIV) and "Anyone who does not provide for their relatives, and especially for their own household, has denied the faith and is worse than an unbeliever" (1 Timothy 5:8, NIV). In many instances, young men are taught a trade even when they are expected to obtain a college education that may not utilize those skills. Many parents teach their sons a trade, send them to a trade school, or have them serve as apprentices for seasoned craftsmen. In many instances, the apprenticeships begin even before a boy reaches primary school. Although the goal of learning a trade is to secure a job, men also often use their skills to earn money in addition to their regular salaries. While wage-earning work has practical value, it further contributes to the *domestic-public dichotomy* or the *private-public contrast* that distinguishes work done in the home from that in the outside world, such as political engagement, trade, warfare, and, of course, wage-earning work (Kottak 2015, 180). Women tend to have greater influence in domestic spheres, while men engage the "outside world" to a greater degree; thus, the domestic-public dichotomy undergirds gender stratification in the African-Guyanese community and the Guyanese community at large (Ortner and Whitehead 1981, 4).

Being a wage earner is such an important male gender role that marital advice in traditional *kweh-kweh* often addresses arduous work and the consequences of financial instability. Before the *kweh-kweh* even begins, elders in the community often interrogate the groom about his preparation for marriage by asking questions like, "Bai, yuh get yuh wuk bench yet?" (Boy, do you already have your workbench?). The term "work bench" is a double entendre for a carpenter's principal workspace as well as the marital bed. In the past, carpentry was one of the first trades that young men were taught; moreover, many men had the responsibility of constructing the principal furniture in their homes, particularly their beds. They would have accomplished such tasks with the help of other men in the community, as was the practice in Africa and during slavery (Smith [1953] 2017; Bush 1990, 107). Although young Guyanese men today have the option of furnishing their homes with store-bought items, self-sufficiency and economic sustenance of the family continue to be core values of male gender socialization in Guyana.

The importance of economic stability on the part of men is also referenced in *kweh-kweh* songs like "Oman Ah Heavy Load" (Women Are Heavy Burdens) (example 3.1). In this song, women are depicted as burdensome, saprophytic creatures who use men and discard them when they are no longer financially stable. While the overt message of the song is desertion due to financial dearth, infidelity is also indexed. The phrase "gwan yuh stchupid man" (go away, foolish man) implies that financial insecurity compels women to seek out more lucrative romantic relationships and to offer their "goods and services" to "real" or "sensible" men who can provide for them adequately. The song objectifies and trivializes women but also highlights an important aspect of African-Guyanese male enculturation whereby real men are supposed to work and provide for their families.

Example 3.1: "Oman Ah Heavy Load"

Creolese: *Oman Ah Heavy Load*
Call: Oman ah heavy load

Response:	Oman ah heavy load/Uh huh
Call:	When yuh money done
Response:	When yuh money done/Uh huh
Call:	Gwan yuh stchupid man
Response:	Gwan yuh stchupid man

English:	*Women Are Heavy Burdens*
Call:	Women are heavy burdens
Response:	Women are heavy burdens
Call:	When you have no money
Response:	When you have no money
Call:	Women say, "Go away stupid man"
Response:	Women say, "Go away stupid man"

African-Guyanese men of the secondary diaspora in the United States (particularly of the migrated diaspora) often express frustration over what they regard as their emasculation. Thus, many are compelled to reevaluate what it means to be a man, and that often involves interacting with women much differently than they did or would in Guyana. This obliges many to modify their cultural schema to fit into new parameters. While economic providence for the family continues to be a requirement of real manhood, it is not as pivotal as it is in Guyana. In the United States, for example, the concept of the breadwinner is complicated by the fact that many women work outside of the home and, in some instances, earn bigger salaries than their male counterparts (Lourenço and Cachado 2012, 55). In some instances, women become the sole wage earners when their husbands or romantic partners lose their jobs or when they are unable or unwilling to find or maintain steady employment. Also, some couples are forced to make employment decisions to save money, which may result in men occupying the traditional female role of "housewife." Scholars like Maxine Margolis (2000) have extensively discussed the ways that attitudes and values regarding gendered work often change in response to changes in economic needs. During the world wars, for example, women entered the workforce in factories and other sectors of society after men were

drafted into war, thereby dispelling the notion of women's inherent unfitness for physical labor and economic productivity (Stoler
1977). These factors affect how African-Guyanese men—who are
expected to be heads of households through wage earning—view
their masculinity. I have discovered that many men find the earlier
phases of such transitions to be emasculating and embarrassing, and
thus many present false narratives about their employment status.
Some explanations I have heard unemployed men give include "run-
ning a business from home," "going to college full time," "working
nights," and not being "straight" (having legal immigration status)
in the United States.

Older African-Guyanese men, particularly those who had jobs
that paid well or held high sociopolitical status in Guyana, often
seem most adversely affected by these changes. In addition to fab-
ricating excuses for why they are unemployed or underemployed,
many give up trying to secure employment altogether, or reject the
archaic standard of the "real man as economic provider." While some
have relinquished control and settled into economically subservient
roles, others have returned home to Guyana to relive their glory
days, sometimes only symbolically, through stories, memories, and
interpersonal relationships.

African-Guyanese-Americans of the secondary (migrated) diaspora who remain in the United States or are otherwise part of the
secondary diaspora are often compelled to deal with established
ideals of the "real man" and the fracture that results from the reality of living in the United States. For many men of the secondary
(migrated) diaspora, also, these new gender dynamics often prove
too oppositional to what they regard as normal; thus, this fracture
in values often results in the dissolution of marriages and romantic relationships. This is not to assume that all African-Guyanese
men hold archaic or stereotypical views of women. In fact, many
African-Guyanese men, particularly younger ones of the secondary (procreated) diaspora and those who have had sustained
exposure to Western values, tend to have more progressive views
on gender. This is also not to minimize or overlook the fact that
many Guyana-born African-Guyanese women, much like their

foreign-born counterparts, worked outside of the home while they were in Guyana but were still expected to fulfill traditional domestic roles. As Pat Ellis argues: "Caribbean women of all classes and races, irrespective of marital status, accept responsibility for child-care and child rearing. Although full-time mothering and house-minding might at one time have been seen to be the ideal, it has never been the norm" (1986, 9). In the United States, however, the stigma often attached to the working woman who earns more than her husband or male counterpart or who is financially independent is greatly diminished, at least in the larger American society. This change in gendered realities, which seems to empower women beyond what some perceive to be their inherent status, often fuels discord in the larger African-Guyanese community. In some instances, also, the economic empowerment of women results in more than a role reversal of wage earner, as many women use their status as wage workers to demean, dominate, and abuse men.

The economics of gender in the African-Guyanese-American community is often put on display at Come to My Kwe-Kwe celebrations, where personal views, Guyanese values, and American realities are simultaneously articulated through music and other ritual enactments. For instance, I observed the ways that attendees at the 2007 Come to My Kwe-Kwe uniquely dealt with this reality. During a brief break, as attendees were preparing for the beginning of the next song, one of the men standing close to the musicians' corner stated, "We gaffa sing 'Oman Ah Heavy Load'" (We have to sing "Women Are Heavy Burdens"). After making that comment, he began singing, "When yuh money done, gwan, yuh stchupid man" (When you're out of money, they say, "Go away, stupid man"). Other men chimed in with their own improvisations: "Gwan, yuh beze man," and "Gwan, yuh suck man."⁴ Upon hearing the men's exchange, individuals standing around the area began laughing, and one of the men exclaimed, "Nah me, nah me, I believe in equal rights; fifty-fifty; me ain tekkin care uh no woman." Other men chimed in the conversation, arguing that, in this new era, gendered responsibilities have shifted; thus, if women "wan' play man" (usurp the place of men), they should be financially responsible for themselves. Although many of the men are sincere in their statements regarding economic contribution and gender equality, I suspect that an even greater percentage of them are using "female empowerment" to escape from a standard they are unwilling or unable to uphold. Interestingly, I have heard similar sentiments expressed by African-Guyanese-American women, especially of the affinal and procreated subcategories, who do not view a man's money as providence or love but as symbolic chains that limit their ability to excel and that endanger their lives. Thus, while they may still embrace the ideal of "man as economic provider," they also view that providence as a double-edged sword.

Domesticating "Proper" Women

An African-Guyanese woman's worth is overwhelmingly judged by her domestic abilities. During Come to My Kwe-Kwe and traditional *kweh-kweh*, the bride is reminded through song and dance that a proper woman cooks for her family and keeps a clean house (Counihan 1999, 13), among other responsibilities. This is not to suggest that men are not domesticated, since many African-Guyanese men are taught (or, as a survival mechanism, learn on their own) to cook, clean house, and do other types of "women's work." For men, domestication is not a gender requirement but a bonus. In fact, young boys who appear to be overly domestic, especially on their own accord, often have their masculinity questioned. Domestication is, however, a crucial evaluator of the good or proper Guyanese woman. From a tender age, girls are taught how to cook, clean house, wash (do laundry), and iron clothes, by modeling older women. Before the Atlantic slave trade, many African women experienced some of the same atrocities in Africa that they would later experience in the primary diaspora in Guyana and elsewhere in the New World. In Africa, women were often subjected to physical and emotional abuse by men, senior wives, sister wives, legal wives, and even other slaves who might have owned them (Robertson 1997, 226). In many instances, women were able to temporarily "restore" their humanity, as it were, by bearing children who were then regarded as freeborn and counted toward the lineage of their father (often the slave owner) (Harms 1997; Strobel 1997, 120). The coping mechanisms slave women used in the primary diaspora in Guyana, and later in the secondary diaspora in the United States, were often transmitted by their ancestors, who were often themselves the victims of intra-African slavery. In many instances, understanding African-Guyanese gender values requires delving beneath the surface of the frivolities at Come to My Kwe-Kwe and examining ritual expressions through the lenses of pre- and postcolonial African traditions, cultural practices of other Guyanese ethnics, religion, and much more. More importantly, to understand how African-Guyanese gendered values have changed, we must also examine what has remained; in the case of women, much of that remnant is intricately connected to the home.

Cooking is one of the principal features of domestication that Guyanese women are expected to master before marriage. Many African-Guyanese girls begin learning how to cook before they enter primary school at around six years old and continue to hone those skills throughout their lives. The skills learned in the home are often refined in the classroom, as most primary and high schools in Guyana include instruction in food and nutrition as part of the academic curricula.[5] Thus, by the time they are teenagers, many young women would have mastered the art of cooking simple and complex cuisines, which are critiqued by relatives, classmates, and other members of the community. As I have mentioned elsewhere, the feedback that women receive is often in the form of ridicule and taunts, such as, "This roti shapes like the map of Guyana" (is misshapen); "Her bakes are hard like the stones that David killed Goliath with"; and "This tastes like 'cookup friend' or 'distant cousin,'" that is, it pales in comparison to the authentic dish (Richards-Greaves 2012). Regardless of the insults or adulation that young women receive, however, many continue to hone their cooking skills with the goal of, one day, feeding their family and pleasing their husband (men).

In an interview, traditional *kweh-kweh* captains (tutors) Lio Britton and "Bertie" Carter discussed some of the domestic advice they offer brides through *kweh-kweh* songs:

Creolese

Don't worry with ahm. Yuh gotta care this man.

You gon marry tomorrow; don't worry with . . . yuh gotta care
    this man.

Yuh must care he; you must love he; do everything fuh he;

Don' worry wid yuh mother; don' worry wid yuh neighbor . . . this
    is your man,

Yuh mekkin' life; love him, care him.

English

Don't worry or stress him. You must take care of this man.

You're going to marry tomorrow; don't worry with . . . you must
    take care of this man.

You must take care of him. You must love him. Do everything
    for him.

Don't worry with your mother. Don't worry with your neighbor.
    This is your man;

You're creating a life together. Love him. Care for him.

Domestication is such an important evaluator of gendered value in
the African-Guyanese community that it is celebrated in the popular Come to My Kwe-Kwe (and *kweh-kweh*) song "Send She Back"
(example 3.2). This song instructs the groom to return an undomesticated wife to her natal home and her nation. While "Send She
Back" is addressed to the groom, it is the undomesticated wife who
is objectified and treated as a defective product that the owner (her
husband) has the right to accept or return at will. As it was, and
still is in many indigenous African marriages on the continent of
Africa, sending a woman back to her natal home is regarded as one
of the greatest insults to the character and value of the bride and
her nation. There was also a period in Guyana's history when men
sent away wives who were undomesticated, unchaste, or regarded
as "useless" in any other way (DeVault 1997, 184).[6] While this practice is not as common as it was forty years ago, around 1980 and
earlier, it still persists. Therefore, in some households, "Send She
Back" provides direct instruction to the groom as well as warnings

to potential brides of their impending fate if they lack domestication. In discussing the content of "Send She Back" and its historical application to Guyana, "Bertie" Carter stated the following:

> And then you have some tunes would say, if the young lady isn't prepared for marriage: if she's not a good housekeeper, and she can't cook and thing and so on; well, she gon gotta go back home!

When a man does not fulfill his responsibilities, the unfulfilled wife and larger society have several weapons in their arsenal to compel such a man to do what is right. Shame and gossip are two of the most basic mechanisms for dealing with a "lazy man" or one who is otherwise incompetent. The insults often begin with the wife, who complains about her husband's behavior before her nation and the larger community and sometimes openly chides him or "gives blow" (engages in infidelity). For example, in the traditional *kweh-kweh* song "Come Away, Oh," sung to the same melody as "Send She Back," the nation of bride advises her to leave her husband for a litany of offences, including "if he beat yuh" (if he beats you), "if he dick too small" (if his penis is too small or if he's impotent), and "if he don' wuk" (if he doesn't work).

Example 3.2: "Send She Back" (Send Her Back)

Creolese	*English*
Call: Send she back, oh	Call: Send her back, oh
Response: Send she back	Response: Send her back
Call: Send she back to she muddah	Call: Send her back to her mother
Response: Send she back	Response: Send her back
Call: If she can't cook	Call: If she can't cook
Response: Send she back	Response: Send her back
Call: If she can't wash	Call: If she can't wash (do the laundry)
Response: Send she back	Response: Send her back

Call: Send she back to she muddah	Call: Send her back to her mother
Response: Send she back	Response: Send her back
Call: Send she back to she muddah	Call: Send her back to her mother
Response: Send she back	Response: Send her back
Call: If she can't wine	Call: If she can't gyrate
Response: Send she back	Response: Send her back

"Send She Back" also references the importance of housekeeping in demarcating proper women from all others. The vignette at the beginning of this chapter offers humorous insight into the practice of wiping floors, one of several domesticated acts collectively regarded as housekeeping. Many of the homes in Guyana have wooden floors, which individuals clean by using a bucket of soapy water, a "floor cloth," a hard brush, and sometimes a scraper.[7] The process of wiping floors includes the following steps: wetting the floor with the soapy cloth, scrubbing it with a brush and scraper, rinsing it with a clean wet cloth, wringing the cloth dry, and then drying the floors. Wiping wooden floors using a bucket and floor cloth is an arduous and often painful task, especially when the house is large and located in a sandy area, such as the mining town of Linden. Even after the floors in these areas are swept clean, they often retain sand and other small particles, which cut into the knees. Properly wiping floors is one of the first chores young women are taught to do, even when they are as young as five years old. Understanding how to use a bucket and floor cloth in the Guyanese community is generally regarded as common sense. Nevertheless, when interrogated further, we observe that common sense is not that common, particularly since cleaning the floors with a bucket and floor cloth is a foreign concept for many young Guyanese of the affinal and procreated segments of the secondary diaspora in the United States. Thus, instead of "common sense," I prefer to use the term "life sense," which refers to the body of knowledge and expertise one acquires from growing up in a particular culture during a specific period of time.

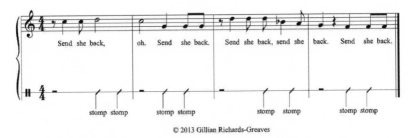

Figure 3.2. Transcription of the song "Send She Back." Transcription by Gillian Richards-Greaves.

Wiping floors is also one of the primary means by which mothers and other adults evaluate a young woman's cleanliness, and thus her readiness for marriage. Adult women often give detailed instructions to young children on how to "wipe floors" and, after a child has finished, conduct a detailed inspection of the cleaned area. When adults deem an area not properly cleaned, they instruct children to rewipe the floors. As a young girl growing up in Guyana, I hated wiping floors, because tiny grains of sand would grate into my knees and cause me much pain. Moreover, kneeling on a rag or other padded surface often proved cumbersome and slowed down the wiping process. Thus, in many instances, I would perform an act known as "dry wiping," which is done by simply wiping the floor with a damp cloth. Engaging in dry wiping also allowed me to finish my chores quickly, albeit haphazardly, so that I could tend to my own personal matters. In more instances than I care to remember, the older women in my family lamented my laziness and warned me that "man gon beat yuh" (your husband will physically abuse you) and "you gon geh blow" (your husband will cheat on you). Many young Guyanese women have received similar warnings from older women who sought to simultaneously warn and protect them.

Using one's feet to wipe the floor is just as egregious an error as dry wiping because it is regarded as a sign of laziness and a lack of domestication on the part of a woman.[8] Moreover, it reflects poorly on the mother and other adult women in a young woman's family, who are responsible for giving the child proper home training. The older women often say that a woman who is too lazy to "bend down and wipe floor" is a woman who is too nasty to be anyone's wife. Thus, when Dr. Rose October-Edun ordered the second bride at the 2014 Come to My Kwe-Kwe celebration to "go down pun yuh knees," she was referencing a key aspect of Guyanese home training.

While the second bride was said to be Guyana-born, she is part of the migrated subcategory of the secondary diaspora in the United States; thus, she would more than likely use a mop instead of a floor cloth and stand rather than kneel if or when she cleaned floors. Nevertheless, in demonstrating the "proper" way to clean floors and in ordering the bride to follow suit, Rose and the Guyanese community were making a statement about their cultural values and reestablishing the boundaries of womanhood in the Guyanese community. Unlike the Guyana-based bride, however, for whom domestic values like wiping floors may be more relevant in deciphering potential "wife material," it merely serves as commentary and fodder for the American-based bride in the Come to My Kwe-Kwe setting. This is not to suggest that Guyanese-American women of the migrated secondary diaspora reject Guyanese domestic values in their entirety, but that they often take advantage of the plethora of other options available to them in the United States, including the option to modify or discard the values of their parents and grandparents. Moreover, in the context of Come to My Kwe-Kwe, where reenactment, jest, jollification, and community building are core objectives, couples tend to accommodate even the most arcane or ridiculous values.

While "Send She Back" is the community's way of instructing the groom and warning the bride, songs like "Me Go Wash Am" (I Will Wash It) allow the bride to demonstrate domestication and dedication to her husband by washing his clothes even under the worst circumstances. The lines "don' kay soapie nah deh" (even if there is no soap) and "don' kay mammy seh, 'no'" (even if my mom says, "don't do it") capture the stereotypical character of the proper (virtuous) woman. Moreover, this song also provides insight into the deep-rooted Guyanese gender value that women are responsible for the deportment of their entire family. Thus, for example, women are often blamed for the unkempt appearance of their husband or children, even when the children are adults.

Example 3.3: "Buy Me Lova Wan Shut"

Creolese: "Buy Me Lova Wan Shut"	*English*: "Buy My Lover a Shirt"
Call: Buy me lova wan shut	Call: Buy my lover a shirt
Response: Meh go wash am	Response: I will wash it
Call: Buy me lova wan shut	Call: Buy my lover a shirt
Response: Meh go wash am	Response: I will wash it
Call: Buy me lova wan shut	Call: Buy my lover a shirt
Don' kay soapie nah deh	Call: Even if there is no soap
Response: Meh go wash am	Response: I will wash it
Call: Don' kay soapie nah deh	Call: Even if there is no soap
Response: Meh go wash am	Response: I will wash it
Call: Don' kay soapie nah deh	Call: Even if there is no soap

Domestication and other gendered ideals in the African-Guyanese community are undergirded by religious values, particularly of the Christian faith, to which many African-Guyanese belong. Women are taught at home and in religious settings that they are the "weaker vessels" (1 Peter 3:7) and that their husbands are the kings and priests of the home. Therefore, they should submit themselves to their husbands and be their "help meet" (Genesis 2:18). Most young women, Christian and non-Christian, would have, at some point in their lives, been told: "Wives, submit yourselves to your own husbands as you do to the Lord. For the husband is the head of the wife as Christ is the head of the church, his body, of which he is the Savior" (Ephesians 5:22–23, NIV). While submission generally encompasses a woman's status and expected behavior in the home and society, the previously mentioned scripture is often used in the context of sex, cooking, and other forms of domestic "service," to quell verbal arguments and physical altercations.

African-Guyanese embrace gendered values of domestication to varying degrees and for diverse reasons. I have observed, however, that while there is a stark division between the attitudes of older and younger generations, the divisions are even more striking when religious values, and type or subcategory of diaspora, are deciding factors. In the primary African diaspora in Guyana, women are generally under the watchful eyes of a larger Guyanese community, which overwhelmingly supports the ideal of the domesticated woman as the proper woman. Even if they are not religious, Guyanese women would have been exposed to these gendered values at home, in public schools, in the media, and in every sphere of society. As such, their processes of enculturation would have included direct and indirect instruction as well as unsolicited advice on cooking, cleaning, submission, and other forms of domestication. Moreover, older women, who grew up in an era when women had less autonomy and who hold more traditional views on marriage, tend to adhere more firmly to established archaic views on a woman's place in society. Academic and economic opportunities and exposure to the larger world, however, often contribute to younger women's exercise of agency in their negotiations and expressions of gender in the Guyanese community. This is never a straightforward process, as many young women find themselves simultaneously in and out of the Guyanese community based on the choices they make from one moment to the next. As Judith Butler noted, "gender is a basically innovative affair, although it is quite clear that there are strict punishments for contesting the script by performing out of turn or through unwarranted improvisations" (1988, 531).

At Come to My Kwe-Kwe, for example, I have observed instances in which young women of the secondary diaspora used the opportunity to renegotiate gender values in the Guyanese community. In some instances, they improvised lyrics of songs to reflect their personal ideals on marriage, and on gender in general. In one memorable instance, I heard young women sing the refrain to "Me Go Wash Am" (I Will Wash It) as "Me nah go wash am" (I will not wash it), because they disagreed with the expressed gendered values they regarded as "stchupidness" (nonsense). The same young women argued that the hardships women are expected to endure in marriage stem from values from "the nineteenth century" or the "the Dark Ages." Floya Anthias states: "Women may be empowered by retaining home traditions, but they may also be quick to abandon them when they are no longer strategies of survival" (1998b, 571; also Bhachu 1988, 61–81). In her research among the Maroons of Suriname, Sally Price (1983; 1984) observed a similar phenomenon, whereby female singers presented their own songs to combat discrepancies between their own self-perceptions and others' views of them (1983, 468). Although the African-Guyanese community has rules some regard as oppressive, many young women often use the Come to My Kwe-Kwe space as a "vehicle both for catharsis and commentary in response to their position in a male-dominated society" (Auerbach 1989, 25). This is not to suggest that the older women agree with every sentiment expressed through *kweh-kweh* songs but that they are less inclined than young women to use the Come to My Kwe-Kwe celebration to make politically charged statements or stances.

Sexuality: Socializing Real Men and Proper Women

Sexual prowess is a crucial evaluator of manliness in the African-Guyanese community. One must demonstrate sexual prowess, often through promiscuous acts, or risk being labeled an anti-man (homosexual) or bewitched, or having one's masculinity otherwise questioned. From the time they are very young, boys learn that if they engage in multiple sexual liaisons at the same time, they could earn the label of "sweet boy." A "sweet boy" is a man who gains the attention and "services" of multiple women, partly by speaking artfully. A sweet boy also dresses attractively, carries himself confidently, speaks articulately (from a cultural perspective), and is regarded as sexually appealing. One's reputation of sexual proclivity and accomplishment is not necessarily based on proven facts but is often established by boasting. Even young men who are not sexually active or promiscuous often strive to be perceived as "sweet boys." This is because the larger Guyanese community generally places men into two divergent subcategories: real men and anti-men.

Even men who are married or are in committed romantic relationships are expected to demonstrate "signs of life," as it were, through acts of sexual prowess. It is not uncommon to hear Guyanese refer to married men who are not openly adulterous as being "under lock and key" (Oladeji 1988, 50). Sometimes, a man's commitment to his romantic partner is also regarded as the result of obeah or witchcraft. In the Guyanese community, many believe that a person can control others through witchcraft. While manipulation through witchcraft applies to all aspects of life, it is frequently referenced in romantic relationships. Moreover, while anyone can use obeah to achieve or maintain romantic relationships, men are often viewed as the victims of such relationships. This might be because women are generally regarded as the ones who have both the need and the means, particularly through food preparations, to engage in the sort of *contagious magic* required to "trap" a man.[9] This adversarial view of male-female relationships also indexes the larger societal view that women *need* men in order to achieve and demonstrate their worth as women, especially by becoming wives and mothers. Nevertheless, using obeah to explain or rationalize a man's fidelity often reflects the society's overarching view of manhood as being inherently linked to sexuality and, more specifically, to unrestrained sexual desires. Even in religious circles, there is less of a stigma attached to men's sexual behavior and indiscretions than to those of women. Thus, while many overtly reject adultery, there seems to be a consensus that it is normal for real men to have overwhelming sexual urges, and therefore to engage with multiple sexual partners (Olayinka 1997).

Sexuality is a key component of Come to My Kwe-Kwe (and traditional *kweh-kweh*), which is evident from the song lyrics that provide advice to the groom about the importance of satisfying his wife sexually to prevent infidelity. Some of the songs also speak directly to a man's African ancestry and thus to his perceived inherent, God-given ability to sexually please a woman. For instance, the song "Biggie So" is an example of the intersection of race and sexuality in the African-Guyanese community. During this song, attendees raise their pinky finger to demonstrate the small size of the genitalia of nonblack males, as they sing, for example, "Chiney man something lilly so, lilly so" (Chinese penis is this tiny). When they sing about the black man, however, they make a fist with one hand while using the other hand to hold the elbow of the fisted hand and wave it, shouting: "Black man something biggie so, biggie so." In this manner, they exaggerate the size of the black man's genitalia as being as large as a human arm. "Biggie So" is often sung by the groom's nation as a way of celebrating their son's masculinity and the strength of their lineage, but it also serves as a warning to the bride about the potential physical harm she might encounter during coitus.

Example 3.4: "Biggie So"

Creolese: "Biggie So, Biggie So"
Chiney man something lilly so, lilly so
Cooley[10] man something lilly so, lilly so
Buck[11] man something lilly so, lilly so
White man something lilly so lilly so.
BUT BLACK MAN SOMETHING BIGGIE SO, BIGGIE.

English: "Big So/Big Like This"
The Chinese man's penis is this big (this small)
The East Indian man's penis is this big (this small)
The Amerindian man's penis is this big (this small)
The white man's penis is this big (this small)
BUT THE BLACK MAN'S PENIS IS THIS BIG!

In the United States, African-Guyanese American men must create newer cultural schema or modify existing ones to accommodate gendered values concerning sexuality. Interestingly, this is the area of diasporic reconstruction that simultaneously offers the most continuity and change. In the larger African-Guyanese community, the assumption of the masculine male who demonstrates sexual prowess in order to prove virility remains consistent and continues to be demonstrated in Come to My Kwe-Kwe. What I have observed is that the fervor with which many African-Guyanese in Guyana sing traditional *kweh-kweh* songs in Guyana to articulate

blackness or Africanness in contradistinction to other Guyanese
ethnicities is compounded in the secondary diaspora in the United
States. In Guyana, they articulate their manliness in opposition
to other Guyanese, with whom, in most cases, they share a similar, albeit not identical, history of suffering and servitude. In the
United States, however, men confront complex societal structures
that seem designed to exclude them from the boundaries of "normal," including masculinity. In this heightened sphere of otherness,
many African-Guyanese-American men draw on their African
ancestry and use it as a key marker of identity. Very often, they
celebrate the stereotypical view of the black man as hypersexual.
While perceived innate hypersexuality is often used by members of
the dominant society as a marker of primitiveness, many African-
Guyanese-American men turn this negative stereotype on its head
and, through song, dance, and other ritual enactments, celebrate it
as a positive attribute. Their behavior seems to assert that masculine
men *are* animalistic. They also often push back against negative
stereotypes associated with black sexuality as expressions of "sour
grapes," in that those who are jealous of the black man's virility or
frustrated by their own lack of masculinity, disparage black men.

While songs like "Biggie So" celebrate the black man's virility,
they also create awkward situations at Come to My Kwe-Kwe rituals, where there is an increased incidence of "strangers and visitors"
(fig. 1.2) or individuals from other ethnic groups. The African diaspora in Guyana usually does not have to be overly concerned with
other Guyanese ethnics because the narratives surrounding race and
sexuality are entrenched in Guyanese cultural discourse and are often
cause for laughter and good humor, not necessarily strife. However,
because Come to My Kwe-Kwe takes place outside of Guyana and
includes diverse iterations of "Guyanese," the number of attendees
from other ethnic groups is often much greater than those at traditional *kweh-kweh* in Guyana or abroad. At the 2007 Come to My
Kwe-Kwe, for instance, attendees were singing and dancing in the
ganda (circle) when the songs became more overtly sexual, with a
focus on the groom. The change in tone occurred with a change of
kweh-kweh captains, as Akoyaw Rudder took over leadership from

Lio Britton. It was like pouring soap into an oil pool, as several individuals of different ethnic groups retreated to the periphery of the *ganda*, clearly embarrassed and some possibly disgusted. Even some African-Guyanese men find the explicit sexual displays to be discomforting. This is not to suggest that men do not enjoy the sexual veneration afforded them through the *kweh-kweh* songs, but for some, it is the publicity that makes the experience uncomfortable.

As with "real men," sexuality is also a crucial evaluator of "proper women." For women, however, the parameters of sexual prowess encompass chastity when they are single, sexual availability (service) to their husbands when they are married, and finally reproduction, the ultimate validation and defense of their womanhood, their nation, and their "race." The notion of the "good girl" who will someday be honored by becoming someone's wife is a crucial aspect of the process of enculturation of African-Guyanese girls. Through direct instruction and observations in the home, in religious settings, at school, and in the larger community, every young, unmarried woman is taught that her husband must be her "maiden man," the one who takes her virginity. Many mothers warn their daughters to remain chaste by using the popular Guyanese proverb, "If yuh mek yuhself grass, horse gon eat yuh" (If you make yourself grass, the horse will eat you); that is, your body and reputation will be destroyed if you behave promiscuously. While a young woman's chaste conduct is primarily intended to protect her reputation, it also safeguards the good name of her mother and her nation. When a young woman is believed to have remained a virgin until marriage, the community celebrates her with phrases like, "Do you know dis gyaal?" (Do you know this girl? Have you heard of her good reputation?); "Dem 'Johnson' gyal a good gyaal" (The Johnson women are good women); "Gyal yuh glorias maanin come" (Girl, your glorious morning has come); and "Listen wuh de bird ah say" (Listen to what the bird says). In the song "Do You Know Dis Gyaal?," for example, the caller highlights the chaste character of the bride and the accomplishments of various members of her nation as he or she asks, "Do you know dis gyaal?" On the contrary, popular folk songs like "Ow, Janey Gyal" (Aw, Janey, Girl), which are now sung at Come to My Kwe-Kwe and traditional *kweh-kweh*, lament the choices of the young woman who becomes pregnant out of wedlock, even before she completes her education or becomes domesticated. Although many African-Guyanese women marry after becoming sexually active, and some never marry, the "virgin bride" and "virtuous [married] woman"[12] remain ideals upheld by the larger Guyanese community.

Example 3.5: "Listen Wuh De Bird Ah Say"

Call:	Early, early wan ma'nin
Response:	Shallah
Call:	Me bin a co-co-ka-dam, oh
Call:	Me see wan lil lilly birdie
Call:	Me pick up lil lilly dutty
Call:	Oh, Congo man listen wuh de bird a say [communal chant]
Call:	Then he push it in further
Call:	Then ah bruck up de wicket[13]
Call:	Then de gyal start to hallah

Example 3.6: "Ow Janey Gyal"

Call:	Ow, Janey gyal
Response:	Janey gyal
Call:	Muma sen yuh ah school
Call:	To learn to read and write
Call:	Hais yuh belly come (3X)
Call:	Who ah de daddy now
Call:	Common cook, yuh cyaan cook [basic cooking, you can't do]
Call:	Common wuk, yuh cyaan wuk
Call:	Common wine, yuh cyaan wine
Call:	Common do, yuh cyaan do

The groom is also lauded for the perceived chaste character of his bride, because, when he is perceived to be his wife's "first man" or

"maiden man," there is a sense of legitimacy surrounding the pater-
nity of the children born to their union. If, however, the husband
or his nation later denies the chastity of the bride, her reputation
may suffer a similar fate to that of an unwed mother or a prosti-
tute. Moreover, like the undomesticated woman discussed earlier
in this chapter, her husband reserves the right to dismiss her from
the marital home. In the past, African-Guyanese women of the
groom's nation engaged in diverse verification tactics—much like
those practiced in precolonial and colonial Africa—to ensure that
the bride was a virgin on her wedding night. One of those tactics
was the inspection of the bedsheet the morning after the wedding
ceremony. If there was blood, the women would hang the stained
sheet out of the window for the entire community to witness it and
to celebrate the bride. If there was no blood, however, they would
cut a hole in the bedsheet and hang it out of the window to let the
world know that the bride was "an open sepulcher."[14]

The importance of chastity is not lost on the secondary diaspora,
but, as with other aspects of the process of *rediasporization*, reactions are multiple and varied. The older women, who remember the
inspections of their marital beds and other examinations of virginity
and who still value those practices, often decry what they regard as
the erosion of decency among young people. Since promiscuity and
masculinity are often used synonymously in the African-Guyanese
community, it is often women's sexuality that is negatively evaluated. An older African-Guyanese man in Guyana, in an informal
interview, asserted: "Dey ain gat no mo virgins in Guyana" (There
are no more virgins in Guyana). As offensive as his statement was,
it is the expressed sentiment of many older Guyanese, particularly
in the United States, who often blame American culture for the
erosion of decency and the "shame" (self-pride) among younger
generations. Religious African-Guyanese are another group who
are generally overtly supportive of the concept of the virgin bride,
even when some community members fall short of that standard.
Nevertheless, in the United States, younger African-Guyanese of the
migrated and procreated segments of the secondary diaspora are
overwhelmingly less stringent about virginity. This is not to suggest

that younger African-Guyanese do not value chastity but rather that they appear to regard coitus as an individual choice, not a community matter. Thus, at many Come to My Kwe-Kwe celebrations, songs about the value of the bride, based on her virginity, often garner lighthearted laughter and teasing instead of judgmental whispers from the community or embarrassment from the groom's nation. In large measure, African-Guyanese-Americans continue to uphold the ideal of the virgin bride, but the community also faces the realities of premarital sex, divorce, rape, and other factors that render the notion of the virgin bride irrelevant. Moreover, more individuals are now aware of the fact that there are other ways, besides sex, in which a woman can lose her hymen, the physical marker of virginity.

Although unmarried women are taught to be chaste, married women are advised to be sexually available and pleasing to their husbands. A woman's inability or refusal to be a wife (in sexual terms) to her husband is often cited as one of the causes for abandonment, infidelity, and domestic abuse. Through songs, dances, and gesticulations in Come to My Kwe-Kwe (and traditional *kweh-kweh*), women are instructed to let their husbands "in." For example, when the two nations meet at the bride's locked gate, the groom's nation requests entry into the bride's compound and, by extension, access to her person, by singing: "Open de door leh de man come in; all ah we ah wan family" (Open the door and let your man in; we are one family now). The phrase "open de door leh de man come in" is understood by the larger African-Guyanese community as a double entendre, with one of the meanings being sexual solicitation.

Show Me Yuh Science

The importance of sexuality in marriage is highlighted in the many risqué songs at Come to My Kwe-Kwe, but the crucial demonstration of sexual prowess is embodied in what I call the *science dance*, performed by the bride and groom throughout the ritual. During the science dance, the bride and groom enter the *ganda* and *wine* (gyrate)[15] separately and with or on each other. The goal of the science dance is for the bride and groom to demonstrate that they are ready for marriage by the mere fact that they can satisfy each other sexually and, by extension, continue their lineage. Thus, while Come to My Kwe-Kwe attendees sing "Show me yuh science" (hence the term *science dance*), the bride and groom are expected to skillfully rotate their pelvic regions, often simulating coitus. If the bride or groom fails to *wine* to the satisfaction of the community, she or he is ridiculed mercilessly and often warned, "Yuh gon geh blow" (You will face infidelity). Sometimes, the audience incites the groom to "show yuh science" (gyrate) by chanting phrases like, "Dem 'Johnson' bai cyaan wine" (Those Johnson men can't *wine*). On occasions when the bride or groom fails to *wine* competently, a member of their nation must enter the *ganda* and *wine* on their behalf in order to redeem their good name. According to Guyanese author and early *kweh-kweh* researcher Kean Gibson: "If the groom cannot show at the gate that he can gyrate he will not be allowed to enter the home. It means he is incapable of continuing the lineage and is therefore 'na good'" (1998, 169). She states further that the person who gyrates on behalf of the bride or groom is sending the message that "if the groom cannot perform his sexual duties someone else will do it for him" (1998, 170). While both men and women are expected to demonstrate sexual competence through the science dance, for a woman, it often centers on service to or satisfaction of her husband, while for a man, it is often couched in the protection of his masculinity, broadly construed. This duality of expectations is captured in the song "Oman Lie Down," which is performed as a call-and-response between the nations of the bride and groom, respectively.

Example 3.7: "Oman Lie Down/Wuh Kinda Man Is Dat?" (bride's nation call)

(teasing from the bride's nation)

Call:	The oman lie down and de man cyaan function;
Response:	Wuh kinda man, he's a beze man/wuk kinda man lika dat

Call: The oman lie down and de man cyaan function;
Response: Wuh kinda man, he's a beze man/wuk kinda man
                   lika dat
Call: The oman lie down and de man nah able;
Response: Wuh kinda man, he's a beze man
Call: Wuh kina man, oh wuh kinda man oh
Response: Wuh kinda man, he's a beze man

Example 3.8: "Oman Lie Down/ Wuh Kinda Man Is Dat" (groom's nation response)

Call: A man like he gon buss up she liver
Response: What kinda man is dat
Call: A man like he gon tear up she pum pum
Response: Wuh kind a man is that . . . lika dah

At the 2015 Come to My Kwe-Kwe, a young man serving as the groom was brought into the *ganda*. I am not sure if he was engaged to the young woman acting as the bride, or if he was Guyana-born, but he seemed to be in his midtwenties and a very willing participant. He had gone through all the other ritual stages and was preparing to "show his science" (gyrate). Once he entered the *ganda*, however, it became clear to the audience that the stereotype regarding black male sexuality, as demonstrated through *wining*, did not hold true for this acting groom. As attendees began singing, "Show me yuh science," everyone turned their gaze to the young groom in the center of the *ganda*. Instead of gyrating his hips, the young man twitched and swayed awkwardly from side to side. His movements caused the women of his assigned nation to spring into action to defend their "son" and restore their honor. They loudly chided him and, raising his shirt, physically moved his hips in a circular motion to get him to "*wine* right." The good-humored young man allowed himself to be contorted into various positions by the women, but to no avail. He just continued swaying like a big oak tree, showing barely any evidence that there were joints in his pelvic region. The crowed laughed, jeered, and criticized the groom and his nation,

Figure 3.3: Older women show the volunteer groom how to "show yuh science" (gyrate) at the 2015 Come to My Kwe-Kwe, Brooklyn. Photo by Gillian Richards-Greaves.

but he carried on. The young man was obviously new to Come to My Kwe-Kwe (and traditional *kweh-kweh*) and to the boisterous, judgmental Guyanese audience, but he was certainly willing to learn about the ritual, even to the point of being scapegoated. By participating in this manner, he allowed himself to be grafted to the African-Guyanese-American community through performance, whether or not he was of Guyanese ancestry.

Very often, the individuals who volunteer to be brides and grooms at Come to My Kwe-Kwe don't hold negative views about the ritual, or simply regard it as nothing more than fun. While the audience members join in the laughter, however, many reject the risqué simulations of sex encompassed in the science dance and other overt expressions of sexuality. "Wutlessness" (worthlessness or vulgarity), "paganism," "bacchanal," and "dry sex" are a few of the labels African-Guyanese-Americans have used to refer to the science dance. Moreover, although both males and females are expected to show their "science," some have expressed disgust at what they perceive to be the debasement and objectification of women. An increasing number of African-Guyanese of the secondary migrated diaspora, particularly older ones, have expressed displeasure with what they regard as the overemphasis on the science dance and on sexuality in general, at the expense of other, "sweeter" aspects of the ritual. They often argue that the ritual is supposed to educate the soon-to-be-married couple, and as such, *wining* should only be a supporting gesture in the ritual, not the staple of the entire ritual. Some also reject the science dance because they view it as a negative representation of African-Guyaneseness. Interestingly, it is the younger people who seem to attend Come to My Kwe-Kwe particularly for the *wining* and overt sexual performances. In some instances, even non-Guyanese youngsters have expressed interest in having a traditional *kweh-kweh* when they get married, partly because of the risqué content and overall fun they experienced at Come to My Kwe-Kwe. Nevertheless, by their presence at Come to My Kwe-Kwe, African-Guyanese-Americans choose to participate in the continued remaking of Guyanese gendered values, even by their rejection of expressions like the science dance. Martin Stokes argues: "Whilst dance is a vital means of gender socialization, and an enactment of masculinity and femininity at ritual occasions such as weddings, it is also an arena in which gender categories can be contested" ([1994] 1997, 22).

African Continuities? Sexual Values in the Diasporas

While demonstrations of sexual prowess celebrate individual grooms and their nations, sexual competence serves a much more crucial role in Guyanese society. Sexual competence indexes virility, which is crucial for the continuation and expansion of any society through biological means. The demonstration of sexual competence and thus potential virility is rooted in an African past and is reminiscent of puberty and marriage rites on the African continent. Many societies in precolonial Africa engaged in coming-of-age *rites of passage*, which functioned to help pubescent boys' and girls' transition from childhood to adulthood. These rites of passage unfolded in secluded settings and were gender specific, such as the Poro (for boys) and Sande (for girls) secret societies in Liberia, Sierra Leone, Guinea, and Ivory Coast (Bledsoe 1980, 46–80; Isichei 1997, 239–60;

Washington 2005, 152–86). These puberty rights are still practiced in contemporary Africa, albeit in more innovative ways. During puberty rites of passage, young people are taught about the responsibilities of adulthood, including providence for one's family (broadly construed) and matters pertaining to procreation. At the end of the rites of passage, the initiates are presented to the rest of society, not as children but as adult men and women. Moreover, they are incorporated back into society as potential spouses or marriage material. According to Onwumere Ikwuagwu: "In Africa, one is considered ripe for marriage after the rite of initiation into manhood has been performed" (2007, 86). At many of these presentations, these newly minted adults are adorned in ways that highlight their beauty and sex appeal, by emphasizing or exaggerating body features deemed crucial to procreation such as breasts, waist, groin, genitalia, eyes, and lips. In many instances, also, young men and women are taught sensual dances, which they are required to perform at their presentations in hope of securing a mate. The *kweh-kweh wining* and other gesticulations are much like the sensual African dances at puberty rites and marriage rites, which inform the larger community and potential suitors that their lineage will not die off. Since the nations of the bride and groom cannot physically inspect the sexual interactions of married couples, they evaluate potential sexual competence or the lack thereof through performances of sexualized dances like the science dance.

Many other ideals expressed during rites of passage in secret societies in Africa can be observed during *kweh-kweh*. In the song "You Shame," for example, the mother tells her soon-to-be-married daughter to wash her *bembe* (vagina) and practice good hygiene to avoid bringing shame (embarrassment) to herself.[16] In this song, the mother argues that she did her job in raising her daughter well, and thus society will judge only the bride for her poor conduct. As the women sing the song, they make a wiping motion in the genital area when they sing "tek wan calabash, wash yuh bembe." This type of interaction between mothers and daughters in Come to My Kwe-Kwe (and traditional *kweh-kweh*) highlights the nature of child-rearing in the Guyanese community, in that it is the mother who generally bears the responsibility for raising children, particularly daughters. Thus, when children behave inappropriately, it is principally the mother who gets a "bad name" (disparagement). Pat Ellis states that "Caribbean women of all classes and races, irrespective of marital status, accept responsibility for child-care and child rearing" (1986, 9). Moreover, the performance of "You Shame" indexes the types of discussions that often unfold between mothers and daughters in the Guyanese community.

Example 3.9: "You Shame, Ah Nah Me Shame"

Creolese

Call:	You shame, ah nah me shame
Response:	Tek wan calabash wash yuh bembe[17]
Call:	You shame, ah nah me shame
Response:	Tek wan calabash wash yuh bembe
Call:	Tek wan calabash wash yuh bembe
Response:	Tek wan calabash wash yuh bembe

English

Call:	It is your shame, not mine
Response:	Take a calabash and wash your genitals [practice good hygiene]
Call:	It is your shame, not mine
Response:	Take a calabash and wash your genitals [practice good hygiene]
Call:	Take a calabash and wash your genitals [practice good hygiene]
Response:	Take a calabash and wash your genitals [practice good hygiene]

Good hygiene, referenced in "You Shame," enables a woman to serve her husband sexually, but the goal of coitus is not only pleasure but also reproduction. In discussing gendered values in Africa, Ikwuagwu states: "The glory of a woman lies on her children, and children are born through the union of man and woman in marriage" (2007, 85). In the African-Guyanese community, as it was and still is in Africa, bearing children is the ultimate validation of one's womanhood (Cutrufelli 1983; Bush 1990, 105). As Barbara Bush notes: "The description of the significance of the mother in slave society correlates very closely with those relating to the mother in West African society where identity comes through motherhood and sterility is a terrible stigma" (1990, 105). It is for this reason that, in the African-Guyanese community, barrenness is often viewed as a curse from God, the result of witchcraft, or bad karma brought about by a woman's misdeeds (Koster-Oyekan 1999). Even when childlessness is the result of the husband's infertility or other medical maladies, it is often initially assumed that the woman is to blame. Although an increasing number of women now get medical assistance for fertility issues, many still blame the "evil mother-in-law" or some other "bad-minded" person for "wukkin obeah" (practicing witchcraft) to shut up their wombs.[18] Some women fast and pray or visit powerful obeah-men or obeah-women to subvert what they perceive to be a preexisting "do" (bewitchment) that is preventing them from conceiving a child.

The general unease surrounding barrenness in African-Guyanese communities has historical roots on the continent of Africa and reverberated with life-and-death consequences during slavery. Childless women in pre- and postcolonial Africa were socially handicapped because they lacked the assistance that children rendered in overwhelmingly agrarian societies, inclusion into certain female spheres, and the emotional and spiritual resolution that comes from the knowledge that children will provide old-age, end-of-life, and afterlife care and the rituals associated with them. During slavery, these African-centered anxieties were compounded by the inhumanities leveled against barren women, who could "expect to be treated like barren sows and be passed from one unsuspecting buyer to the next" (White 1985, 101). However, the overriding stigma surrounding childlessness is gradually waning, particularly in the African-Guyanese-American community. In fact, the stigma of barrenness is itself becoming a stigma associated with ignorance and meanness.

An increasing number of African-Guyanese women are viewing reproduction as only one aspect, albeit an important one, of their identity. For many of them, childlessness is not a curse from God or the result of bewitchment by bad-minded people, but instead a conscious personal choice on their part. Those who desire to be mothers but face infertility often embrace the age-old African and African diasporic practice of becoming *othermothers* to the children of relatives, friends, and strangers. Othermothers are *fictive kin*,[19] women who informally adopt children and assume responsibility for their economic providence, discipline, personal care, and other factors associated with child-rearing, even when the children continue to live with their *bloodmothers* (biological mothers) or other *consanguineal kin* (blood relatives) (Bush 1990, 86). During slavery, African-Guyanese engaged in the practice of "giving a child" to someone, who then became an othermother or, less frequently, an *otherfather* (Edwards [1801] 2017). Children were given to others when parents had multiple children and paltry finances, when a parent fell ill or died, when the child was asked for by another person, and for various other reasons. The act of giving children and the service of othermothers was not only practiced in Guyana but was also common among other African diasporic groups in the Caribbean and the United States (Pollitzer 2005, 133).[20] In discussing the importance of othermothers among African-Americans, Patricia Hill Collins states:

> Children orphaned by sale or death of their parents under slavery, children conceived through rape, children of young mothers, children born into extreme poverty or to alcoholic or drug-addicted mothers, or children who for other reasons cannot remain with their bloodmothers have all been supported by othermothers, who . . . take in additional children even when they have enough of their own. (2003, 319)

Many African-Guyanese women also legally adopt children. Even in legal adoptions, however, the overwhelming preference seems to be for the children of relatives over strangers. While African-Guyanese women in the primary and secondary diasporas may have differing views on childbearing and even adoption, they seem to embrace the pervading sentiment that, by having children, they will have someone to care for them when they are old. Thus, while factors like economics and migration may cause African-Guyanese women to have more progressive views on fertility and childbearing, the practicality of life in the Guyanese community (and the larger black community) anchors their views on mothering in a more conventional African-Guyanese framework.

Although bearing children authenticates womanhood in the African-Guyanese community, the birth of male children is especially valued. This is observed in *kweh-kweh* songs like "Bin' Yuh Belly" (Bind Your Belly; example 3.10), during which the mother of the groom is told to "gird her loins," as it were, in anticipation of the pain she will feel over the loss of her "wan" (only) son to marriage. The "binding" in this song might also refer to the use of a common piece of cloth or to the intense abdominal pain women are said to experience at the loss (via separation or death) of a child; however, this concept might also have deeper roots in an African past. In pre- and postcolonial Africa, young women's waists were bound or adorned with colorful beads, particularly after the completion of their puberty rites. The waist beads served several functions including the enhancement of the beauty of the reproductive areas, protection from bad spirits, the provision of enticement or excitement for men, and even proof of rape, in cases where they are broken. In the broader African diaspora, women continued to wear waist beads, as evidenced by findings during the excavation of the African Burial Ground in New York City (Frohne 2015, 131–41). In Guyana, women of my grandmother's generation wore the *baji-rang*,[21] a type of loincloth or breechclout composed of a waistband or waist beads with an attached piece of cloth that runs between the legs. In an interview, Ms. Gladys, a middle-aged Ewe woman from Ghana, stated that the waist beads are "the beauty of a woman." She stated further that even when a woman dies, she must wear beads, because "to be a complete woman, you have to put on the beads" (interview, June 26, 2017).

The reasons surrounding the preference for male offspring are multiple and varied, but the women I spoke with cited biblical texts, issues with child-rearing, assistance with physical labor (particularly the kind that can earn wages), financial security, and the continuation of the family name or lineage. While many religious women, particularly Judeo-Christians, view the birth of sons as God's way of singling out women for special blessings (Exodus 13:2), others claim that boys are easier to raise because they need fewer amenities to survive and thrive. Moreover, sons are coveted because they cannot get pregnant and "bring shame" to the family. Living in a society that practices patriliny also makes boys preferable, since the family name (lineage) is traced through males, and males generally occupy higher socioeconomic strata in society. This preference predates colonial Africa and continues today. According to Bolaji Olukemi Olayinka, among the Yorubas,

> [w]omen are seen and regarded as appendages of men. A woman's role as a wife not only includes child bearing but she must also ascertain the production of a male offspring. Failure to achieve this means her inability to ensure the husband's immortality. (1997, 216)

Example 3.10: "Bin' Yuh Belly"

Creolese

Call:	Bin' yuh belly fuh yuh wan bai pickney
Response:	Bin' yuh belly tonight, tonight
Call:	Bind yuh belly fuh yuh wan bai pickney
Response:	Bin' yuh belly tonight, tonight

English

Call:	Bind/strap your belly for your only son
Response:	Bind/strap your belly tonight, tonight
Call:	Bind/strap your belly for your only son
Response:	Bind/strap your belly tonight, tonight

Another connection between Africa and the diaspora regarding sexuality concerns *polygyny*, whereby a man has multiple wives at the same time.[22] In precolonial Africa, polygyny was practiced as a way of demonstrating virility and wealth and ensuring the continuation and expansion of one's lineage. Although polygynous marriages and the large numbers of children that emerged from them were crucial to the functioning and wealth of agrarian communities, many in Africa today still regard the practice as a sign of a man's wealth and fertility. This is not to overlook the role of Islam in helping to propagate and undergird polygyny in many parts of Africa, particularly in the northern regions of the continent. I also do not minimize the role of enslavers in creating polygynous-type relationships through the forced breeding of enslaved Africans to produce more slaves, buffer the slave population, and increase their own wealth. This is, however, an acknowledgment that polygyny existed before slavery and Islam and had several manifest (expressed) and latent (covert) functions throughout Africa, and that it continues to be practiced today (Iliffe 1995; Fortes and Evans-Pritchard [1940] 1987).

During slavery, informal polygyny continued in Guyana and in the African diaspora at large because enslaved Africans remembered the nature of marriages on the continent; witnessed the informal continuation of polygyny in Guyana and other areas where Africans were enslaved (Pollitzer 2005, 131, 169); and in many instances found polygynous relationships to be crucial for their survival. According to Barbara Bush: "Much evidence exists in contemporary literature which indicates that slave masters were, in effect, more aware of the significance of the slave family and the existence of marriage forms which did not conform to the modern European model than a superficial examination of their writings would suggest" (1990, 84; see also Long [1774] 2010). Informal polygyny is still practiced today by many African-Guyanese, although they might not label their relationships as such. Thus, while monogamy is the legal form of marriage in Guyana, many men engage in long-term sexual and domestic relationships with multiple women at the same time.

On Gendering Domestic Violence

In the African-Guyanese community, and in the larger Guyanese community, domestic violence is also a gendered value. At the core of domestic violence in the Guyanese community is enculturation, a process during which domestic violence is normalized within and without the home through proverbs, scriptures, jokes, and practical experience. In many instances, as Pat Ellis notes, "[a]ttitudes previously reinforced the societal belief that violence in the family was a private matter between a man and a woman and that outsiders should not interfere" (1986, 8). Young children learn from adults in society that hitting and other types of abuse is a "normal" part of romantic relationships. One of ways that normalcy is attached to domestic violence is through proverbs like "teeth and tongue must bite" (the teeth will bite the tongue), which "advises the couple that disagreements, including physical abuse, in marriage are normal and should be expected" (Richards-Greaves 2016b). A similar proverb, "Man weapon a-he fist, woman weapon a-he tongue" (A man's weapon is his fist and a woman's weapon is her verbal abuse) (Speirs 1902, 26), upholds domestic violence by embracing stereotypical views on men's physicality and women's loquaciousness. This latter proverb support bell hooks's claim: "Patriarchal violence in the home is based on the belief that it is acceptable for a more powerful individual to control others through various forms of coercive force" (2000, 61).

Compounding the attitudes toward domestic violence are the community's reactions to domestic violence cases, in which the victim is often blamed for her plight, even by other women, who ask questions like: "What did she do to him" (Haug et al. 1987; Benjamin 1988; Messner 2003). Sometimes, even the victims themselves ask their abusers to provide a reason for the abuse, as if a response would justify the abuse or assuage their suffering. Even when community members speak out, they don't necessarily condemn abuse in general but excessive abuse, asking questions like, "Why he hit her like that" (to that degree or so viciously).

During the Come to My Kwe-Kwe ritual, domestic violence is addressed through songs like "Hear, Auntie Bess Ah Hallah" (Hear, Auntie Bess Is Hollering) and "Sancho Lick 'e Lova Pon de Dam" (Sancho Beat His Lover on the Dam). In "Hear, Auntie Bess," domestic violence is only inferred, as the question "Wuh she hallah fah" (Why is she hollering?) is never answered by the song lyrics. The answer is left to the listener's imagination. Another implied explanation for Auntie Bess's hollering is a sexual one; but even from a sexual standpoint, the way Auntie Bess is said to holler signifies discomfort, pain, and possibly abuse. "Sancho Lick 'e Lova Pon de Dam" is a bit more straightforward in addressing domestic violence. In this song, Sancho is the man or husband who either licks (hits) his lover while on the dam, or he licks (body-slams) his lover on the dam, causing her to holler, "Murder!" When her cries draw the attention of the police, Sancho is told by the community of onlookers, "Boy, you better run." As humorous as this may seem on the surface, it is the reality of too many Guyanese women, who are abused or murdered only to have the perpetrators escape, often with the support of relatives and friends. "Sancho Lick 'e Lova Pon de Dam" is sung in traditional *kweh-kweh* as well as Come to My Kwe-Kwe, but it was originally a folk song that the average Guyanese child in Guyana would have learned from a young age. Thus, when it is sung at Come to My Kwe-Kwe in the United States, it often has a bipartite function of wedding commentary and nostalgia.

Example 3.11: "Hear, Auntie Bess Ah Hallah"

Creolese
Hear Auntie Bess,
Hear, Auntie Bess
Hear, Auntie Bess ah hallah
Wuh she hallah, wuh she hallah, wuh she hallah fah?

English
Hear Auntie Bess,
Hear, Auntie Bess
Hear, Auntie Bess is hollering
What is the reason she is hollering?

Example 3.12: "Sancho Lick 'e Lova Pon de Dam"

Creolese
Sancho lick 'e lova pon de dam and de gyal ah hallah, murdah (2x)
Bip bap, police ah come and de gyal ah hallah, murdah

English
Sancho beat his lover on the dam and the girl hollered, "Murder!"
Now, the police are coming, and the girl is still hollering, "Murder!"

Nevertheless, an increasing number of African-Guyanese-American women, including those who sing the "Sancho" song, are openly addressing the problem of domestic violence, even in seemingly benign *kweh-kweh* songs. They often openly discuss disturbing song lyrics in the context of past experiences with abusive relatives and romantic partners, and what they regard as the complicit behavior of the larger Guyanese community. Beyond discussions on violence, members of the African-Guyanese-American community have also begun creating official and unofficial social and economic networks to support victims of domestic violence. While the support for victims is gaining momentum, there is still much to be done to change Guyanese gender values that underscore or minimize the gravity of domestic violence.

Conclusion

Several factors shape gender values in the African-Guyanese community, including African continuities (retentions), creolization, religious doctrines, and migration, but the process of enculturation involves direct and indirect instructions that overwhelmingly focus on socializing boys to be "real men" and girls to be "proper women." The gender roles assigned to real men and proper women are countless and diverse but include economic providence, sexual prowess, and leadership on the part of men; and various types of "service" on the part of women. Domestic violence is also a gender value in the African-Guyanese community; it is a widespread practice that is normalized through everyday behavior, folk songs, proverbs, and traditional *kweh-kweh* (and Come to My Kwe-Kwe) music. These gender values are established in the primary African diaspora in Guyana but are complicated in the secondary diaspora in the United States, which is composed of distinct subgroups who identify as African-Guyanese (fig. 1.2).

In the secondary *rediasporized* diaspora, what it means to be a
real man or a proper woman is reconceptualized to accommodate
changing cultural values, financial and legal realities, and other
constraints. As more African-Guyanese embrace women's equality
or face the reality that women in America can be, and sometimes
are, equally or more economically stable than men, they modify
the parameters of the real man to accommodate the wage-earning,
economically independent woman. Those who adapt to these newer
conditions must relinquish some of the gender values established
in the primary African diaspora in Guyana; those who do not often
find themselves at odds with younger members of the secondary
diaspora and overarching gender values in the United States. In
an analogous manner, domestication, sexual prowess, and other
female gender values must be reassessed as women increasingly
work outside the home. Thus, the domestic-public dichotomy that
is at the core of gendering in the African-Guyanese community is
rendered a faulty standard in the *rediasporized* African-Guyanese-
American community.

African-Guyanese-Americans are also becoming increasingly
vocal about the domestic violence epidemic that shaped many of
their lives and continues to infest Guyana. Nevertheless, real changes
to domestic violence must begin in the home with the resocialization of children. This means encouraging parents to discard the
"boys will be boys" mentality, which minimizes physical, verbal, and
emotional violence and aggressiveness, especially toward females. At
the crux of resocialization, however, must be the systematic reeducation of adult women and men, particularly community leaders
including clergy and schoolteachers. Such reeducation must include
the reconceptualization of women not as appendages of men but
as complete and independent human beings. From an early age,
also, boys and girls must be taught the harmful effects of physical
violence. Teaching restraint to all genders is especially important,
because many girls are conditioned to be victims through values
embodied in Guyanese sayings like "he beats me because he loves
me," often provoking nonviolent men to be abusers. Thus, teaching
and modeling positive acts of affection should also be a part of

the reeducation process. Law enforcement officials must receive training in identifying domestic violence cases, and offenders must be deterred with severe punishment. Pat Ellis observes: "In the Caribbean, as in other parts of the world, strategies to deal with violence against women within the law are either non-existent or grossly inadequate" (1986, 8). Therefore, providing support systems for abused women such as shelters, childcare, and job training would afford many women the opportunity to leave abusive situations. Ultimately, tackling domestic violence from these vantage points will facilitate more positive gender values in both the primary and secondary diasporas. These revised gender values will be reflected in Come to My Kwe-Kwe through improvisations of older *kweh-kweh* songs and in the composition of newer songs.

In the context of Come to My Kwe-Kwe, established African-Guyanese gender values are reinterpreted or altogether rejected through music, dance, and other ritual performance. In this audience, established Guyanese gender roles and stereotypes form the foundation of expression. However, in the new diaspora, men and women reevaluate songs and sometimes improvise them, based on newer realities or values. Even when they sing the songs as is, it is with the understanding that, unlike with their foreparents, the songs do not define their values or determine their behavior or future. In some instances, songs that would have enjoyed pervasive improvisation, albeit from an overtly sexual perspective, are now modified to accommodate the changing composition of the audience and function of Come to My Kwe-Kwe. Ritual expressions are thus a vehicle for education about the past, an opportunity for celebration, and, for some, ideals by which to live. *Rediasporization* is an intense and ongoing reconceptualization, reassertion, readjustment, and display of the gendered self in a constant state of flux.

4

"Beat de Drum and de Spirit Gon Get Up"
Music, Dance, and Authenticity in *Rediasporization*

When bomba drum a come, nah flounce go meet am
GUYANESE PROVERB

Dance ah battam, look ah tap
GUYANESE PROVERB

At the 2007 Come to My Kwe-Kwe *celebration, traditional kweh-kweh guru Lionel "Lio" Britton was flown in from Guyana to teach the audience how a real (authentic) kweh-kweh is performed. Lio quickly realized, however, that his training and expectations conflicted with those of the African-Guyanese American audience. While dancing, Lio expressed annoyance after he observed that there were individuals still sitting in their seats. He ordered them to "get out of those chairs and participate!" A few individuals joined the ganda, but the majority did not budge. They just seemed to be taking it all in. A woman in the audience, who possibly knew Lio back in Guyana, yelled, "Lio, start singing and we gon get up." Switching songs, Lio sang, "Vee-yo, gangara" (unknown vocables), and the dancers responded, "Nah me wan ah veo gangara" (I am not the only one). They sang this song only for a few minutes before Lio, once again, began to chide the attendees,*

Figure 4.1: Musicians prepare to perform at Come to My Kwe-Kwe, Brooklyn, August 31, 2018. Photo by Gillian Richards-Greaves.

but this time on a more personal level. Speaking directly to the woman who had earlier told him to "start singing and we gon get up," Lio ordered, "Patsy, get up from that chair!" She quickly replied, "Beat the drum and we gon get up." Ignoring Patsy, Lio continued to sing "Vee-yo, gangara" for a few more minutes. Realizing that Lio was not paying her any attention, Patsy shouted, "Beat the drum and the spirit gon get up" (beat the drum and the spirit, loosely interpreted, will be awakened) (Richards-Greaves 2013; Richards-Greaves, forthcoming).

Introduction

Guyanese music and dance encompass a plethora of musical genres and styles from around the world, by Africans, Europeans, East Indians, and Amerindians (indigenous Guyanese), and including creolized expressions that result from the blending of diverse musical expressions over centuries of acculturation in Guyana. Additionally, musics from the Caribbean, Latin America, the United States, and other regions of the New World played a significant role in shaping Guyanese music and dance, and the identities associated with the various genres. A survey of Guyana's musical styles from the precolonial era to the present reveals a diverse body of music that includes ethnic folk songs like shanties (work songs from the hinterlands; Cambridge 2015, 85), European classical music (22, 47), urban militia bands (21–22), festival music like masquerade or centipede music (Ahyoung 2013; Cambridge 2015, 24), American jazz (Cambridge 2015, 30), Trinidadian calypso (69), British patriotic songs (75), political protest songs (43), and trade union demonstration songs of the 1960s (21, 24, 26). While acculturation, perceptions of race, and historical events like World War II shaped Guyana's musical fabric, religious groups including Muslims, Hindus, and Christians also played a crucial role in this process (Cambridge 2015, 24). The musical instruments used in producing Guyanese music and dance are also diverse and include European musical instruments (Cambridge 2015, 31); Amerindian bone flutes, reed whistles, and rattles (36); East Indian *tassa* drums, harmoniums, and *majeeras* (Cambridge 2015, 34–35; Manuel 2015); and African banjos, drums, and *shak shaks* (a type of rattle) (Brown [1876] 2010, 139). Since gaining independence in 1966, and particularly after the country's economic downturn from the late 1970s through the late 1980s, Guyana has experienced a consistent waning, and in some instances the complete demise, of many musical styles, most notably European classical music. Nevertheless, pervading musical genres—such as life-cycle ritual songs like those performed at the East Indian (Hindu) marriage ritual called Matticore (Dig Dutty) and the African-Guyanese *kweh-kweh* marriage ritual (Cambridge 2015, 34)—are sustained by the ethnic groups that perform them.

In the African-Guyanese community, music continues to occupy a crucial place in everyday life because it facilitates "an enhanced mode of communication beyond the petty power of words—spoken or written" (Gilroy 1993, 76). African-Guyanese make music to express joys, sorrows, and hopes; to remember, and to forget; to encourage themselves in times of hardship; to lighten the burden and monotony of work; and to execute diverse rituals. Music is, therefore, an integral part of African-Guyanese children's enculturation, which begins when they are in the womb and continues when they are infants and young children. Parents and teachers also provide academic instruction through song and dance, as they teach children multiplication tables, mathematical formulas, poetry, patriotic songs, Guyana's history, and much more (Cambridge 2015). Moral values and religious dogma are also imparted through liturgical music, such as chants, choruses, and hymns (Hyles 2014, 44–45; Cambridge 2015, 24). Ultimately, music is an important medium through which African-Guyanese inform the world and themselves of who they are.

Africans in Guyana, like other African diasporic groups that emerged out of slavery, also used music to provide direct and coded commentary on various experiences and situations (Liverpool 1994; Burnim 1985a; Burnim 1985b). As discussed extensively by Vibert Cambridge in his monograph *Musical Life in Guyana* (2015), music also enables African-Guyanese to make direct and indirect political commentary. The music enslaved Africans made was informed by an African past as well as by their experiences in the New World. Although forcibly separated from the African continent and important ritual and performance contexts of music making, the enslaved drew on memories and an accompanying knowledge base to create culturally relevant music. The music they made reminded them of the past, sustained them through hardships, and enabled them to communicate their deepest emotions and aspirations. More importantly, the music Africans created in the Guyana reflected the multifaceted nature of their emerging diasporic identity.

Several scholars have interrogated the crucial role that music plays in the complex relationships between diasporas and their homelands, particularly in "linking homeland and here-land with an intricate network of sound" (Slobin 1994, 243). Very often also, dance and other expressions are encompassed by the term "music" because they occur in the context of overarching musical performances, which subsume them (Hanna 1988; Baumann 1990; Thomas 1993; Béhague 1998; Downey 2005; Osumare 2010; Reed 2003). Ethnomusicologists have been particularly astute about interrogating how diasporic musical expressions highlight and maintain connections between former and current homelands by helping diasporic groups to recount historical events (Duran 2015, 27–44;

Melville 2015, 209–26); recall past experiences and relationships (Dorson 1971; Shelemay 1998); express the sadness that results from separation and the longing to return (Zheng 2010; Schramm 1999); preserve languages and cultural and religious systems (Naff 1985; Mori 2003; Gregory 2000; Sandoval 2008; Shelemay 2015); make overt and coded commentary on diverse situations they face (Epstein 1977; Norfleet 2015; Rosenbaum 1998); and reconstruct a sense of place or belonging in their new homelands (Slobin 1994, 243–51; Nguyen 1995; Summit 2000; Morley 2001, 425–48; Richards-Greaves 2015). More importantly, music is one of the ways that diasporas negotiate diverse identities that simultaneously bind people to former and current homelands by articulating their complex existence (Allen, Ware, and Garrison [1867] 1971; Baumann 1990; Cunningham and Nguyen 2003; Reed 2016). Gender (Sugarman 1997), race (Burnim 1985a; Apter 2002), class (Campbell 1988), and nationalism (Baily [1994] 1997; Lesser 1999; Dudley 2004; Alvarez 2008) are a few of the diverse, overlapping identities that diasporas uniquely negotiate through music and dance (Leante 2004; Epstein 2015). However, less explored in academic literature are the multilayered, multidimensional relationships that develop between various levels of diasporas (primary, secondary, and others) and the musics they create. Also, less examined are the unique ways that music facilitates *rediasporization*.

This chapter examines the process of *rediasporization* through the lens of music and dance at Come to My Kwe-Kwe celebrations in New York City. My examinations of music and dance focus on the repertoire, form, content, and linguistic elements of Come to My Kwe-Kwe songs as well as the execution of the traditional choreographed ritual dance and freestyle dances. The longitudinal research project on Come to My Kwe-Kwe reveals the complex ways that African-Guyanese use music to comment on and display who they perceive themselves to be. It also allows for the charting of musical changes that have taken place and continue to take place in Come to My Kwe-Kwe, as African-Guyanese work to canonize the music and other ritual performances of the event as a means of establishing and policing the boundaries of their doubly hyphenated

African-Guyanese-American community. It is therefore imperative
that this chapter also address issues of authenticity that come to
the fore in Come to My Kwe-Kwe, as dancers, musicians, and other
participants innovate ritual elements to accommodate ritual novices
and experts alike or reject innovations for more archaic expressions
of tradition (Middleton 1990, 127).

Traditional *Kweh-Kweh* Music and *Diasporization* in Guyana

There are several musical expressions through which African-
Guyanese articulate individual and group identities, but the music
of the quintessentially African-Guyanese *kweh-kweh* ritual offers
unique insights into African continuities and processes of *diasporization* in Guyana. Traditional *kweh-kweh* music encompasses
singing, dancing, and the playing of formal instruments as well as ad
hoc or "found" instruments, which are naturally occurring objects in
the environment or other objects used as instruments (Seeger 1958,
52; Borde 1973, 45; Dudley 2002, 18; Campbell 2012). As discussed in
the introduction, music highlights and demarcates each of the *kweh-
kweh* ritual segments, which include a procession, a meeting at the
bride's gate, the hiding of the bride, the negotiation of the bride price,
and the communal circular dance with members of both nations.
For instance, the greeting song "Goodnight, Ay" is typically sung by
members of both nations during the meeting at the gate and at the
beginning of the festivities (fig. 4.2). Traditional *kweh-kweh* songs
cover a wide range of topics that collectively address matrimony;
thus, songs about sex, domestication, Guyana's history, and Africa are
all performed in the context of *kweh-kweh* and reference gendered
expectations in marriage (table 4.1).

  Kweh-kweh singing is executed in call-and-response form, with
calls given by a *kweh-kweh* captain (sometimes referred to as a
raconteur or tutor) and responses provided by *kweh-kweh* attendees.
The calls of songs are often improvised pervasively by the captain,
while responses remain virtually unchanged.[1] *Kweh-kweh* songs are
sung in Creolese, Guyana's English-based creole language, which

© 2013 Gillian Richards-Greaves

Figure 4.2: Transcription of the song "Goodnight, Ay." Transcription by Gillian Richards-Greaves.

also includes syntax and other linguistic features from African languages, Amerindian (Arawakan) languages, Hindi and Bhojpuri, and European languages.[2] The songs are also sung using the chest voice and a raspy or buzzing timbre, characteristic of singing in precolonial sub-Saharan Africa (Hast et al. 1997, 139–68). A former *kweh-kweh* captain I refer to as M. C. discussed the timbre of *kweh-kweh* singing in the following manner: "*Kweh-kweh* is not sweet singing, it's not nice voice. You ain't got no emphasis on no diction and pitch. It's just raw, you know, [singing] 'Yuh nah know wah yah do'" (M. C., interview, 2005). Most of the songs sung at *kweh-kweh* are regarded as "traditional" songs, which emerged in the context of the wedding-based *kweh-kweh* ritual; however, the *kweh-kweh* repertoire also includes Guyanese folk songs, African popular music, and Caribbean genres like calypso, reggae, and soca. Even when non-traditional songs are performed at *kweh-kweh*, they tend to address racial and matrimonial issues.

Regardless of the types of songs being sung, traditional *kweh-kweh* singing is largely a communal enactment that allows any person to shape the direction of the ritual by calling out "Batto!" (pronounced bat-toe) during the singing. As I have explained elsewhere: "Batto! is an audible command or signal to the *kweh-kweh* community (including the captain) to terminate the singing in progress. Batto! also affords the caller the authority, opportunity, and responsibility to 'raise' (start) another song of his or her choosing. Thus, when batto! is called, everyone stops singing and waits for the caller to raise the next song" (Richards-Greaves 2013). An

Table 4.1. Selected Kweh-Kweh Song List and Categories

Song Categories/Types	Musical Examples	Related Ritual Segments	Ritual Performances
Preprocession celebratory songs (individual nations)	"Lilly Gyal"; "This Time Nah Laang Time"	Nations gather at separate venues or at a single location to sing and dance prior to the procession.	Singing of folk songs and kweh-kweh songs; celebrating a son or daughter; eating and drinking.
Procession songs	"Coming Down with a Bunch of Roses"; "Come to My Kweh-Kweh"; "Close Yuh Bedroom Window"	(1) Procession to the home of the bride or groom.	Walking, singing, waving (palm) tree branches, or "a bunch of roses."
Confrontation /meeting songs	"Open the Door Let the Man Come In/ All Ah We a Wan Family"; "Come Leh Awe Go Way"	(2) Meeting at the gate or door.	Through song, the groom's nation requests permission to enter the bride's premises. Pouring libation.
Greeting songs	"Goodnight, Ay"; "Nation"; "Come to My Kweh-Kweh"	(3) Families/nations of the bride and groom meet and greet each other in song.	Singing, hugging, and other forms of greeting. (Pouring libation.)
Searching /seeking songs	"Ah Wonder Whey Me Lova Gaan"; "Search Am Go/So Find Am"; "Com Leh Awe Go 'Way"	(4) Hiding of the bride; searching for the bride.	The groom and his nation search for the bride, who has been hidden somewhere on the premises prior to the opening of the door or gate. When they can't find the bride, they threaten to leave or "go 'way."
Bride-price songs	"Ah Who Go Stan' Am?"; "Twenty Dallah Cyaan Buy Dis Gyal"; "Dis ah we Tadjah"	(5) Buying of the bride (exchange of bride price). Conclusion of the bride-price negotiation.	After the bride is found, she is covered with a white sheet and made to sit on a chair. The bride's and groom's nations then engage in the symbolic exchange of the bride-price in the form of money, alcohol, or other goods. At the conclusion of the bride-price exchange, the groom's nation celebrates by hoisting the bride in her chair and dancing her around.

Song Categories/Types	Musical Examples	Related Ritual Segments	Ritual Performances
Celebratory invitational songs	"Come to My Kweh-Kweh"; "Lilly Gyal"	(6) The *kweh-kweh* celebration in full swing. Collective singing and dancing by representatives from all sides.	Forming the *kweh-kweh* circle *(ganda)*; pouring of libation to welcome or appease the ancestors.
"Science" songs	"Show Me Yuh Science"; "'Oman Lie Down and de Man Cyaan Function"	(7) "Science" dance	Bride and groom *wine* (gyrate) alone and with/ on each other to demonstrate sexual prowess.
Celebratory "general" kweh-kweh songs	"Seetyrah"; "Bamboo Fiyah [Fire]"	(8) *Kweh-kweh*.	Singing, dancing, eating, talking, mingling, etc.
Farewell songs	"Gyal Yuh Glorious Maanin' Come"; "Here Aunty Bess Ah Hallah"; "Las' Wan"; "Tomorrow Ma'nin Yuh Ah Go Away"; "Goodbye, Janey, Goodbye"; "Come Away"	(9) Saying goodbye.	Cleaning up, singing, dancing, greeting, making final wedding arrangements.

environment of communal singing also provides a safe space for *kweh-kweh* participants to address sex and other matrimonial issues. In the African-Guyanese community, candid discussions between parents and children about sex are rare and sometimes regarded as taboo. Even though educators who are tasked with the responsibility of providing sex education often address such topics in the classroom, parents may resort to proverbs and other forms of coded language to gauge the topic of sex with their children (Richards-Greaves 2016a). Thus, for many, the *kweh-kweh* ritual might be the first time they hear their parents and respected adults in society openly address sexual matters. In the past, sex was addressed in traditional *kweh-kweh* with songs that used coded language and accompanying risqué gestures. Recently, it has become commonplace for *kweh-kweh* participants, particularly younger ones, to discard the use of coded language altogether for more explicit language, partly because they believe that younger generations lack the skills needed to decode and understand proverbial speech. However, even in cases where communal singing involves more overtly risqué lyrics, singers are somewhat protected by established societal norms at *kweh-kweh*, including: (1) *kweh-kweh* is grown-folk business (an adult affair) because it addresses sex and other matters of marriage; (2) "*kweh-kweh* nuh get bad word" (there's no foul language in *kweh-kweh*), partly because it is grown-folk business; and (3) *kweh-kweh* takes place in the dead of night and generally excludes young (prepubescent) children.

Kweh-kweh singing is accompanied by traditional *kweh-kweh* dance, which is performed in a circle that moves counterclockwise to a rhythm in common time (4/4 meter). The choreographed movements of the dance include the stomping or shuffling of the feet, the contorting of the upper body, and, in the case of women, the swaying of skirts from side to side. At regular intervals during the dance, participants stop moving and dance in place. It is during this stationary period that the bride and groom are placed in the *ganda* (performance center), where they are expected to "show yuh science" or demonstrate sexual process by *wining* (gyrating) alone and with each other. During the science dance, the *kweh-kweh* community offers commentary on the sexual abilities of the bride and groom, their impending marriage, and, by extension, the continued survival of the larger Guyanese community.[3] If either the bride or groom does not *wine* to the satisfaction of the attendees, the *kweh-kweh* community verbally disparages them, forcing a representative from their nation to enter the *ganda* and *wine* on their behalf. Some older Guyanese have argued that having someone else *wine* on one's behalf indexes failure and sends the message to the community that if a man or woman does not do their "job" in the bedroom, someone else will do it for them (Gibson 2003). Adrienne Kaeppler argues that dance highlights "invisible" or embedded systems in a society (2000, 118), and this aptly applies to music and dance performances in traditional *kweh-kweh* and Come to My Kwe-Kwe rituals. For African-Guyanese, the preponderance of sex-related songs, coupled with skillful *wining*, indexes sexual prowess and, by extension, one's ability to procreate, ensuring the continued survival of the community (Gibson 1998,

169). Moreover, in the eyes of the Guyanese community, procreation validates one's femininity or masculinity. Therefore, having a close relative or friend *wine* on one's behalf is a way of reclaiming one's pride, redeeming the nation's good name and safeguarding the continued existence of the larger community.

The singing and dancing at traditional *kweh-kweh* is generally accompanied by drums, body percussion (particularly the stomping of feet), and ad hoc ("found") instruments such as bottles and spoons, and buckets and sticks. More recently, however, keyboards and other formal instruments have been added to the instrumentation, particularly in the United States. The playing of instruments at *kweh-kweh* is a largely gendered activity in that musicians are males, while women participate in the communal singing and dancing. Many older African-Guyanese view the presence of instruments, particularly drums, as an affront to tradition, because they believe that the rhythmic accompaniment at *kweh-kweh* should be provided by the feet and "found" instruments only (Lionel Britton and Ian "Bertie" Carter, interview, New Amsterdam, Guyana, 2009). The argument against the use of instruments in *kweh-kweh* indexes an earlier period in Guyana's history when enslavers banned the use of drums for fear that the slaves might use them to communicate their plans for insurrection and other subversive acts against enslavers (Handler 1982, 17). After the banning of drums, African-Guyanese used their feet and "found" instruments to provide the heavy duple-meter rhythms of the traditional dance. Thus, rhythms produced by hitting a glass bottle with a metal spoon or a plastic bucket with a stick became familiar sounds in traditional *kweh-kweh* rituals in Guyana. The practice of using "found" instruments as musical accompaniment or creating "something from nothing" was common in precolonial Africa and continues today (Afolayan 2004, 240). Some well-known examples of such musical innovations in the African diaspora include the *steelpan*, which originated in Trinidad and Tobago (Liverpool 1994; Dudley 2004), and the *diddley bow* (Gillaspie 2006, 268–69), homemade drums, flutes, and guitars of early African-American bluesmen and blueswomen from the Mississippi Delta region in the southern United States (Lomax 1979).

African Continuities in Traditional *Kweh-Kweh* Music in Guyana

In addition to "found" instruments, traditional *kweh-kweh* (and the reenacted Come to My Kwe-Kwe) has many musical features that are arguably *African continuities*, both in form and function. The diffusion of African continuities to Guyana occurred in the minds, mouths, and muscle memory of enslaved Africans (Waterman 1971, 227–44; Nketia 2005). In addition to the *kweh-kweh* ritual, African continuities are also embodied in African-Guyanese religious rituals like *comfa* (Gibson 2001, 1), *mami wata* (Gibson 1996; Drewal 2008), and *obeah* (Browne 2011); and in life-cycle rituals like the prewedding *kweh-kweh* ritual (Richards-Greaves 2013) and *'nansi 'tory*, a funerary rite that eulogizes the deceased through oral narratives that aggrandize their life and accomplishments (Bauman [1977] 1984, 74).[4] Over time, the manner in which African-influenced rituals were executed changed as Africans in Guyana experienced acculturation through their interactions with Amerindians, East Indians, Europeans, and other ethnic groups. Thus, several factors, including the separation of enslaved Africans from the African continent and the historical contexts of musical and cultural performances; their forced assimilation into European cultures; and cultural mixings with other ethnic groups in Guyana, facilitated musical innovations in crucial life-cycle rituals like the traditional *kweh-kweh* ritual. Thus, the *kweh-kweh* ritual simultaneously exhibits African musical continuities, elements from other Guyanese ethnicities, and hybrid or *syncretic* ritual expressions that developed in Guyana. It is, however, the African continuities—including communal singing, the use of drums, the counterclockwise moving circle, and the interconnectedness of music and dance—that are central to the negotiation of African group identities and cohesiveness, which are so essential to processes of *diasporization* (Hanna 2001, 165–66; Sublette 2004, 57).

Communal singing is an African continuity that continues to be practiced in *kweh-kweh*. Although communal singing is also a *cultural generality*, many scholars have noted its pervasiveness in Africa and its integral role in everyday life in pre- and postcolonial sub-Saharan Africa (Agawu 2016). Communal singing on the

African continent and in the African diaspora functions in numer-
ous ways, including enabling participants to provide commentary
on or to critique a situation or person, thereby limiting the risk of
individual culpability for the act. Communal singing also serves
to lessen the tedium of work by facilitating a steady rhythm and
synchronizing movements during tasks and taking the mind off
the activity at hand (Work 1998, 38; Gioia, 2006).

A key feature of communal singing that further connects Africa
and its diasporas is call-and-response, which allows the entire community to actively participate in the singing. In the *kweh-kweh* ritual,
call-and-response helps to sustain the energy level of the performance by creating what Doede Nauta (1972) refers to as a "feedback
loop" between the captain or leader and other attendees. The feedback from the audience also serves as an approval or commentary on
the quality of the performance, which can further influence the manner in which the captain proceeds, if he proceeds at all. Moreover, the
refrains in each *kweh-kweh* enable participants to establish a musical
foundation upon which the captain develops elaborate narratives
about the bride, the groom, and their nation. In effect, the feedback
loop created from the call-and-response communal singing renders the division between the performer and the audience virtually
nonexistent (Burnim 2001; Richards-Greaves 2015).

African musical continuities in *kweh-kweh* are also observable in
the seemingly inherent connectedness of music and dance (Nketia
1981; Reed 2016). Although music in pre- and postcolonial Africa
accompanied work and other activities during which dancing was
not possible or allowed, ritual music was overwhelmingly accompanied by dance. The connectedness between music and dance is partly
influenced by the communal nature of music making in precolonial
Africa, in which the metaphorical distance between the performer
and the audience was narrower than in European musical expressions. This is not to overlook the fact that skilled musicians such as
djelis often entertained audiences with solo performances, but to
emphasize that ritual music was often functional in that it facilitated
entertainment, agency in the spirit realm, and other activities that
required communal participation. Even when a primary musician

is the center of music production, the audience in attendance is still expected to provide feedback and support in the form of singing, clapping, dancing, and verbal affirmation.

Drums constitute another key African continuity in traditional *kweh-kweh*. Although Africans were initially separated from their drums due to slavery, they retained the knowledge of drum making, the techniques of playing the drums, and the rhythmic patterns played on the drums. Thus, in Guyana and around the world, the Enslavement African Diaspora continues to make conga drums, *djembes*, and other types of percussive musical instruments out of the materials they encountered in the New World. Africans in Guyana, for example, continue to make drums from hollowed-out tree trunks and animal hides, plastic pipes, buckets, and other synthetic materials. The *djembe*—which has become a unique musical symbol of pan-Africanism (Charry 2000; Polak 2005; Flaig 2010)— continues to occupy a central place in *kweh-kweh*. Although their African heritage continues to be a crucial wellspring for music composition, African-Guyanese drum making and drum playing are also shaped by sustained cultural contact with Amerindians, Europeans, East Indians, and other ethnic groups.

The performance of dances in a counterclockwise-moving circle is another African continuity that is observable in traditional *kweh-kweh* and Come to My Kwe-Kwe. Ring dances and games—such as "Colored Girl in the Ring," "Limbo Sah-Lay," and, in the past, *yama pele*—are key features of African-Guyanese children's enculturation. Ring games and dances are also prevalent in other segments of the Enslavement African Diaspora (Stuckey 1988; Stuckey 2002; Rosenbaum 1998). Some of the ring games and songs are of European origin, some of African origin, and some, New World compositions. Nevertheless, many ring games include songs with words, phrases, and syntaxes from African languages, which the users themselves may or may not understand. When ring games involve physical movement in a circle, participants generally move in a counterclockwise direction. Similarly, when ring games involve the passing of objects within an immobile circle, participants pass the objects to their right, thus creating a counterclockwise movement of the objects in the circle. The counterclockwise dance

Figure 4.3: A drummer from the village of Buxton, Guyana, tightens the membrane of his homemade drum at a traditional *kweh-kweh* in Georgetown, Guyana, 2009. Photo by Gillian Richards-Greaves.

in *kweh-kweh* and Come to My Kwe-Kwe is very similar to circular dances in other African diasporic groups, such as the ring shout among the Gullah Geechee in the southern United States (Stuckey 1988; Stuckey 2002; Rosenbaum 1998). Counterclockwise dances are also practiced by indigenous peoples of the United States and by other groups but are especially pervasive in the musical traditions of Africa (James 2000; Henderson 2009). Although many African-Guyanese understand that the counterclockwise-moving circle in the *kweh-kweh* ritual is an African continuity transmitted to them by their ancestors, many are unaware or even unconcerned about the deeper significance of the circle or its counterclockwise movement to African cosmology or their perpetuation of it.

In African cosmology, the circle represents the continuity of human life. Among Bantu-Congo peoples, there are four crucial points on the circle that represent the four key events or phases of life, which are "pregnancy, birth, maturity and death" (Fu-Kiau 1994, 23; Fu-Kiau 2001; Abímbólá 1994, 100–116). At each stage within the circle, a person fulfills a specific function in the maintenance of balance in the social and spiritual order of a society. From the African cosmological perspective, also, death is not regarded as a finality but a transition into another phase or realm of existence—that of the ancestors (Kanu 2013, 533–55). Thus, while the ancestors no longer dwell in the physical realm, they are included in prayers, rituals, and daily activities, as they are responsible for assisting, guiding, blessing, and even punishing the living. In the *kweh-kweh* ritual, the continuity of life after death is represented not only by the circle but also by the pouring of libation to include the ancestors in the ritual proceedings.

Come to My Kwe-Kwe and African-Guyanese *Rediasporization* in New York City

African musical continuities that feature prominently in traditional *kweh-kweh* and play a key role in the process of African-Guyanese *diasporization* are further reinterpreted and utilized in the American context to facilitate African-Guyanese-American *rediasporization*. Through music, the captain (leader) demonstrates his virtuosity in singing, textual improvisation, and storytelling as well as his skill at drumming or playing other instruments. Music also demarcates each stage of Come to My Kwe-Kwe, allowing attendees to recount childhood memories in Guyana; advise, chide, or tease the bride and groom and their nation; and, in the process, comment on Guyanese values. In the secondary diaspora, however, Come to My Kwe-Kwe music also functions as a leveling mechanism that compels the old, the young, the Guyanese born, the "foreigner," and the stranger to orally conform to, or at least confront, an established notion of African-Guyanese-Americanness. Thus, although African-Guyanese-Americans continue to perform traditional (wedding-based) *kweh-kweh* songs at Come to My Kwe-Kwe, several factors have facilitated unique changes to the music and the traditional choreographed dance, including: (1) the physical features of the performance space; (2) the repertoire; (3) the instrumentation; (4) the composition of the audience; and (5) the function of the ritual itself.[5]

Since 2011, Come to My Kwe-Kwe has been held in the ballroom of Saint Stephen's Lutheran Church in Brooklyn. The fluorescent lighting in this ballroom creates a relatively well-lit performance space where everyone's deportment is visible to everyone else. However, traditional *kweh-kweh* in Guyana historically unfolded in the dead of night with limited lighting, partly because of a lack of or inadequate electricity. The opacity of the ritual performance space was further underscored by the adult content addressed in the ritual. The relative darkness at traditional *kweh-kweh*, particularly in the primary diaspora in Guyana, provides a real and symbolic mask for singers addressing sensitive topics, dancers gyrating or performing sexualized dances, and performers demonstrating risqué gestures. Even contemporary expressions of traditional *kweh-kweh* in Guyana and the United States take place with much less lighting than the Come to My Kwe-Kwe venue affords. The lighting of the performance space at Come to My Kwe-Kwe is a significant development, because coitus is one of the principal topics addressed, just as it is in traditional *kweh-kweh*. Thus, at Come to My Kwe-Kwe, the well-lit performance space may adversely affect the composition of the audience and the participation levels of attendees, who might be apprehensive about participating in risqué performances that are recorded and publicized on the internet. Moreover, since young, prepubescent children are sometimes present at Come to My Kwe-Kwe, the well-lit performance space is particularly problematic for older African-Guyanese-Americans, who tend to maintain conservative values and who view the content of Come to My Kwe-Kwe as too mature or risqué for children.

The relatively small performance space and its fixed location also affect the music and dance at Come to My Kwe-Kwe. Although a traditional *kweh-kweh* proper unfolds at a bottom house, tent, or other fixed location, the outdoor procession and other ritual elements at traditional *kweh-kweh* allow for greater usage of physical space and community involvement than Come to My Kwe-Kwe. Thus, for example, during the "searching for the bride" segment in traditional *kweh-kweh*, participants are often compelled to move beyond the central performance space (*ganda*) to search closets, houses, cars, and storehouses in yards to find the bride. However, because the church's ballroom is the only performance space utilized at Come to My Kwe-Kwe, ritual segments must be drastically shortened. The procession, for instance, must be shortened to fit the time it takes the attendees to walk from the front of the hall to the back. Additionally, the places the bride can hide are limited and confined to the hall, thus diminishing both the amount of time the groom and his nation must spend searching for her and the excitement often associated with that endeavor. Consequently, the diminished search time, like the shortened procession, affects the types and number of songs performed as well as the duration of each performance. The captains at Come to My Kwe-Kwe must choose songs that best capture and highlight the ritual segment at hand in the relatively short period of time allotted. The limited space also requires Come to My Kwe-Kwe captains to forego the elaborate improvisations of songs, which is a crucial element of traditional *kweh-kweh*. This omission is notable because improvisation allows song leaders to demonstrate their virtuosity and wit, recount history, and provide commentary on the bride, the groom, and their respective nations. Ultimately, the shortening of the singing during ritual segments adversely affects the layering or thickening of the performance that is achieved through the storytelling embedded in those improvisations.

As it is with the performance space, instrumentation also affects the *soundscape* (Shelemay 2015, 8) at Come to My Kwe-Kwe rituals, where singing and dancing are primarily accompanied by drums and synthesizers.[6] The synthesizer, with its preprogrammed beats, often determines the key in which each song is sung, while the drummers set the tempo. This is in stark contrast to traditional *kweh-kweh* instrumentation in the primary diaspora in Guyana, where the stomping of feet sets the tempo and adds to the aesthetics of the performance. At Come to My Kwe-Kwe, the tempo set by the drums and synthesizer is generally faster and the rhythmic patterns different from those set by the singers and their stomping feet in traditional *kweh-kweh*. The resultant sound, therefore, mirrors calypso, soca, and other forms of Caribbean dance music and Afropop, as opposed to the communal call-and-response commentary characteristic of traditional *kweh-kweh*.

The instruments at Come to My Kwe-Kwe create a lively and celebratory atmosphere, but, as mentioned previously, they are also often a source of annoyance and even discomfort for older African-Guyanese-Americans, who view the instruments as disruptive to the flow and sweetness of the ritual. They argue that tempo should be established by the captain and accentuated and improvised by the dancers, who stomp, shuffle, and kick their feet in time while contorting their bodies. The dancers are therefore compelled to adjust their steps to accommodate the faster tempo or to discard the traditional dance altogether for more freestyle dances. Moreover, the sound of the drums, and the amplified instruments and captains' voices, drown out the voices of the other attendees and the rhythmic stomping of their feet during the choreographed ritual dance. Thus, the introduction of formal instruments into the performance wrests the power of melodic and rhythmic decision-making from dancers, who must adapt their movements to an established beat.

Complaints that many older African-Guyanese-Americans have about the presence of musical instruments in the Come to My Kwe-Kwe ritual are often compounded by Christians' perceptions of drums as vessels of African spirituality, specifically as vehicles of spirit possession (Charry 2000). For many African-Guyanese Christians, drums are not just musical instruments but vessels of spiritual power, which, if played in a certain way, can take control of the minds of weak and unsuspecting listeners and compel them to behave out of character. African-Guyanese often talk about feeling lightheaded, as though they are approaching an altered state of consciousness, when hearing the beat of drums. Many often express a desire to dance to the rhythm of drums but fear losing control of their mental faculties. This fear is compounded by the fact that Faithists and other African-Guyanese who openly incorporate African drumming in their rituals also embrace African magico-religious practices like *comfa* and obeah.[7] The power of the drum was referenced in the vignette at the beginning of the chapter when Patsy shouted to Lio, "Beat the drum and the spirit gon get up." While the "spirit" may refer to Patsy's own energy or excitement level, it also indexes a spiritual awakening that African-Guyanese associate with drumming. Many view drums as a remnant of their African heritage and thus a symbol of backwardness and pagan identity. This negative view of drums among African-Guyanese (in Guyana and abroad) is underscored by Christian doctrine on blackness (Africanness), particularly the "myth of Ham" (Johnson 2004). Even African-Guyanese who are not Christians tend to associate drums with Africanness, and thus with evil. These negative views on drums were solidified during centuries of indoctrination during which enslaved Africans and their descendants were taught to equate Africanness with darkness or sin. Thus, the negative perceptions of drums held by many African-Guyanese transcended the instruments to include all African-derived cultural practices. Akoyaw Rudder, *kweh-kweh* captain, master drummer, and member of the Santería religion, explained the negative attitudes of African-Guyanese toward drums in the following manner:

> Well the drums, the goatskin is alive. The tree, according to the Africans, is alive. And all those forces are put together, and remember now, we are African people, and the drums [are] our roots. It's within our soul, our body, and that's part of us that you can't just tear away. Some people react to it favorably and some people don't. So therefore, when those who are light-headed [who have a weak spirit; are easily overcome spiritually] . . . soon as they hear the drum tap they ready to shake; they start to shiver. . . . There's a communication with drums and self and soul. So once that communication is right, your music, your ancestors, you have your ancestors with you. (Akoyaw Rudder, interview, November 23, 2005)

Nevertheless, an increasing number of African-Guyanese-Americans who rejected the use of drums in traditional *kweh-kweh* in a Guyana context have begun to tolerate, embrace, and even defend the use of drums at Come to My Kwe-Kwe celebrations, for diverse reasons. Some view the presence of drums in the American context as a necessary evil—as a means of driving the performance and sustaining the excitement level, particularly when attendees are not actively participating in the ritual segments. Since around 2005, also, an increasing number of African-Guyanese have become vocal about embracing drums as a symbol of their African heritage. For some of these individuals, embracing Africanness became important after they were displaced from Guyana, and it became expedient for them to articulate an ethnic identity that distinguished them from other Guyanese ethnics in the United States. Many also regard drums, particularly the *djembe*, as a symbol of pan-African identity that unites peoples of African descent within and beyond the United States. Thus, when played in the context of Come to My Kwe-Kwe, drums feature prominently in the process of *rediasporization* by connecting African-Guyanese-Americans to *home*—both Africa and Guyana.

The instrumentation at Come to My Kwe-Kwe also shapes the repertoire, much like the performance space, discussed previously. Very often, the songs chosen are catchy and popular, but they do not necessarily allow for elaborate improvisation or the development of a narrative, as is common in traditional *kweh-kweh*. The leaders and audience at Come to My Kwe-Kwe prefer to lean toward fast-paced medleys that include traditional *kweh-kweh* songs, Guyanese folk songs, and other genres that fit the mood and sustain the jollification. Regardless of the genre, however, Come to My Kwe-Kwe repertoire tends to draw heavily on more risqué songs like "Biggie So" (example 3.4) and "Two Lolo." Because of changes to the repertoire and traditional dance in Come to My Kwe-Kwe, many older African-Guyanese regard the newer performances as inauthentic, because they lean too heavily on risqué songs and *wining* rather than on the intricacies of the ritual.

Example 4.1: "Two, Lolo, Two Lolo"

Creolese
"Mighty Lo" got two lolo
Wan in he face and wan in he waist
"Mighty Lo" got two lolo

English
Two penises, two penises
"Mighty Lo" has two penises

Although the performance space and instrumentation shape the nature of the musical performance, the composition of this diaspora's diaspora also plays a crucial role in shaping the music at Come to My Kwe-Kwe. As discussed in chapter 1, the African-Guyanese diaspora in the United States is composed of the *migrated diaspora*, the *procreated* or *reproduced diaspora*, the *affinal diaspora*, and visitors and strangers (fig. 1.3). For this reason, Come to My Kwe-Kwe leaders work to ensure that everyone gets a basic understanding of how traditional *kweh-kweh* will be interpreted in this new setting before the ritual begins. Thus, at the beginning of every Come to My Kwe-Kwe ritual, dancer Dr. Rose October-Edun, master drummers Akoyaw Rudder and Winston "Jeggae" Hoppie, and other leaders provide an overview of the traditional *kweh-kweh* ritual and teach attendees the choreographed dance steps of the traditional dance. Throughout the performance, they also provide guidance and instruction to attendees on the proper execution of ritual practices. This type of direct, public instruction generally does not take place at traditional *kweh-kweh*, where attendees are familiar with the proceedings or fall in line after observing other, more seasoned participants.

In 2007, the generational differences in musical performances was put on full display when self-proclaimed *kweh-kweh* guru Lionel "Lio" Britton was invited by the Guyana Cultural Association in New York to be the guest captain (or tutor, as he calls it) at that year's Come to My Kwe-Kwe. Lio, who was in his late seventies at the time, stated that the sweetness of the ritual lies in the leader's ability to extemporize the lyrics of each song in a manner that creates a detailed narrative about the bride and groom and their matrimonial responsibilities. He also argued that the only instrumentation in the ritual should be the stomping feet against the floor and the use of "found" instruments. However, at Come to My Kwe-Kwe he encountered an audience who had paid an entry fee to attend the event and had grown accustomed to the type of entertainment provided by master drummers Akoyaw and "Jeggae," and other members of the Kwe-Kwe Ensemble. Thus, from the beginning of the ritual until the end, there was a sort of tug-of-war between Lio and the American-based captains and performers, as both sides promoted their own view of authenticity. For Lio, authenticity requires strict adherence to an archaic form of traditional *kweh-kweh* (Moore 2002, 211). From his perspective, also, authentic music and dance performances are those of "the folk" (ordinary people), characterized by "no sham, no got-up glitter, and no vulgarity" (Boyes 1993, 26). However, captains like Akoyaw view Come to My Kwe-Kwe as space where young Guyanese, visitors, and *kweh-kweh* novices can learn about African-Guyanese culture and have fun in the process. Moreover, many seasoned *kweh-kweh* participants often overlook the risqué language and behavior because the ritual provides "a legitimate social occasion when people in the community can behave in a way that is contrary to expected patterns" (Edwards 1982, 188). Thus, Akoyaw and other performers in the American context view their interpretations of traditional *kweh-kweh* as equally authentic as Lio's, because they are African-Guyanese and they maintain the overall structure of the ritual. From their perspective, the changes to traditional *kweh-kweh* that occur in Come to My Kwe-Kwe do not destroy the ritual but ensure its survival by keeping it relevant, especially among younger generations. Akoyaw argued further:

> When young people get involved with stuff, you have to take it and jump with it. Don't just criticize, you have to encourage them, and it's our culture. Too many times, the Guyanese culture is just being swept under the rug. I'm glad that the young people—and

all the Guyanese—that their eyes are open. They're seeing the light.
(Akoyaw Rudder, interview, November 23, 2005)

As they teach the audience to sing the songs, perform the ritual
dance, and execute ritual segments, Come to My Kwe-Kwe leaders
are also teaching attendees how to be African-Guyanese. While a
national Guyanese identity is articulated through songs, stories,
and proverbs that are all performed in Creolese, an African identity is demonstrated by using drums and "found" instruments, and
by wearing dashikis, long skirts, head wraps, and other African-
influenced clothing. More implicit negotiations of African identity
are achieved when performers reference villages in Guyana as a
means of asserting the authority or claiming the authenticity of
Come to My Kwe-Kwe ritual practices. This is partly because these
villages are where enslaved Africans lived and performed traditional *kweh-kweh*. After emancipation, formerly enslaved Africans
purchased the villages and established communities with money
they earned doing odd jobs and selling the produce they cultivated
during their free time (Covey and Eisnach 2009, 76; Ishmael 2013,
98–99). Moreover, during and after slavery, villages like Buxton,
Hopetown, and Victoria, to cite a few, remained strongholds of
African continuities such as burial societies (Smith 1956, 10, 265;
Moore 1995, 116); informal banking in the form of *susu* or *throwing
box* (Smith 1956, 89; Allsopp 1996, 556; Wilson 2008, 234); and many
of the religious and secular rituals mentioned previously.

Conclusion

African-Guyanese-Americans constitute a secondary diaspora that
uses music and dance to demarcate the boundaries of their community and articulate ethnic identities. While they perform Guyanese
folk songs and other types of music in their everyday lives, the
music of the quintessentially African-Guyanese traditional *kweh-
kweh* ritual serves as the primary vehicle for cultural education and
entertainment in Come to My Kwe-Kwe celebrations. In this new

performance context in the United States, however, performers are compelled to innovate traditional music and dance to accommodate the needs of this eclectic community as they undergo the process of *rediasporization*. The innovations in music and dance are shaped by the performance space of the Come to My Kwe-Kwe venue, the instrumentation, the composition of the African-Guyanese-American community, and the function of the ritual. Nevertheless, even as African-Guyanese-Americans innovate the music and dance of traditional *kweh-kweh*, they continue to hold onto the crucial aspects of the traditional ritual, which simultaneously binds them to past (Africa and Guyana) and present (United States) homelands.

In many ways, music and dance at traditional *kweh-kweh* and Come to My Kwe-Kwe reflect processes of acculturation and creolization that have resulted from long-term, sustained interactions of African-Guyanese with other ethnic groups in Guyana and, later, the United States. However, many of the central features of Come to My Kwe-Kwe music and dance exhibit African continuities in both form and function. Some of these features include the communal call-and-response form; the use of coded language, particularly during singing, to address sensitive or risqué topics and to provide matrimonial advice; the counterclockwise-moving circular dance, executed with a lowered upper body and stomping feet, thus creating a two-against-three rhythmic pattern when coupled with the rhythm of the singing; and the use of drums that are said to energize performers, partly by imbuing them with spiritual power. African-Guyanese-Americans often emphasize the creolized elements of music and dance in Come to My Kwe-Kwe to highlight a national Guyanese identity, but draw on African continuities to articulate black (African) identities.

While African-Guyanese-Americans embrace Come to My Kwe-Kwe as "we ting" (their own cultural practice), many reject newer expressions, which they regard as inauthentic. The incorporation of instruments, particularly drums, is one of the primary markers of inauthenticity. For some older African-Guyanese, authentic instrumentation involves the stomping of the feet against the floor and the use of "found" instruments. In their view, drums, synthesizers, and other formal instruments deprive the performance of its sweetness by overwhelming the rhythms produced by the feet, subverting the pervasive and often humorous improvisations of the captain, and limiting the responses of attendees. Moreover, many regard drums as symbols of African spirituality, which is oppositional to Christianity and, thus, evil (DeVale 1989, 85; Case 2001, 44). The drums and other instruments are also blamed for inauthenticity in dance performances at Come to My Kwe-Kwe, which some regard as divergent from traditional *kweh-kweh* dance, and as excessively explicit. One older captain argued that the young people are not interested in learning the proper way to do the ritual because they only want to form a line and *wine*. For older Guyanese and religious persons who reject musical innovations, authenticity is rooted in the longevity of performance practices as well as in their distinction from *African continuities* (Africanisms or African retentions); these criteria are, however, often contradictory, since older practices often feature more Africanized conventions.[8]

For most African-Guyanese-Americans, however, Come to My Kwe-Kwe is not about an adherence to archaic notions of authenticity or tradition; it is about creating and sustaining community through cultural performances. For many who participate in Come to My Kwe-Kwe, music "evokes and organizes collective memories and present experience of place with an intensity, power and simplicity unmatched by any other social activity" (Stokes [1994] 1997, 3). Thus, many African-Guyanese-Americans attend Come to My Kwe-Kwe with the sole intent of enjoying themselves in the time allotted. For those who have never attended a traditional *kweh-kweh* and those who are disconnected from Guyanese cultural practices, Come to My Kwe-Kwe provides a unique and welcome respite in a society where they are bombarded by cultural differences. In the United States, many feel compelled to construct and display Guyanese identities that distinguish them from Indo-Guyanese and other Guyanese ethnics, and black identities that differentiate them from African-Americans, black Africans, Afro-Caribbean people, and others. As they move around in the circle, they may or may not adhere to the traditional *kweh-kweh* dance steps or sing in the key established by the keyboard, but their engagement in this reinterpretation of the ritual roots them in their current homeland (the United States) and binds them to two ancestral homelands (Guyana and Africa). Their performances may facilitate irrevocable changes to *kweh-kweh* music and dance, but their continued reinterpretation of the ritual ensures its continued survival. In essence, the performance of music and dance at Come to My Kwe-Kwe facilitates the broadening of the scope of relevance of traditional *kweh-kweh* to include cultural education and ethnic boundary maintenance in the *rediasporized* community.

5

"Borrow a Day from God"
Navigating the Boundaries of Race and Religion
in *Rediasporization*

Shroud nah gat packit, coffin nah gat ledge

<small>GUYANESE PROVERB</small>

*In 2007, traditional kweh-kweh guru Lionel "Lio" Britton was flown
in from Guyana to teach African-Guyanese at Come to My Kwe-Kwe
how to properly execute the ritual. I was introduced to Lio by Dr.
Vibert Cambridge, the president of the Guyana Cultural Association
in New York City. Not long after, Lio introduced me to his friend and
"right-hand man," who was also a skilled kweh-kweh guru, whom I'll
refer to as "Clive." After I asked Lio's permission to take his photograph,
he instructed me to also include his friend in the picture. However,
as soon as I was about the take the photo, Clive covered his face and
turned his body away from the glaring eye of my lens. I was a bit
confused but did not take Clive's photo. After Come to My Kwe-Kwe
began, I noticed that Clive, who was a skillful and comical kweh-kweh
dancer, avoided the cameras at all costs, even turning his back when
necessary. I was baffled that someone who was introduced as an assistant or a sidekick to the evening's main act (Lio) would be so bashful.
A few days later, when I asked Lio about Clive's antics, he explained*

Figure 5.1: Ira Leona "Lady Ira" Lewis—entrepreneur, humanitarian, philanthropist, culture bearer—pours libation at the beginning of Come to My Kwe-Kwe as musicians look on; Brooklyn, August 31, 2018. Photo by Gillian Richards-Greaves.

that his friend was an accountant in his Seventh-Day Adventist church and was attending Come to My Kwe-Kwe on the Sabbath. According to Lio, Clive stated that when he has to attend events on the Sabbath, he will "borrow a day from God."

Introduction

Religious diversity is a defining characteristic of the Guyanese community, as most Guyanese claim some form of religious affiliation and view their religious values as crucial to enculturation and their very existence (Hill 1996; Stephanides and Singh 2000; Gibson 2001; Bissessar and La Guerre 2015, 75–80). A significant percentage of the Guyanese population embraces established Old World religions like Christianity, Hinduism, and Islam, but Guyana's religious fabric is also composed of agnostics, atheists, shamans, and those who practice newer, more syncretic religions such as Faithism and Rastafarianism (Guyana Bureau of Statistics 2012, 34). There is also an underlying correlation between race (ethnicity) and religious affiliation (Guyana Bureau of Statistics 2012, 32–34). Thus, for example, East Indians overwhelmingly identify as Hindus and Muslims; Amerindians and Chinese embrace Christianity and indigenous religious practices; and African-Guyanese practice Christianity, Faithism, Islam, Rastafarianism, and indigenous African religions, among others. Religion is so important to Guyanese culture that religious dogma undergirds most societal values, particularly those pertaining to race, class, gender, politics, and education (Glasgow 1970; Rabe 2005; Bissessar and La Guerre 2015, 75–80). Parents, teachers, clergy, and other leaders in society often use scriptures, songs, stories, proverbs, and other sources to instill and reinforce religious values in young children and members of the Guyanese community at large (Wilson 2008; Cambridge 2015; Richards-Greaves 2016b).

Among African-Guyanese, religious values shape individual and collective perspectives on race and blackness. These religious values essentially divide the population into two overarching religious categories or groups: (1) Christians, who make up the religious majority; and (2) "Africanists," who openly embrace their African heritage regardless of other religious affiliations. Under the umbrella of "Christians" are individuals who identify as Anglicans, Catholics, Faithists, Pentecostals, Presbyterians, and Seventh-Day Adventists, among others (Wilson 2008, 162–66; Cambridge 2015; Bisnauth 1996). "Africanists" are a more heterogeneous group that includes individuals who identify with one or more religious sects as well as those who claim no religion. Thus, groups like the Faithists, who embrace Christian doctrinal practices as well as African practices like obeah—"an Afro-Caribbean complex of spiritual healing, harming, and divination" (Browne 2011, 453)—can be categorized as both Africanists and Christians. Therefore, African-Guyanese religious values not only shape their views on race (ethnicity) but also affect how or whether they engage with African-influenced cultural and religious practices and practitioners.

This chapter examines the ways that religious doctrines, particularly those pertaining to "good" and "evil," influence

African-Guyanese views about their African heritage and their engagement with Come to My Kwe-Kwe. The chapter delves beneath the surface of individual religious stances to examine how African-Guyanese religious views on *kweh-kweh* ritual elements have remained relatively static or changed in a new performance context. Thus, this chapter demonstrates the strategies that African-Guyanese-Americans employ to negotiate multiple identities uniquely shaped by embedded, increasingly shifting religious values in a community experiencing *rediasporization*.

Theologizing "Good" and "Evil" in African-Guyanese Religious Practices

Christianity and the "Myth of Ham"

African-Guyanese practice diverse religions, but they overwhelmingly identify as Christians. Christianity was largely introduced to Guyana by British enslavers during the Atlantic slave trade. The British drew on the religious doctrine of the Anglican Church (the Church of England) to enact and enforce laws (Paton 2009, 1–18; Browne 2011, 453; Rugemer 2018, 102–20; Cambridge 2015); to establish economic, educational, and sociopolitical institutions (Gibson 2001; Costa 1994, 77); and to exert control over the slave population using ethnocentric notions of "civilization" (Bush 1990, 102; Thompson 2003, 35). Because the Anglican Church controlled just about every civil and social institution in Guyana, joining the church was, for a long time, the only way for blacks to achieve economic and social advancement during and after slavery (Cambridge 2015; Gerbner 2018, 31–49). Furthermore, embracing Christianity was one of the only ways for blacks to achieve a sense of basic humanity or "civilization" in the eyes of Europeans, who generally regarded them and their African traditions as animalistic, barbaric, and evil (*Daily Argosy* 1931, 7; Allen, Ware, and Garrison [1867] 1971; Epstein 1977; Payne [1891] 2018, 125–30). While British Anglicanism became the face of Christianity in Guyana for many years, other

Christian denominations such as Catholicism, Presbyterianism, and Pentecostalism were eventually established in the country due to immigration, international missionary outreach, and evangelism (Seamone 2013; Marina 2016; Gerbner 2018).

Each sect of Christianity has its own canon, but there are over-arching tenets of faith that unite the diverse bodies of Christian denominations. Some of these doctrines include the creation of humankind; the virgin birth of Christ, his crucifixion and resurrection; and salvation from sin (Stagg 1962, 80). Christian religious principles are largely seen as uplifting to humanity; however, some African-Guyanese and religious scholars alike regard crucial Christian doctrines as oppressive and detrimental to African peoples and cultures. For example, Judeo-Christian doctrine teaches that after the flood that destroyed the earth, humanity was reestablished through the lineage of Noah's three sons, Shem, Ham, and Japheth. However, Ham, translated as "heat," "burned" and "dark" and regarded as the apical ancestor of black people, was cursed by his father to a life of servitude to his brothers Shem and Japheth (Genesis 9:18–28). This view of humanity is often labeled by those who embrace black liberation theology as the "myth of Ham" (Goldenberg 2003; Johnson 2004, 4). Black liberation theologians argue that any religion that espouses any form of enslavement or oppression of black people is a bondage religion and thus must be discarded (Cone [1970] 2010; Cone and Wilmore 1993). Sylvester Johnson argues that the "myth of Ham" causes black people to be "beleaguered by the burden of acting out a double script, lining the roles of both the people of God and the children of Ham—heathens" (2004, 11). Because Christian values are so deep-rooted in the African-Guyanese community, even individuals who embrace other religions or identify as atheists or agnostics often also practice or are familiar with Christian principles. Christian dogma is so entrenched in the Guyanese community that African-Guyanese themselves cite these doctrines to support their rejection of African cultural and religious practices.[1]

Christian values appear overwhelmingly at odds with Africanness, but there are significant differences in the way that established

Christian denominations like Anglicanism and Catholicism, and newer Christian denominations like Pentecostalism and Seventh-Day Adventism, respond to African-influenced traditions (Thomas 2014, 34). The doctrinal teachings and the clergy of more established Christian denominations tend to be less directly controlling of the personal lives of parishioners, apart from required religious liturgy. Because of this relative separation between religious and personal spheres, African-Guyanese members of these denominations tend to be more amenable to or accommodating of Africanized practices, particularly those practiced discreetly. In fact, many Faithists and others who practice syncretic religions were raised as Anglicans, Catholics, or members of other mainstream Christian sects. The relative ease with which African-Guyanese in established Christian denominations accommodate African and Christian practices may also be due to the fact that older people remember a time when simultaneously embracing African continuities and Anglicanism, for instance, was a matter of daily survival, of existing in a world where what was necessary for one's emotional health transcended established Christian doctrines about "good." Christians of established denominations may also embrace African continuities because of the commonalities they observe in seemingly disparate religious systems, such as in the roles of Catholic saints and African *orishas* or deities (Murphy 1993; De La Torre 2004). As Paul Zeleza noted: "Religion and music have been among the most crucial elements of cultural exchange. The traffic in religious ideas, institutions, and iconography, encompassing the African derived religions, Islam, Christianity, and Judaism, has been particularly intense and an important aspect of the African diasporic experience, identity, struggle, agency, and linkages with Africa" (2008, 19). Moreover, established Christian denominations are also becoming more accommodating because they are facing diminishing membership due to aging populations and large numbers of young people leaving these churches to join more vibrant Pentecostal churches or to reject Christianity altogether (Guyana Bureau of Statistics 2012, 34).

New World Christian denominations such as Seventh-Day Adventism, Jehovah's Witnesses, and Pentecostalism tend to espouse more rigid views of "good" and "evil," and what constitutes "the church" (believers) and "the world." Additionally, the values undergirding these distinctions are expected to be practiced by adherents within and without the church and are often monitored by fellow church members and leadership alike. One of the worst things, for instance, for an African-Guyanese Pentecostal Christian to be accused of is "wukkin' obeah" (practicing witchcraft), which encompasses a range of practices, some having nothing to do with African continuities (Bisnauth 1996). Beating drums (particularly in a drum circle), lighting candles or incense, praying to anyone or anything outside the Christian realm, and practicing any non-Christian rituals are some of the many reasons that individuals have been accused of "wukkin obeah." A person accused of "wukkin' obeah" can be excommunicated from the church, ridiculed in the community, and ostracized by close friends and relatives. Even when such accusations turn out to be false, the indictment often lingers long after the accused is deceased. Because of Christian dogma, African-Guyanese themselves tend to categorize African cultural and religious traditions as "evil" or "of the world"; thus, keeping these elements out of their personal lives and religious worship often takes precedence. It is no surprise, then, that Christians often openly reject Come to My Kwe-Kwe (and traditional *kweh-kweh*) because they view it as a residual stain of their African "Hamitic" heritage. By rejecting Africanness and embracing a "slave religion," African-Guyanese Christians inadvertently and overtly affirm the "merits" of slavery (Martin 1990; Gerbner 2018, 3). It is important to note, however, that the Africanness that African-Guyanese Christians reject is often not overt religious rituals but instead cultural expressions such as *wining* (gyration) and risqué language, which they regard as quintessentially African and vulgar.

In the United States, African-Guyanese Christians continue to embrace their Christian faith, but many are also compelled to discard or reinterpret some or all aspects of Christian dogma to accommodate their changing lives and beliefs. In their discussion of changes to Hinduism that results from migration, Inês Lourenço and Rita Cachado argue that "[t]he transformation of traditions always results from processes of adjustment to the circumstances found in the new places of settlement" (2012, 54). In many instances, African-Guyanese's more nuanced approach to Christianity stems from a confrontation of race and racial matters in the United States that requires them to rethink the religious teachings they previously accepted, particularly those pertaining to blackness or Africanness. Also, while many quickly find new church homes, their need to articulate uniquely African-Guyanese-American identities often influences them to turn to African-influenced Guyanese practices they might have overlooked or disparaged in Guyana. Additionally, the influences of members of the *procreated diaspora* (American-born children) and *affinal diaspora* (non-Guyanese spouses) further complicate the religious fabric of the African-Guyanese-American community (Lourenço and Cachado 2012, 54–55). Moreover, the changes taking place in the personal lives of African-Guyanese-Americans often require them to forego established religious doctrines—especially those pertaining to gender roles, church attendance, and Africanness—to accommodate employment and other personal needs, and to adjust to becoming members of a secondary diaspora.

African Continuities in African-Guyanese Religions

African-Guyanese I categorize as Africanists openly embrace African-influenced practices. Although Africanists embrace diverse religions, an increasing number of them claim no religion at all. One of the most visible groups of Africanists are the Faithists, who identify as Christians but also embrace indigenous African religions, Hinduism, Amerindian religious practices, and other religious dogmas and rituals they deem functional (Mintz and Price 1976, 19). The Faithist sect is an outgrowth of the Jordanites, a Christian faction that emerged in 1882 under the leadership of Joseph MacLaren, a Grenadian, and Bhagwan Das, an East Indian-Trinidadian. It was MacLaren's evangelism trip to Guyana that resulted in the conversion of Nathaniel Jordan in 1917, whose followers were later called "Jordanites" and "White-Robed Christians" as a reference to the long white robes they wore (Gibson 2001, 55–56; Roback 1974). The splintering of the Jordanites gave rise to the Faithists, who continued many Jordanite practices such as the wearing of white robes, worshipping on the Sabbath, and an emphasis on Old Testament doctrines (Gibson 2001, 57). The Faithists also added ancestor worship to their tenets of faith, which is referenced in the Old Testament although not generally practiced in contemporary Judaism (Gibson 2001, 57). Unlike most Christian churches, in which the pastor or leader is male, the highest-ranked leader in the Faithist church is a female called a "Mother." The syncretic nature of the Faithist church is observable in its blend of Christian and African rituals and symbols, including the singing of Christian hymns, the burning of incense, and the use of the *djembe* drum as the principal instrument in worship, for instance at the Faithists' Divine Apostolic Mystical Order of Saint Mary in Buxton, Guyana. Despite their adoption of syncretism, the Faithists' overt, enthusiastic embrace of African-influenced practices like obeah often results in their marginalization from Christian circles and from the larger African-Guyanese community.

Because Faithists view their African heritage as the essence of their religious experience, they regard self-knowledge as the foundation of true salvation. Africanists who embrace Christianity often reinterpret the "myth of Ham" in ways that reject the premise of Ham or the black race being cursed. Moreover, they often argue that these interpretations of scriptures were promoted by enslavers to justify enslavement and the continued subjugation of black people (Cone 1997, xv–xviii; Gnuse 2016, 65). Thus, from an Africanist perspective, knowing oneself requires an understanding of African history and culture that predates European colonization and the Atlantic slave trade, and historical narratives that demonstrate the genius, suffering, triumphs, and, more importantly, the complexities of African cultures. Africanists also argue that knowledge of one's African self generates self-pride, which inspires a sense of urgency on the part of African-Guyanese to celebrate and protect African cultural and religious practices. In a 2009 interview, Eric Phillips, an Africanist and the director of the African Cultural and Development Association in Guyana, stated:

We had great civilizations way, way, way beyond slavery. Slavery was four hundred years. Africans have been on this continent and this world as the first people, fifty-five thousand years and so we are trying to tell our young people that we had great civilizations whether it's Nigeria, Zimbabwe, South Africa, Egypt—the cradle of civilization—and Nubia; you can go all across Africa: Mali, you have the great libraries of Timbuktu, so we have an incredible culture.

Africanists also argue that the embrace of one's African heritage must involve the interrogation and embrace of known African continuities in the Guyanese community, such as magico-religious practices like *comfa*, obeah, and *mami wata*; life-cycle rituals like *'nansi 'tory*,[2] traditional *kweh-kweh* and Come to My Kwe-Kwe; and Afrocentric celebrations like Emancipation Day, which commemorates the end of the Atlantic slave trade.

Comfa is a generic term used to describe the manifestation of spirits (Gibson 2001). *Comfa* was "originally used to refer to the worship of the Watermamma [*mami wata*] spirit" (Gibson 2001, 1; also Moore 1995, 138; Asantewa 2016).[3] In African-Guyanese culture, *comfa* is also used to refer to the religion of Spiritualism or Faithism, in which spirit possession plays a significant role (Gibson 2001, 1). Thus, for instance, when the beating of drums causes a person to become spiritually possessed or to enter "altered states of consciousness" (Aldridge and Fachner 2006), that person is said to "ketch *comfa*" (Gibson 2001, 1), which causes them to "dance *anta-banta*" or dance on their head while in a trance-like state. The term *comfa* may also be a derivative of or have roots in the Akan word *akomfo*, which means "priest/ priestess" in the Akan Akom tradition and refers to human vessels or representatives of *abasom* (deities). The *abasom* of the *akomfo* function similarly to *mami wata* in *comfa* in that they are consulted by adherents who seek good fortune or relief from life's ills, such as barrenness (Manoukian 1964, 56; Opokuwaa 2005). Even though there are striking similarities between African-Guyanese *comfa* and the Akan *akomfo* (Akom tradition), it is likely that the magico-religious practices of other African ethnicities may have also influenced the practice of *comfa* in Guyana (Pérez y Mena 1998; Fandrich 2007).

The word *obeah*, referring to another magico-religious practice and African continuity, is said to be a derivative of the Twi word *obeye*, "used to describe the *won* entity that is within the witch— that is, anything that can work but is not seen" (Gibson 2001, 16; see also Moore 1995, 142–43). However, derivations of the term *obeah* referring to similar practices are observed among the Igbos of Nigeria and among other African ethnicities (Williams 1932). Obeah practitioners, called obeah-men and obeah-women, are local shamans who use their knowledge of the use of herbs to cure diseases or harm individuals (Harley 1941; Bush 1990, 154–55). As mentioned previously, African-Guyanese often indiscriminately categorize African-influenced or unexplained practices as obeah to disparage them and discourage others from practicing them. The negative attitude that many African-Guyanese express toward obeah reflects the sustained efforts of enslavers, who sought to eradicate African cultural practices by demonizing them and inflicting harsh punishment on those who practiced them (Browne 2011, 451–80; Paton 2012). Although obeah is overwhelmingly regarded as an African tradition, Amerindians, East Indians, and other ethnic groups in Guyana also engage in magico-religious practices referred to as obeah (Case 2001). Kean Gibson (2001) states: "The planters and administrators feared *obeah* because it was a source of power and unity for Blacks." Obeah was a source of power because the obeah-man was viewed as an "agent employed in the execution of vengeance," which was often leveled against the planter class (Gibson 2001, 17). Even African-Guyanese Christians and others who verbally reject obeah sometimes visit the obeah-man or obeah-woman discreetly to seek assistance when they face life crises that seem insurmountable (members of the Divine Apostolic Mystical Order of Saint Mary, interview, 2009; Fernández Olmos and Paravisini-Gebert 2011, 211). For many African-Guyanese, *comfa*, obeah, and other magico-religious African continuities provide a deep sense of angst not only because they are contrary to their religious beliefs but also because these practices delve into unknown African spiritual realms, which many regard as dangerous with retributive outcomes (Paton 2015, 41, 283).

When Africanists migrate to the United States, the angst surrounding African magico-religious practices continues to shape
their engagement with African-centered practices, as many try to
distinguish themselves from people who practice the "black arts."
Nevertheless, because of the diversity of African ethnicities in the
United States, especially in urban areas like New York City, many also
find more options for worship, and more freedom to do so. Groups
such as the Faithists often form alliances with Santeros (worshippers of Santería), adherents of Candomblé, and others who practice
Afrocentric syncretic religions (Murrell 2010; Fernández Olmos and
Paravisini-Gebert 2011, 9–11).[4] In fact, many African-Guyanese, such
as master drummer and practitioner of Candomblé Akoyaw Rudder,
find greater diversity of religious practices an increased opportunity
for African religious expressions. This allows them to form alliances
with other worshippers and musicians from whom and with whom
they learn more about the connections between African practices on
the African continent and in African diasporas. Moreover, through
their tireless embrace and showcasing of African traditions in the
United States, Africanists often create opportunities for once hardline
Christians to become Africanists, even if only part time or temporarily. It is therefore not surprising that Africanists constitute the
principal performers and musicians at Come to My Kwe-Kwe, who
work tirelessly to promote African-Guyanese culture and educate
others. It is the overwhelming need to articulate uniquely African-
Guyanese identities in the United States that compels many to turn
to African-influenced Guyanese practices for the first time or to
reexamine practices they already engage in from new perspectives.
Nevertheless, for diverse reasons, including religious and personal
values and saving face, African-Guyanese in the United States often
feel compelled to modify their religious beliefs and attitudes to
engage in some or all of Come to My Kwe-Kwe.

"Borrow a Day from God"

For many African-Guyanese-Americans, particularly Christians like
"Clive," mentioned in the vignette at the beginning of this chapter,

participation in Come to My Kwe-Kwe requires them to "borrow a day from God" when the event conflicts with religious observances like the Sabbath. Kwe-Kwe Nite takes place on Friday, when most people are off from work and can stay out into the wee hours of the morning. Additionally, changing the day of Come to My Kwe-Kwe to accommodate Sabbatarians would be unfeasible, since that would cause greater disruptions to the lives of more people than would celebrating on Friday evening. Moreover, most Seventh-Day Adventists would likely forego such an event rather than violate the Sabbath. Thus, Seventh-Day Adventists who choose to participate in Come to My Kwe-Kwe are compelled to ignore the stipulations of the Sabbath to do so. However, because of their dedication to their faith, many also devise ingenious ways to repay the day they borrowed from God to participate in Come to My Kwe-Kwe by observing Sabbath rituals on other days.

It is not only Sabbatarians who borrow a day from God but also Guyanese who view participation in Come to My Kwe-Kwe as contrary to their religious or moral values on any day of the week. In their case, borrowing a day from God is an even more symbolic gesture than that of Sabbatarians, as it does not apply to Friday and Saturday, on which the Sabbath is observed, but to every day of the week. For these individuals, attending Come to My Kwe-Kwe renders the day distinct, more sacrilegious than other days of the week. From their perspective, even if Come to My Kwe-Kwe were held on a Wednesday, that day would have to be set aside to engage in practices or behave in ways they regard as ungodly. Thus, by participating in Come to My Kwe-Kwe, they are robbing God of time that would have been committed to his service, even if that "service" is simply their proper deportment. The seemingly apologetic attitude that some African-Guyanese have toward participation in Come to My Kwe-Kwe and other African-influenced practices indexes a deep-rooted anti-African indoctrination that became entrenched in Guyanese culture during slavery and that persists today. Thus, even as they claim Come to My Kwe-Kwe as "we ting" (our thing) in the complex process of *rediasporization*, they still find it necessary to justify the time they take from their Christian walk to celebrate their blackness, as if those aspects of their identities are diametrically opposed.

African-Guyanese-Americans who borrow a day from God often participate in Come to My Kwe-Kwe in a manner that might be regarded as more subdued or restricted than that of other revelers. Thus, for instance, when Clive, mentioned in the vignette above, performed the ritual dance in a circle, he avoided the gaze of the camera. Even though he was introduced to the audience as the assistant or sidekick of the main tutor, he performed as though he wanted to ensure that there was little or no record of his performance that would outlive the evening. Thus, as he skillfully improvised the traditional *kweh-kweh* ritual dance in the circle, he systematically and strategically turned his back to the camera in a way that created smaller embedded circles within the larger *ganda*. In addition to avoiding my camera, Clive also tried to achieve limited visibility by dancing in a space that was farthest from the upraised stage where media personnel were gathered. Even though he claimed to have borrowed a day from God, Clive still demonstrated a high degree of caution in how he used the day, by attempting to mask his identity and, by extension, his presence at Come to My Kwe-Kwe.

A Day to (Mis)Behave

One of the principal reasons that African-Guyanese-Americans find it necessary to "borrow a day from God" to participate in Come to My Kwe-Kwe is to act "outta ardah" (out of order) or behave in a manner many view as vulgar or contrary to proper decorum (Edwards 1982, 188; Cowley 1998, 95, 172). The "misbehavior" that many cite encompasses the performance of risqué songs, dances, and gestures used to advise, instruct, and critique the acting bride and groom, and to provide humor for the community. Because Come to My Kwe-Kwe (like traditional *kweh-kweh*) is focused on marriage, sex often receives a disproportionate amount of attention, compared to other topics. Some songs about sex, like "Biggie So," celebrate the groom's virility, particularly as a slight to nonblack men. Celebrants use their entire forearms to symbolize the girth of the black man's genitalia, while singing, "Black man something biggie so, biggie so." Over the years, the performance of "Biggie So" has decreased, possibly to accommodate the diverse audience that includes men of other ethnicities or races.

While songs like "Biggie So" have decreased in frequency over the years, the performance of songs that instruct the bride and groom to remain sexually available to each other has remained consistent. Coitus is viewed as spousal "service" that the bride and groom are mandated to provide for each other, and the songs warn that the neglect of this crucial "service" could cause a person to "get blow" (becoming the victim of infidelity). Thus, during the science dance, when the bride and groom are placed in the *ganda* to demonstrate sexual prowess by gyrating alone, and with and on each other, the audience sings, "Show me your science" (gyrate). During this time, as the bride and groom gyrate, the audience evaluates their performance and provides feedback, such as "Dem 'Johnson' boi cyaaan wine" (The Johnson men cannot gyrate) or "Duh gyul gon geh blow" (That girl will be cheated on). Some African-Guyanese regard the science dance as nothing more than "dry sex." Moreover, in the context of Come to My Kwe-Kwe, in which the "bride" and "groom" are volunteers who may not be involved in a romantic relationship or even know each other, the idea of them performing activities reserved for engaged or married couples is unsettling to some. Some individuals who attend the ritual on borrowed time may accept that Come to My Kwe-Kwe is a respite from the daily rigors of strict deportment and thus should be enjoyed, or at least entertained. Others may, however, choose to avoid such demonstrations by remaining on the periphery of the performance space until the risqué segments of the ritual have concluded. Nevertheless, there are African-Guyanese who find the science dance personally distasteful but choose to marginally participate in this aspect of their culture by moving closer to get a better view of the performance, recording the event, or simply laughing along. Ultimately, how religious African-Guyanese-Americans choose to use their borrowed day varies from year to year, person to person, and even from one performance to the next in a single evening.

In addition to risqué songs and dances, explicit gestures are another reason some African-Guyanese feel the need to borrow a day from God to engage in Come to My Kwe-Kwe. During many gestures, the male and female genitalia are referenced or overtly celebrated, as in the song "Biggie So." In the song "You Shame," the bride is warned by her mother and the women in her community to practice good hygiene. The bride is further admonished that the potential shame or embarrassment that results from poor hygiene will be hers alone if she does not "tek wan calabash, wash yuh bembe" (take a calabash and wash [her] vagina). As they sing this song, participants use the palms of their hands to make a wiping motion close to the genital area to demonstrate how the bride should wash herself. Even though the language in this song is relatively coded in that *bembe* is used to refer to the vagina, the singing and accompanying gestures work in tandem to unmask the word and expose its meaning to the larger community. Moreover, during the singing of many other risqué songs, participants strip away the proverbial language for more colloquial or "raw" language, which many regard as inappropriate for everyday speech or for use in public spaces. In this context of openness, many who borrowed a day from God to join the proceedings are compelled to quickly decide how they will engage with this aspect of their culture. It is not uncommon to see participants move in and out of the *ganda* based on the song being sung or the accompanying gestures. As they navigate performance spaces at Come to My Kwe-Kwe, African-Guyanese engage in a series of checks and balances established and maintained by religious dogma and the need to negotiate ethnic identities.

In some instances, religious aspects of Come to My Kwe-Kwe, such as the pouring of libation to welcome the ancestors, pose greater personal conflicts for African-Guyanese than risqué songs, dances, and gestures. Libation can be loosely translated as "food for the dead," and, among African-Guyanese, it takes many forms (Nehusi 2015). For instance, the Faithists and others who engage in African-influenced religious practices sometimes offer libation to the ancestors in the form of cooked meals, fruits, and vegetables. However, a more common form of libation, particularly at traditional *kweh-kweh* and Come to My Kwe-Kwe, is the pouring of alcoholic beverages or water. In many African cultures, the pouring of libation is done using palm wine, whereby in the past, African-Guyanese used "bush rum" (Achebe 2011; Nehusi 2015, 18, 160). The practice of offering libation is rooted in African cosmology, which regards life as a cycle in which the living, the dead, and the unborn exist in different states and play crucial roles in the lives of the living (Mintz and Price 1976, 45; Mbiti 1970, 278–79). The pouring of libation is so common in the African-Guyanese community that many, including devout Christians, do so without much introspection. Thus, for instance, men drinking at rumshops often pour some of their alcohol on the ground before taking their first sip; women baking wedding cakes also pour some alcohol on the ground and in the corners of the home to welcome the ancestors and solicit their assistance and protection (Richards-Greaves 2016b). For many, particularly Christians, the pouring of libation and other practices that delve into the spirit realm of African traditions are regarded as too African or pagan for enlightened or "saved" individuals to participate in. The mention of ancestors or the pouring of libation to welcome them often causes visible unease among some participants, who eagerly wait for such aspects of the ritual to elapse. Even though some may privately participate in the pouring of libation or other African-centered religious rituals, the public engagement in such practices increases the risk of them being accused of engaging in ancestor worship, or worse, "wukkin' obeah." The angst associated with the pouring of libation is often heightened when the utensils used are earthy or indigenous, such as the calabash (dried, degutted gourd) used by Ira Leona ("Lady Ira") Lewis, a culture bearer in the Guyanese community, in figure 5.1.

A Day to Be African-Guyanese in America

African-Guyanese-Americans who borrow a day from God to attend Come to My Kwe-Kwe often spend their time actively negotiating ethnic identities by modifying their participation in the ritual to suit their religious values, or by reinterpreting religious dogma to accommodate the ritual. For these individuals, Come to My Kwe-Kwe is about manipulating the literal and figurative spaces to negotiate situational African-Guyanese-American identities that are simultaneously Guyanese, African, religious, sacrilegious, and more. Some Christians, like Mrs. R. from Brooklyn, whom I interviewed in 2005, is one such individual who reinterprets the scriptures to accommodate her performances. Mrs. R. is a deaconess in her local church and thus has certain doctrinal standards to uphold. However, she is from the village of Buxton in Guyana, known for its passionate embrace and protection of African cultural practices (Richards-Greaves 2013). Moreover, Mrs. R. regards her Christian faith and African heritage as complementary aspects of her life. This is due in large part to how she was raised—to be responsible for the knowledge of and participation in both African and Christian practices. Even though Mrs. R. regards Come to My Kwe-Kwe (and traditional *kweh-kweh*) as a time for jollification, she uses biblical scripture to highlight and validate the more crucial role of the ritual as a medium for older women to provide matrimonial instruction to younger women. Overlooking others' perceptions of ritual performances as "vulgar," Mrs. R. argues that the Bible states: "The older women must teach the younger." The scripture Mrs. R. references is drawn from the book of Titus:

> Likewise, teach the older women to be reverent in the way they live, not to be slanderers or addicted to much wine, but to teach what is good. Then they can train the younger women to love their husbands and children, to be self-controlled and pure, to be busy at home, to be kind, and to be subject to their husbands, so that no one will malign the word of God. (Titus 2:3–5, NIV)

While some African-Guyanese reinterpret the scriptures to suit their performance, others like "Clive," who danced on the periphery of the *ganda*, modify their performance to accommodate their religious convictions. In most instances, their performance modifications have minimal impact on the larger celebration because they do so on the periphery of the performance space and, for the most part, go unnoticed by the larger audience. This is primarily because Come to My Kwe-Kwe is a staged event in which the focus is primarily on the principal performers executing the ritual, who often occupy center stage. In some instances, African-Guyanese come only because Come to My Kwe-Kwe is a Guyanese event, which they seek to support with their presence and money. Thus, they may sing the responses to the calls of traditional *kweh-kweh* songs but abstain from singing more risqué lyrics like "A woman in jail, and she put she *pum pum* (vagina) for sale"; and "two lolo" (two penises). In some instances, also, attendees participate in the communal singing but improvise different words to reflect their views on gender, religion, and other values. Some also participate in the choreographed ritual dance that moves in a counterclockwise circle, while others stand on the sides of the hall and dance in place, partly because they do not want to be seen engaging in the ritual. Whether they are dancing in the circle or on the periphery, singing traditional words or improvising new ones, African-Guyanese-Americans often find themselves confronted by embedded religious values that influence their perception of their ethnic selves. Thus, as they maneuver their bodies, their values, and the performance space to accommodate the complex of their identities, African-Guyanese-Americans facilitate changes to the ritual and articulate identities that reflect a *rediasporizing* community.

Conclusion

Religion underscores the fabric of Guyanese culture, often reflecting the ethnic diversity of the Guyanese people. Christianity, Hinduism, Islam, Faithism, Rastafarianism, and a plethora of indigenous and syncretic religions shape Guyanese values on race, gender, class, and much more. Religious indoctrination primarily takes place in the home but is also reinforced in houses of worship, in academic and political institutions, and in every sphere of society. There is also a positive correlation between "race" and religion in that, for instance, East Indian-Guyanese overwhelmingly identify as Hindus while African-Guyanese generally identify as Christians. In addition to undergirding societal values and laws, religious dogma also shapes self-perceptions, particularly regarding race or ethnicity. Moreover,

religion-informed self-perceptions also affect individuals' relationships with cultural elements in society.

Among African-Guyanese, Christian doctrines about human
origins and good and evil often result in negative perceptions of
their racial (African) selves. The "myth of Ham"—which claims that
black people are the descendants of a cursed ancestor and son of
Noah, Ham, and that they are themselves thus cursed—serves as the
theological crux of the debasement of African peoples and cultures.
The negative views on blackness vary in intensity depending on the
Christian sect and its relations with its members outside of liturgical proceedings. Thus, for instance, mainline Christians such as
Catholics and Anglicans tend to be less stringent than Pentecostals
in policing the deportment of their members outside of the boundaries of the church. In fact, many of the gatekeepers of African
cultural practices in the African-Guyanese community in Guyana
and abroad are current members of mainline Christian groups,
or former members who parted ways with the church to embrace
Faithism and other syncretic religions. These African-Guyanese are
not only Christians but also "Africanists" who study, protect, and
propagate African history and culture in the Guyanese community,
in an attempt to negotiate identities, police ethnic boundaries, and
ensure that their culture does not "finish off" (Oakdale 2004, 78).

It is not surprising, then, that Africanists' view of the intersections
of religion and race differ from the view of those who embrace the
"myth of Ham." They regard salvation as an act of self-love that moti-
vates people to learn about and embrace the complexities of their
African heritage, particularly those cultural and religious elements
that epitomize African genius and resilience. These African cultural elements that are practiced by Africanists include obeah, *comfa*
(like the Akan *akomfo*), and *mami wata*. Because of their embrace
of African religious traditions, Faithists and other Africanists are
often labeled indiscriminately as obeah-men and obeah-women or
practitioners of witchcraft. Nevertheless, African-Guyanese from
all walks of life frequently consult the practitioners of indigenous
African religions when they are faced with difficulties in life, particularly in cases involving incurable diseases (Fernández Olmos

and Paravisini-Gebert 2011; Paton 2015). While many may discreetly visit the local shamans at night or in clandestine locations to avoid being detected by the larger community, Africanists, who are systematically ridiculed for engaging in such practices, continue to act as *culture bearers* (Burnim 1985b; Patton 2013, 74) and gatekeepers of their African heritage.

In the secondary African-Guyanese diaspora in the United States, both Christians and Africanists often feel compelled to reevaluate their religious values as they undergo the process of *rediasporization*. Some Christians continue to wholeheartedly reject African cultural and religious practices for more rigid interpretations of "righteousness" and "sin," while others find diverse ways to engage these practices. Africanists must also adjust, but they tend to find more allies and opportunities in the process than they did in Guyana. In the context of Come to My Kwe-Kwe, the complex of religious values and ethnic identity negotiations collide with varying outcomes. Some who embrace African-Guyanese culture but reject the religious undertones of the ritual, such as the beating of drums or the pouring of libation, might remain on the periphery of the *ganda* or participate in select practices. Others who might seek the mental reprise from religious doctrines that bind them to their faith and prevent them from embracing their Africanness reinterpret scriptures to suit the performances they participate in. For many, however, participating in Come to My Kwe-Kwe requires them to "borrow a day from God" to sing, dance, and gesticulate in a manner they would ordinarily regard as "outta ardah" (unseemly), particularly on the Sabbath. In effect, in the context of Come to My Kwe-Kwe, African-Guyanese-Americans "borrow a day from God" to negotiate identities that allow them to be simultaneously black (African) and religious beings.

6

Conclusion:
Wholly Fractured, Wholly Whole
Innovating "Traditions" and Reconstructing Self
in Come to My Kwe-Kwe Rituals

When a rooster goes for a walk, he does not forget his house
AFRICAN (DAN) PROVERB (CITED BY DANIEL REED)

Don't mind how bird vex, it can't vex with tree
GUYANESE PROVERB

Migration and Fracturing

This book examined how African-Guyanese in New York City participate in the Come to My Kwe-Kwe ritual to facilitate *rediasporization*, the construction and solidification of a diaspora's diaspora. It specifically examined the process of *rediasporization* using culinary, gendered, religious, and expressive arts frameworks. Each chapter explored the strategies that African-Guyanese employ to mitigate the physical, emotional/psychological, and cultural fractures that result from the disruptive process of migration. By

Figure 6.1: Drummers from the Guyana Folk Festival's Kwe-Kwe Ensemble accompany Jaliya Kafo, a Gambian ensemble (foreground), as they perform instructional songs from the *maniota* (traditional Gambian wedding); Come to My Kwe-Kwe, Brooklyn, August 31, 2018. Photo by Gillian Richards-Greaves.

examining Come to My Kwe-Kwe performance over a period of almost two decades, I have demonstrated how African-Guyanese straddle three "homelands"—Africa, Guyana, and the United States—in an effort to articulate conceptualizations of being and belonging that are simultaneously racial, gendered, religious, nationalistic, fractured, "whole." Through food, music and dance, African attire, and diverse ritual expressions, African-Guyanese in New York City establish ethnic boundary markers that communicate to the world who they are and who they're not (Guest 2018, 156). Thus, this book has highlighted the ways that African-Guyanese-Americans negotiate complex, overlapping identities in their new homeland by combining elements from the past and present and utilizing or reinterpreting them in ways that ensure group survival by facilitating *rediasporization*.

This book has also demonstrated how migration positions African-Guyanese in the United States as cultural "others," compelling them to negotiate differential identities. Thus, for example, while they are of African descent (black), African-Guyanese in the United States must articulate racial identities that distinguish them from African Americans, Afro–West Indians, black Africans, and other peoples of African descent. Even as they carve out racial identities within the larger African diaspora, African-Guyanese must also find ways to unify the unique factions or embedded sub-diasporas within the larger African-Guyanese community in the United States. Thus, as demonstrated in chapter 1 (fig. 1.4), the term "African-Guyanese diaspora" is a heterogeneous group that includes individuals who migrated from Guyana (*migrated diaspora*), their children (*procreated diaspora*), their spouses (*affinal diaspora*), and others regarded as strangers and visitors. Moreover, the African-Guyanese diaspora is composed of individuals of different age groups and varying expertise and interests in Come to My Kwe-Kwe and its antecedent, the traditional (wedding-based) *kweh-kweh* ritual. Because of this diversity, Come to My Kwe-Kwe has become increasingly important in the African-Guyanese community in New York City, in large part because it constitutes a sort of compound ethnic boundary marker that encompasses other crucial ethnic boundary markers such as food, music and dance, dress, and religious and gender values.

Negotiating Identities in a *Rediasporizing* Community

One of the principal feats of *rediasporization* is the process of gelling, which requires that a community move beyond an imagined community to a tangible one that does the same things, at the time, and in the same space—that they know each other. For African-Guyanese, this *knowing* takes place in the context of Come to My Kwe-Kwe. As people of African-Guyanese descent, Come to My Kwe-Kwe attendees provide a logical solution, because the celebration is a reenactment of traditional *kweh-kweh*, a uniquely African-Guyanese ritual. In the context of this ritual, they highlight "African" practices such as the pouring of libation, the negotiation of the bride price, the counterclockwise choreographed *kweh-kweh* ritual dance, the pervasive call-and-response in singing, and the preparation of *conkee* and other African-influenced foods. However, as an ethnic group in the United States, African-Guyanese are often compelled to reinterpret many of the African continuities (African retentions) and Guyanese values and practices to accommodate a new homeland, new information (education), changing lifestyles, and newer members of the African-Guyanese-American community. Come to My Kwe-Kwe creates a space where this heterogeneous community can actively negotiate identities that are multiple, overlapping, and complex.

For many African-Guyanese, what it means to be of African descent (black) takes on new meaning, significance, and urgency in the United States. Thus, while Come to My Kwe-Kwe revolutionizes traditional *kweh-kweh* to accommodate this secondary diaspora, the Guyana Folk Festival Committee works to maintain or increase the authenticity of the ritual by emphasizing its African elements and their connections to similar processes among other African diasporic groups. For example, since the inception of Come to My Kwe-Kwe in 2005, the pouring of libation has become a more elaborate process each year, so much so that the 2018 celebration began with a concise explanation of libation, followed by the use of a calabash instead of a water bottle and the cultivation of a more sacred space for the act. However, one of the more tangible ways that African-Guyanese-Americans link their practices to the African continent is by collaborating with African immigrants living in New York City. At the 2018 Come to My Kwe-Kwe celebration, for example, the Guyana Cultural Association hosted Jaliya Kafo, a Gambian ensemble from the Bronx. Jaliya Kafo was composed of four members who are of the Mandinka ethnic group: Salieu Suso, the leader and kora player; Abdoulaye Toure, the balafon player; Alhaji Saho, a *djembe* player; and Aunty Zeena, an elderly singer and the only female in the group. During Come to My Kwe-Kwe, the group performed the Mandinka wedding ritual called *baasumung*, which, like the traditional (wedding-based) *kweh-kweh* ritual, takes place the night before a wedding and includes songs that provide advice and warnings primarily to the bride. While men were present at the reenacted *baasumung*, it was principally women who executed the ritual, including the playing of the water drum (a large upturned

calabash gourd in a bucket of water) and the singing of matrimonial songs. With the assistance of one of her male counterparts,
Aunty Zeena also shared some of the advice that would be given to
a bride at a typical Gambian wedding, called a *maniota*. Beyond the
demonstration of an indigenous African marriage ritual, however,
African-Guyanese were able to experience a taste of the Mandinka
language by singing the responses to Aunty Zeena's calls. As Aunty
Zeena sang the instructional songs, African-Guyanese attendees
noted the striking similarities between *baasumung* and *kweh-kweh*
songs. While the cultural commonalities between Gambian and
Guyanese wedding ritual practices were readily observable, the
differences could not be overlooked. Thus, for example, before demonstrating their circular dance, the visiting Gambian group dressed
the bride in a *manifano*, the traditional wedding attire, akin to a
kaftan with an extra wrapper and a headband (fig. 6.2). After the
circle stopped moving, the ensemble instructed her to bow before
her husband. After the volunteer bride rose from her knees, the
African-Guyanese women in the audience quickly and loudly que-
ried whether the groom was also going to bow before the bride.
It was evident that the Gambian group was caught off-guard by a
question that would be inapplicable in Mandinka culture, but they
accommodated the African-Guyanese audience and had the groom
bow before the bride. Nevertheless, by collaborating with African
groups from the continent, African-Guyanese-Americans can revise
Come to My Kwe-Kwe (and traditional *kweh-kweh*) practices to
align with what they regard as more "authentic" African practices.

While Come to My Kwe-Kwe creates an opportunity for African-
Guyanese-Americans to return to their African "traditions," it
also creates a space for the established practices of the traditional
kweh-kweh ritual to be celebrated, challenged, revised, and fractured to accommodate the innovative functions of the ritual, new
performance spaces, and the needs of a *rediasporizing* community.
As demonstrated throughout this book, Come to My Kwe-Kwe
functions to provide entertainment, education, and community
for African-Guyanese who have a certain level of experience with
Guyana and the traditional ritual. Moreover, since Come to My

Figure 6.2: A volunteer bride dressed in a *manifano*, the wedding attire of a traditional Gambian (Mandingo) wedding called a *maniota*. Photo by Gillian Richards-Greaves.

Kwe-Kwe is confined to a ballroom with limited space, the ritual segments and accompanying music must all be modified to accommodate the performance, the heterogeneous group of people, and competing events taking place during the Labor Day weekend. The innovations to traditional *kweh-kweh* that take place during Come to My Kwe-Kwe affect just about every aspect of the ritual and often cause rifts in the African-Guyanese community between individuals who espouse strict adherence to archaic iterations of traditional *kweh-kweh* and those who promote and support innovation. Nevertheless, African-Guyanese-Americans who engage in Come to My Kwe-Kwe celebrations do so with the understanding that, as they move forward and change in the process of *rediasporization*, their cultural practices must also change to accommodate or serve the community.

Guyanese food literally fuels Come to My Kwe-Kwe and is one of the "performances" that simultaneously demonstrates the resilience of Guyanese culture and the changes taking place in the secondary African-Guyanese diaspora in the United States. As discussed in chapter 2, "Where's the Cookup Rice?," African-Guyanese manipulate the diversity of cuisines collectively labeled "Guyanese food" to highlight ethnically diverse national (Guyanese) identities as well as racial (black or African) identities. Thus, the Come to My Kwe-Kwe menu often includes *channa*, fish cakes, black pudding, and *pholourie* (fig. 2.2), which reflects the diversity of the Guyanese people; however, it also often highlights African-influenced cuisines like *conkee*, cookup rice, and *metemgee*. As African-Guyanese-Americans celebrate Come to My Kwe-Kwe, they examine each item on the menu to ensure that it adheres to preestablished notions of "authentic" Guyanese food, *kweh-kweh* food, and ultimately African food. While many evaluate authenticity based on the appearance, aroma, and taste of each cuisine, beneath the surface, authenticity also lies in the food's ability to mend fractures by arousing the senses and connecting attendees with meals, people, experiences, and geographies of the past and present.

While the foods served at Come to My Kwe-Kwe reflect the traditional *kweh-kweh* menu and theme of the Guyana Folk Festival, economic factors also shape the menu and participants' engagement with the foods, which must be purchased. Moreover, food consumption at Come to My Kwe-Kwe is also greatly affected by the changing desires or tastes of individual Guyanese, who are increasingly modifying their diet due to increased dietary education, health concerns, and other factors. From this perspective, *rediasporization* is a gastronomic process that encompasses the cuisines, the experiences and memories associated with them, and the changes they nourish or facilitate in the secondary African-Guyanese diaspora in the United States.

Some of the most visible and consequential changes taking place in the African-Guyanese community in the United States as a result of *rediasporization* affect gender values. Chapter 3, "Wipin,' Winin,' and Wukkin,'" explored the ways that African-Guyanese gendered values, largely underscored by an African past and religious values, are articulated through song texts, proverbs, and physical gesticulations at Come to My Kwe-Kwe. Specifically, this chapter examined how Come to My Kwe-Kwe music and dance help to reinforce gender stereotypes of the hardworking, wage-earning male and the virtuous, domesticated female. Through music and dance, the bride and groom are advised to protect their nations' honor by adhering to established gender roles, and to protect their future marriage by satiating each other's sexual desires. The gendered advice, instructions, and chiding provided through song and dance facilitate the continued survival of the community by the increase to one's nation through procreation, and are expressed in songs like "Biggie So" (example 3.4) and *wining* (gyrating) during the science dance. Thus, deviating from gender norms can have consequences, including infidelity, a wife's dismissal from the marital home, and the loss of face in the community on the part of the couple and their nation. However, African-Guyanese-Americans often deviate from established gender norms because of economic advancement, necessity, and shifting views on gender. These factors also influence individuals to discard or innovate segments of the traditional *kweh-kweh* repertoire that espouse domestic violence or values that are archaic or injurious to women. Thus, for instance, Come to My Kwe-Kwe attendees refuse to sing songs like "Hear, Auntie Bess" (example 3.11) and "Sancho Lick 'e Lova Pon de Dam" (example 3.12), which many believe reference or celebrate domestic violence against women. Women have also actively revised the lyrics of "Me Go Wash Am" (I Will Wash It) to become "Me Nah Go Wash Am" (I Will Not Wash It) to reflect their rejection of the notion that women must provide unwavering service to men, even when it is disadvantageous for them to do so. The reassessment of African-Guyanese gender norms and expectations reflects personal experiences and choices, increased education (knowledge) and resources, and agency for self-determination in a new homeland. Being part of a *rediasporized* community affords many the literal and figurative protection they need to articulate diverse, innovative, and even contrary gender values. Moreover, Come to My Kwe-Kwe, which is not tied to a specific nation (family), reduces the potential for loss of face for the violation or innovation of gender norms.

Come to My Kwe-Kwe music and dance performances also provide unique insight into the process of *rediasporization* and the innovative changes taking place in the African-Guyanese community in the

United States. As explored in chapter 4, "Beat de Drum and de Spirit Gon Get Up," music and dance drive the celebrations and underscore most other ritual performances at Come to My Kwe-Kwe. It is through music and dance that African-Guyanese views on gender, race, religion, sexuality, nationality, and other values are expressed, reevaluated, celebrated, and rejected. Moreover, it is through music that African-Guyanese create strong corporeal bonds with Africa, Guyana, and the United States. However, to accommodate this secondary diaspora, Come to My Kwe-Kwe captains and the Kwe-Kwe Ensemble of dancers, drummers, and musicians often perform non-Guyanese or non-*kweh-kweh* songs; modify the repertoire to accommodate shorter ritual segments in relatively confined performance space; sing fast-paced medleys instead of elaborately improvised song-stories; use synthesizers and other pitched instruments; reject proverbial speech for more colloquial language that some regard as crude or vulgar; and tend to privilege *wining* as expressed in the science dance and other improvised dances at the expense of the choreographed ritual dance. While some argue that musical innovations in Come to My Kwe-Kwe erode African-Guyanese culture, others focus on how these changes facilitate the longevity of the ritual and the inclusivity of the diverse factions of the African-Guyanese diaspora. Moreover, there is a dialectical relationship between the innovations to Come to My Kwe-Kwe music and dance and the *rediasporized* African-Guyanese-American community.

The changes taking place in the *rediasporized* community also affect religious values. As demonstrated in chapter 5, "Borrow a Day from God," religion influences African-Guyanese views on race, gender, and nearly every other identity in this community and affects how they engage with African-influenced practices. Although they embrace diverse religions, African-Guyanese overwhelmingly identify as Christian. However, since one of Christianity's underlying beliefs is the Hamitic or inherently cursed nature of blacks, often referred to as the "myth of Ham" (Goldenberg 2003; Johnson 2004, 4), African-Guyanese often feel compelled to engage in the *situational negotiation of identity* (Guest 2018, 157), which allows them to separate their blackness (race) from their God. The "myth of

Ham" further creates a racial-religious fracture during Come to My Kwe-Kwe, where African-influenced practices occupy center stage. Because Come to My Kwe-Kwe allows for a diversity of expressions under the umbrella of "African-Guyanese," attendees stand on the periphery of the performance space, actively revise song lyrics, forego participation in ritual elements they regard as too African or too risqué, embrace practices they regard as benign or easily improvised, and devise other strategies to assuage the effects of the racial-religious fractures they experience. An increasing number of African-Guyanese in the *rediasporized* community have also begun modifying their religious values to sanctify the ritual, even if it means temporarily "borrowing a day from God" to participate in ritual practices they regard as pagan or behave in ways they generally view as ungodly, "outta ardah" (out of order), or unseemly.

Old Becomes New, New Becomes "Traditional"

Come to My Kwe-Kwe is a reenactment of traditional *kweh-kweh* that some African-Guyanese regard as detrimental to the traditional ritual. Some older African-Guyanese also express concern that the changes displayed at Come to My Kwe-Kwe will delegitimize the ritual as an ethnic boundary marker by making it less African and less Guyanese. Thus, although Come to My Kwe-Kwe maintains the overarching structure of traditional *kweh-kweh*, some view the innovations to the ritual as detrimental to its continued authenticity and survival. The ritual innovations in Come to My Kwe-Kwe to a certain degree render traditional *kweh-kweh* archaic, possibly serving to hasten its demise. However, by performing Come to My Kwe-Kwe—which the Guyana Folk Festival Committee now promotes as Kwe-Kwe Nite—African-Guyanese in the United States are keeping traditional *kweh-kweh* alive, if only in name.

Although many African-Guyanese embrace traditional *kweh-kweh* as uniquely African and Guyanese, and as such "we ting" (our thing), many may never have the opportunity to attend a traditional ritual. Thus, Come to My Kwe-Kwe, which has been celebrated at the

Guyana Folk Festival in New York City since 2005, has become the only *kweh-kweh* that many African-Guyanese are familiar with. For many, the ritual practices they learn at Come to My Kwe-Kwe have become etched in their minds as "traditional" *kweh-kweh*. In fact, I have spoken to African-Guyanese who attended "traditional" *kweh-kweh* after first being exposed to Come to My Kwe-Kwe and who felt that the latter made more sense and was more fun. In fact, many older African-Guyanese who grew up participating in traditional *kweh-kweh* regard Come to My Kwe-Kwe as the place where traditional *kweh-kweh* resides, or at least the "new" traditional *kweh-kweh*. African-Guyanese in the United States don't have to wait for some-one to get married before they can "dance *kweh-kweh*" because Come to My Kwe-Kwe provides ritual consistency, clarity, and jollification.

On several occasions, middle-aged or older African-Guyanese expressed that they did not experience traditional *kweh-kweh* while growing up in Guyana or the United States. In some instances, it was because they grew up in Guyana's capital city of Georgetown, where *kweh-kweh* celebrations are uncommon. However, many of these individuals also explained that they had been restricted from participating in traditional *kweh-kweh* by adults (particularly Christians) who sought to protect them from African and risqué practices. Therefore, in the context of Come to My Kwe-Kwe, mem-bers of the migrated diaspora often find themselves in the same position as the procreated diaspora, affinal diaspora, and visitors and strangers, experiencing an aspect of Guyanese culture for the first time or trying to learn more about it. For novices as well as those who are experts on traditional *kweh-kweh*, authenticity rests in the propagation of Guyanese culture, particularly as it pertains to edifying the next generation.

As it promotes Come to My Kwe-Kwe, the Folk Festival Committee works to ensure that the entire *rediasporized* commu-nity of African-Guyanese-Americans is equipped with the tools to participate in the proceedings at each stage of the ritual. Thus, for instance, the Kwe-Kwe Ensemble of performers begins Come to My Kwe-Kwe celebrations by providing an overview of traditional *kweh-kweh* and demonstrating the choreographed dance. As the drummers play a slow, polyrhythmic beat, Dr. Rose October-Edun and the other dancers dance in a circle while demonstrating the "stomp-stomp-kick" steps of the traditional *kweh-kweh* dance and inviting attendees to participate. Throughout the ritual, also, the ensemble pauses to explain upcoming segments and to encourage attendees to join in. The instruction provided by the ensemble is relevant not only to members of the procreated diaspora and to visitors and strangers, but also to members of the migrated diaspora who were never exposed to the traditional ritual in Guyana.

For many African-Guyanese-Americans, Come to My Kwe-Kwe is a time to look, feel, and *be* African by wearing African attire, playing African instruments, and engaging in the practices handed down to them by their ancestors. More importantly, Come to My Kwe-Kwe creates a space where traditional *kweh-kweh* experts and older Guyanese can evaluate and comment upon the performances of their peers and the younger generations to ensure that they are getting it right. Beneath the consistent articulation of identities and the policing of ethnic boundaries lies self-preservation. An increasing number of African-Guyanese support Come to My Kwe-Kwe to keep it alive for the next generation in order to prevent complete assimilation. Master drummer and captain Akoyaw Rudder argues in support of Come to My Kwe-Kwe and the changes taking place in the ritual in the following manner:

> It's our culture. We should not let our culture just vanish or dwindle under us. You see, when young people get involved with stuff, you have to take it and jump with it. Don't just criticize, you have to encourage them, and it's our culture. Too many times, the Guyanese culture is just being swept under the rug. I'm glad that the young people, and all the Guyanese, that their eyes are open. They're seeing the light.

Many African-Guyanese in America are unconcerned with a view of authenticity that focuses on the degree of oldness or on individual ritual practices, but instead regard Come to My Kwe-Kwe as crucial to the gelling and continuity of the African-Guyanese American community.

African-Guyanese-Americans who engage in Come to My Kwe-Kwe celebrations do so with the understanding that, as they move forward and change in the process of *rediasporization*, their cultural practices must also change in order accommodate or serve the community.

I suspect that over time, Come to My Kwe-Kwe will surpass traditional *kweh-kweh*, which is a relatively isolated event, in importance and relevance in the Guyanese community. In fact, younger generations who might be interested in continuing this tradition are able to access videos on YouTube and social media to learn about *kweh-kweh*. However, the media they harvest will more than likely show iterations of Come to My Kwe-Kwe. Even older African-Guyanese in Guyana and the United States are turning to Come to My Kwe-Kwe to learn about their heritage. I experienced this phenomenon first-hand during my dissertation research in Guyana, when I interviewed a middle-aged African-Guyanese man regarded as a *kweh-kweh* expert. During our interview, he explained to me that, due to the infrequency of traditional *kweh-kweh* performances in Guyana, he had forgotten many of the songs he had sung in his youth. Thus, he often turns to recordings of Come to My Kwe-Kwe that friends bring from the United States and videos he sees on YouTube to "see" how to do a "proper" traditional *kweh-kweh*. He represents an increasing number of Guyanese in the United States and Guyana who are embracing Come to My Kwe-Kwe as the standard, or at least as *a* standard. Wedding-based (traditional) *kweh-kweh* continues to be practiced, but in the *rediasporized* African-Guyanese community in the United States, Come to My Kwe-Kwe is increasingly viewed as "authentic." More importantly, for many African-Guyanese-Americans, Come to My Kwe-Kwe is now their "tradition." This is largely because Come to My Kwe-Kwe facilitates the mending of fractures created by migration and the *rediasporizing* process. It also enables African-Guyanese-Americans to individually and collectively gather the seemingly disparate elements of their identities and their community to negotiate cultural difference, belonging, and wholeness. In effect, Come to My Kwe-Kwe allows African-Guyanese Americans to pick up the pieces.

EPILOGUE

Picking Up the Pieces

Father eat sour grapes, children's teeth set on edge
GUYANESE PROVERB

Her name is *Dia* but her new family calls her "*D*."

She belongs to no one, because she belongs to everyone.

Dia was born in a quiet village where she lived with her parents, siblings, and a large extended family. She spent her early childhood days singing, dancing, playing games like *oware*, and observing marriage rituals from afar. But today, Dia lives in a faraway land she now calls home. Physically, she looks the same, but on the inside, she is different. Complex. She doesn't remember her original name and she no longer speaks the languages of her people, but deep down on the inside she knows who she is. The muscles in her feet remember the dances; her mouth salivates at the taste of the old songs; her hands recall the rhythms of the drums; and her mind is fortified with the chants and prayers of her ancestors. Somehow, she knows who she is.

Dia's carefree life was upended when her best friend, Nana, abruptly left town in the middle of the night. When Dia asked her mother, "Where is Nana?," her mom replied tersely, "She went to live with her mother's people in a faraway village." Through the whispers of adults, however, Dia learned that her friend Nana had gone to pay off the debts of her parents. You see, Nana's parents had borrowed money from her uncle when Nana's father became ill, and promised to repay the loan after two full moons. When Nana's parents could not repay their debt, her uncle demanded payment in the form of labor. Nana's mother resisted her uncle and begged for more time, but he came late one night and snatched Nana away. Nana was the oldest of five children and a constant source of help for her mother. So, Nana's mother was left to provide for her remaining young children and to care for her sick husband without the help of her eldest daughter. Dia missed Nana sorely, but at least she had other friends in the village—or so she thought.

Not long after Nana left, other relatives came from far away and snatched children from Dia's village to "pay off debts"—or so they claimed. Sometimes, parents willingly gave their children to the debtors because they thought they would see them again after their debt was settled. At other times, their children were stolen without their knowledge. One by one, Dia's friends left the village, kicking and screaming and pleading with parents and relatives to reconsider their decision. Many of Dia's friends were afraid that they would never return home; some were afraid of the unknown villages they were traveling to; and some were saddened by what they viewed as their parents' rejection. Dia heard from relatives that her friends were treated badly in the new villages.

Nana was forced to marry her uncle and debtor and become his fourth wife. Nana knew that she should not get married before completing her puberty rites, but she had no choice. These puberty rites were designed to help a child transition emotionally, physically, and psychologically from childhood to adulthood, with the support of the of entire community of the living and the blessing and seal of the ancestors. Thus, getting married before the puberty rites were performed would anger the ancestors and bring bad luck upon oneself. So, on her "wedding night," she attempted to run away by escaping into the forest. She was caught and sorely beaten. Death, she thought, would be better than marriage to a man who was older than her father.

Nana later settled into married life with her brutish sister wives, who forced her to do most of the chores and sometimes beat her.

Nana's situation worsened after she had her first child, a son. He was fat and plump with rosy cheeks, like he had been eating good *fufu*, and his skin glistened like he had been bathed in palm oil. Most importantly, he was a son. Every man in Nana's new community wanted sons, but Nana's sister wives only had daughters. It seemed like Nana's status in her home had drastically changed overnight—her husband seemed to value her, and her sister wives envied her.

Back in Dia's village, children continued to be taken away, but a new phenomenon was also developing. New kinds of debtors began showing up and taking the villagers away. These new debtors were not from Dia's village or her country. They didn't look like her, talk like her, or believe in the religion of her ancestors. They were *strangers*. The strangers sold beautiful beads, cloth, jewelry, and weapons, which the locals purchased. Some of the wares the strangers peddled included intricately handwoven fabrics to be used as head and body wraps, brightly colored rugs, glass beads and metal earrings, machetes, and guns. Sometimes, local villages took the strangers' merchandise and paid them later. When the villagers could not pay their debts, they stole their neighbors' children and gave them to the strangers, who then took them away. Dia began to live in constant fear that her relatives or neighbors might one day snatch her, too.

Then that horrible day came.

The chief of Dia's village took beautiful cloth and trinkets from a group of strangers and, in turn, gave them access to the homes of the villagers. The strangers came when the villagers were asleep and seized all the healthy young men and women. Dia was not spared. The strangers tied them up and burned their village, killing the old, the sick, and the very young.

The chief died that day.

The captured villagers were forced to walk for miles in the scorching heat to a distant village by the sea. On the way, many people from other villagers were added to the march. Like Dia and her people, they, too, had been captured. Each time new villagers were added, Dia tried to comfort them, but they did not respond. They simply stared searchingly at her face, trying to read her observable emotions. They could not understand her language. They spoke different languages. When they tried to communicate with gestures, the strangers yelled at them and beat them. As they trudged along on their way to the village by the sea, some villagers became sick, some died, and some were killed.

After what felt like an eternity, the villagers reached their destination. "Why would they treat us so badly and bring us to such a beautiful place?" Dia wondered.

In the part of the village facing the coast stood a beautiful, gigantic, two-story castle where the strangers spent much of their time doing whatever pleased them. The top story of the castle had a large veranda that wrapped around the entire circumference of the castle, where the strangers relaxed and looked out upon the rest of the world. Strange enough, the top story also had large, black cannons. One of the strangers boasted that the cannons were put there to "defend the castle from attacks from bad men." The castle was protected by the Great River on one side and gigantic walls on the other three sides. Each side of the castle had large windows with beautiful designs in them, except the side that faced the sea; that side had large windows on the top floor but no windows on the lower level. The outside of the castle as well as its protective walls were white like a diviner's chalk. Coconut trees, burdened with their fruit, lined the outside of the palace's protective walls and even reached the shores of the Great River.

The villagers were marched to the dark, cold dungeon in the bowels of the castle, and shackled. With limited mobility, they ate what little food they were given and relieved themselves in the same place. They moaned, they prayed, they fought, they died, all the while hoping for a speedy end to their trauma. The trauma did not end. It was there in the dungeon that the strangers began beating those who resisted, even killing some of Dia's friends. It was also in the dungeon that the strangers began touching the young village girls in strange ways. Sometimes the strangers chose young women and took them to their quarters. Dia would listen in horror to their blood-curdling screams. As she witnessed the hell around her, she thought, "I prefer death."

Dia never got the "privilege" of dying!

One day, as some of the strangers "walked" the villagers to keep them healthy, another stranger, a male, stood on the balcony of the castle and pointed at Dia. She did not know what he said or what he wanted because she could not understand his strange language. A short while later, the stranger's guards came and forcefully took her to the upper levels of the castle. The smell of roasted meat; beautifully painted walls with portraits of people, possible the strangers' kin; shiny floors made of sturdy wood; large beds with embroidered bedding; vases with colorful, fresh flowers . . . Beautiful! Before she knew what was happening, the stranger grabbed her by the arm and proceeded to tug at her clothes. She slugged him across the face and began a fierce fight for her life, but she was no match for the bigger, stronger stranger. He ripped her clothes to shreds and raped her.

Dissonance. "How could such a beautiful place house such atrocities?"

After what seemed like forever, the villagers were forced from the dungeon, through a narrow doorway. Daylight. They were then forced to make a short walk to a waiting ship. Once again, a beautiful structure with the bowels of hell beneath. Dia limped in pain from the beating and violation of her body, her clothes tattered, her mind clouded. "When will it end?" she wondered.

The ship stayed at sea for what seemed like forever, and many of the villagers died during that time. Sometimes they committed suicide. Sometimes they were thrown overboard by the strangers, who killed them or disposed of them because they were sick. The ship was worse than the dungeon of the castle because it was cold and rocked constantly, making the villagers sick. Dia and the other villagers sat shackled for most of the day, but sometimes they were taken on deck and "danced." This was to ensure that they remained healthy for later use by the strangers. On the ship, Dia experienced many more instances of rape and other kinds of physical and emotional abuse. It was on the ship that she learned to "go into her head"—where she was free to do or be anything—to cope with the horrors she witnessed and experienced.

After many, many months, the ship carrying the villagers and the strangers reached land. As the villagers were marched from the ship in stocks, they wailed. Sadness, loss, pain, and confusion flooded their minds at once. They were separated from their loved ones, their ancestral lands, and their villages, but the strange land seemed eerily familiar. The weather was warm, the water was black, the trees were green, and the animals knew her. Grabbing ahold of her tattered clothes, Dia teetered off the huge ship, feeling battered and nauseous. It was not much longer before the older women discovered that Dia was pregnant. She had completed her puberty rites, although she had not been "sealed" (qualified) for marriage in the traditional way. But through rape, she was thrust into womanhood.

The strangers forced pregnant Dia to work on large plots of land, where she planted cocoa, cotton, indigo, rice, sugar, and other crops. They forbade her from speaking her language, performing rites of passage, or practicing religious rituals. Over time, she gradually forgot some things. The strangers mocked Dia for having no land, no language, no lineage—no culture. Since Dia's parents had died in the village fire set by the strangers and she had no siblings, she was an orphan in the strange land. The older women adopted Dia as their own daughter and helped her with her work in the fields. When Dia gave birth to a daughter she named Ani, the older women mothered the child. Over time, the villagers learned words and phrases from each other's languages and from the languages of the strangers who had captured them. As time went on, they used their new pidgin language to communicate, to sing, to remember, and to resist.

After a long while, the villagers regained their freedom.

After many years, some of the strangers died and the rest moved to unknown places. Dia traveled to a faraway land hoping to find greener pastures—and to rest.

Surprise.

Dia's relatives from a neighboring village in her old homeland also traveled in search of new opportunities. After deliberating among themselves, Dia's relatives decided to seek her out. Dia instantly recognized her relatives, but they did not know her. She was old now. After Dia recited the names of her ancestral lands and her kinsmen, her relatives acknowledged her identity. They did not accept her. Her clothes were tattered, her language was different,

A view from atop Elmina Slave Castle. Photo by Gillian Richards-Greaves.

and she embraced strange religious beliefs. Notwithstanding their role in Dia's trauma, they declared, "You are not one of us! Don't wear *our* clothes. Don't speak *our* language. Don't call *our* village your home." Dia ignored her relatives and continued to mend her tattered clothes, to speak the words she recalled from her ancestral language, and to perform the rituals she remembered.

Dia continued to live!

The residual violence is observable in Dia's clothes, in her language, and even in her deportment. Dia continued to push forward. She was determined to pick up the pieces of her life and to put them back together as best she could. She knew that after she had mended her clothes that had been tattered during the rape, the evidence of the trauma would still be noticeable. She knew the marks of violence on her body mapped her life experiences. She knew that when she bent over to pick up the pieces, strangers and relatives alike would disparage her for being an "empty shell" and having no home. But Dia has survived much worse, and she is determined to retrieve every possible yarn.

Dia will create her own brand of authenticity that uniquely incorporates the past, the present, and the future. She stands resolutely, faces her critics, and affirms: "I am *Dia Spora!*" Her determination, her resilience, her ingenuity, and her very life send one ultimate message:

To the buyer: *Let me pick up the pieces!*
To the seller: *Let me pick up the pieces!*
To the silent: *Let me pick up the pieces!*
And, to their beneficiaries: *Let me pick up the pieces!*

I pick up the pieces.

Glossary

acculturation: The exchange of cultural features that results when groups come into continuous firsthand contact; the cultural patterns of either or both groups may be changed, but the groups remain distinct (Kottak 2015, 312).

affinal diaspora: Individuals who become members of a diasporic group through marriage.

African continuities: Practices (cultural, linguistic, musical, religious, etc.) that are arguably of African origin, even if they have been modified slightly or grossly as a result of acculturation and other forms of cultural contact.

apical ancestor: A common ancestor from whom a lineage or clan has descended.

assimilation: The processes through which minorities accept the patterns and norms of the dominant culture and cease to exist as separate groups (Guest 2018, 166).

baasumung: A wedding ritual of the Mandinka people of Gambia, primarily executed by women.

bajirang: A type of loincloth or breechclout composed of a waistband or waist beads with an attached piece of cloth that runs between the legs. Older African-Guyanese women as well as East Indian women wore *bajirangs*.

balafon: A type of African xylophone that has sixteen to twenty-seven keys and uses gourds as resonators.

batto! (pronounced *bat-toe*): An audible command or signal to the *kweh-kweh* community (including the captain) to terminate the singing in progress. Batto! also affords the caller the authority, opportunity, and responsibility to "raise" (start) another song of his or her choosing.

bembe: An old term for vagina.

black cake: A dark fruitcake popular in the Caribbean. It is particularly eaten at Christmastime, and is used as a wedding cake. The term "black cake" is also used to refer to someone who is a "third wheel" or acts as a point of obstruction in a romantic relationship.

body percussion: The use of the body as a percussive instrument to produce rhythms. This includes stomping, clapping, and patting the mouth or body with the hands.

calypso: An older form of music in Trinidad and Tobago through which singers (calypsonians) comment, often humorously, on social issues and life in general.

Candomblé: A syncretic religion in Brazil, largely formed from the merging of Catholicism and indigenous African religions during slavery.

channa: Chickpeas, often boiled until soft and seasoned with spices to create an Indian delicacy.

chow mein: A yellow noodle of Chinese origin, prepared in Guyana and other parts of the Caribbean.

coalpot: A locally made cooking utensil made of iron. Guyanese often claim that food cooked on a coalpot tastes "sweeter" or more flavorful than that cooked on gas or electric stoves.

coded language: A way of speaking that involves the use of words, phrases, and concepts that mask overt meanings and leave the interpretation up to the listener.

code switching: A switching back and forth between one linguistic variant and another depending on the cultural context (Guest 2018, 107).

comfa: A generic term used to describe the manifestation of spirits. *Comfa* was "originally used to refer to the worship of the Watermamma [*mami wata*] spirit" (Gibson 2001, 1). In African-Guyanese culture, *comfa* is also used to refer to the religion of Spiritualism or Faithism, in which possession plays a significant role.

conga drum: A staved, single-headed drum from Cuba.

conkee: A meal made with boiled and seasoned cornmeal wrapped in banana leaves (akin to tamales).

contagious magic: "Ritual words or performances that achieve efficacy as certain materials that come in contact with one person carry a magical connection that allows power to be transferred from person to person" (Guest 2018, 379).

cookup rice: A dish made with rice, peas or beans, coconut milk, meats, and vegetables.

Creolese: Guyana's English-based creole language, which also includes syntax and other linguistic features from African languages, Amerindian (Arawakan) languages, Hindi and Bhojpuri, and European languages.

creolized: Expressions that have resulted from the blending of disparate elements, resulting in the construction of newer, unique constructs.

cultural generality: A cultural pattern or trait that exists in some but not all societies (Kottak 2015, 314).

culture bearers: Individuals, particularly of a given culture group, who help to maintain and pass on that culture (Patton 2013, 74).

dance *anta-banta*: To dance on one's head while in a trance-like state during the *comfa* ritual.

diasporization: The process of becoming a diaspora, which involves separation from a homeland, the act of remembering, cultural mixing, and the formation of a new community.

diddley bow: A one-string folk instrument that emerged in the southern United States, primarily in the Mississippi Delta region.

diffusion: The borrowing of cultural traits between societies, either directly or through intermediaries.

***djembe*:** A goblet drum that originated in West Africa.

domestic-public dichotomy: The contrast between women's role in the home and men's role in public life, with the corresponding social devaluation of women's work and worth.

***dougla*:** The term *dougla* is derived from the Bhojpuri and Hindi word *doogala*, meaning "two-necks," which historically referred to a mixed-raced (East Indian and black) person; however, today the term is used to refer to any mixed-raced person who is partially black.

enculturation: The social process by which culture is learned and transmitted across generations (Kottak 2015, 313).

ethnic boundary marker: "A practice or belief, such as food, clothing, language, shared name, or religion, used to signify who is in the group and who is not" (Guest 2018, 156).

ethnography/ethnographic research: Fieldwork conducted in a cultural setting.

ethnomusicologists: Individuals who study music as culture and music in culture. Historically, ethnomusicologists have focused their study on non-Western musics.

Faithists: A syncretic religious group of believers who worship on the Sabbath, wear white robes, and embrace a blend of religious practices from indigenous African religions, Christianity, Hinduism, and other faiths.

five fingers: Starfruit (*Averrhoa carambola*), used to make local beverages and dried fruits for black cake (dark fruitcake).

forced assimilation: The use of force by a dominant group to compel a minority to adopt the dominant culture.

"found" instruments/found sounds: Naturally occurring objects in the environment or other objects used as musical instruments, such as bottles and spoons, and buckets and sticks.

fufu: Starchy African meal made with boiled and pounded tubers like cassava, plantains, and yams.

ganda: The performance circle at a *kweh-kweh* ritual in which the dancing takes place (Warner-Lewis 2003, 328).

Ïgba Nkwü: A wine-carrying premarriage ceremony practiced by the Igbo of Nigeria.

Jaliya Kafo: A Gambian ensemble of musicians and performers who live in the Bronx.

kweh-kweh: An African-Guyanese prewedding ritual that emerged among enslaved Africans in Guyana. Also known as *karkalay, mayan, kweh-keh,* and *pele.*

leveling mechanism: A custom or social action that operates to reduce wealth disparity and bring standouts in line with community norms.

life history: A form of interview that traces the biography of a person over time, examining changes in the person's life and illuminating the interlocking network of relationships in the person's community.

longitudinal research: Long-term study of a community, region, society, culture, or other unit, usually based on repeated visits (Kottak 2015, 315).

majeera: A pair of small hand cymbals, used as traditional percussive instruments in Indian music.

maladaptive: An adjective describing "cultural traits, patterns, and inventions [that] threaten the group's continued survival and reproduction and thus its very existence" (Kottak 2015).

mami wata: Often depicted with the head and torso of a woman and the tail of a fish, *mami wata* is water goddess or deity worshipped in many indigenous religions in Africa and the African diaspora as a giver of good fortune.

manifano: Traditional wedding attire of the Mandinka people of Gambia.

maniota: A traditional Mandinka wedding.

Matticore: Also known as "Dig Dutty," a prewedding ritual among Hindus in Guyana.

metemgee: Also known as *metegee* and *metem*, a Guyanese one-pot meal made with tubers and boiled in coconut milk, with meats, dumplings, and spices.

migrated diaspora: The segment of a diasporic group that actually migrated from a previous homeland and settled in a new one.

'nansi 'tory: A funeral rite based on the concept of "Anansi" that eulogizes the deceased through oral narratives that aggrandize his or her life and accomplishments.

nation: In the *kweh-kweh* ritual, the relatives, friends, and other representatives of the bride and groom, who sing and dance on their behalf.

native ethnographers: Individuals who conduct research in the groups to which they belong.

obeah: A complex of Afro-Caribbean magico-religious practices that involve spiritual healing, harming, and divination; used synonymously with witchcraft.

orishas: Deities in the syncretic Santería religion that emerged among slaves in Cuba.

othermothers: Women who informally adopt children and assume responsibility for their economic providence, discipline, personal care, and other factors associated with child-rearing, even when the children continue to live with their bloodmothers (biological mothers) or other consanguineal kin (blood relatives).

pepperpot: Guyana's national dish, made with cassareep (a by-product of the cassava root), meats, peppers, and spices and served with bread, rice, or cassava bread, the preference of many Amerindians.

pholourie: An Indian delicacy that is made with flour, yellow split peas, and spices.

Poro: A secret society for boys in Liberia, Sierra Leone, Guinea, and Ivory Coast, where boys undergo puberty rites of passage and are taught how to be men.

procreated diaspora: Members of a diasporic group who were born in a new homeland (hostland) to parents from a previous homeland.

rediasporization: The process of creating newer diasporas from existing or established ones.

reggae: A style of Jamaican popular music that originated in the 1960s among Rastafarians.

reproduced diaspora: Members of a diaspora who are children of the migrated diaspora, born in the new homeland.

rite of passage: A category of ritual that enacts a change of status from one life stage to another, either for an individual or for a group (Guest 2018, 371–83; van Gennep 1960).

roti: A type of Indian flatbread.

Sande: A secret society for girls in Liberia, Sierra Leone, Guinea, and Ivory Coast, where girls undergo puberty rites of passage and are taught how to be properly socialized women.

Santería: A syncretic religion that emerged among enslaved Africans in Cuba and later spread to various parts of the world. The religious practices of Santería are largely shaped by the Lucumí tradition of the Yoruba people of Nigeria, Catholicism, and other religions.

science dance: A dance performed by the bride and groom in which they *wine* (gyrate) to demonstrate sexual prowess.

shak shak: A type of rattle made with gourds.

situational negotiation of identity: The shifting of an individual's self-identification with a particular group according social location (Guest 2018, 157).

soca: A type of popular dance music that emerged in Trinidad, particularly performed during Trinidad's carnival season.

sorrel: *Hibiscus sabdariffa*; a species of hibiscus used to make local beverages.

soundscape: Aspects of a musical environment ranging from a single musical tradition to all the sounds heard in a particular place (Shelemay 2015, 9).

steelpan: The national instrument of Trinidad and Tobago, made from an oil drum that is dented and tuned to produce different chromatic pitches.

susu: Also known as "throwing box," a type of informal banking that involves the systematic pooling and "drawing" (collecting) of funds from a set number of participants.

syncretic: Adjective describing the blending of cultural, particularly religious, elements that results from acculturation or the long-term contact and interaction of ethnic groups.

taboo: Set apart as sacred and off limits to ordinary people; prohibition backed by supernatural sanctions (Kottak 2015, 317).

***tassa* drum:** A conical or bowl-shaped Indian drum played in Trinidad and Tobago, Guyana, and other Caribbean countries with large East Indian populations (Manuel 2015).

timbre: The unique quality of sound that arises from a particular voice or instrument that distinguishes it from others.

tricultural: Being of or belonging to three distinct culture groups or nationalities.

water drum: A large, upturned calabash gourd in a bucket of water that is beaten with sticks to produce percussive sounds like a drum. The water drum is played at the *baasumung*, the Mandinka wedding ritual.

wining (from the verb "to *wine*"): Gyrating. *Wine* is a possible colloquialization of the verb "to wind" (to go around). *Wining* is used in the English-speaking Caribbean to mean gyration, which, in the context of the African-Guyanese traditional *kweh-kweh* and Come to My Kwe-Kwe, symbolizes sexual prowess.

yama pele: A vibrant, choreographed dance that was performed by African-Guyanese during slavery and well into the twentieth century. It involves skipping and jumping while the dancer slaps out rhythmic patterns on his thighs and other parts of his body. The type of body percussion demonstrated in *yama pele* is reminiscent of *patting juba* in African-American culture (Brown 2015, 25–27). When performed in traditional *kweh-kweh* (and Come to My Kwe-Kwe), *yama pele* songs are sung in Creolese and include unidentified words, phrases, and vocables. Prior to the 1960s, young African-Guyanese children and youths spent the evenings of the preparatory phase of *kweh-kweh* playing ring games such as "Colored Girls in the Ring" and "Yama Pele," which mirror the adult *kweh-kweh* ritual in some regards (Richards-Greaves 2013, 8).

Notes

Chapter One

1. With the different labels associated with *kweh-kweh* come slight variations in performance practices; however, overarching ritual segments and performative aspects of *kweh-kweh* are largely consistent throughout Guyana.

2. There are variations in the way *kweh-kweh* has been spelled, including *kwe-kwe*, *queh-queh*, and *que-que*. I have chosen to spell *kweh-kweh* phonetically because scholars in African languages generally spell the word with an initial *k*. Additionally, by spelling *kweh-kweh* with an *h* at the end, I emphasize the aspiration heard at the end of word when Guyanese pronounce it.

3. The term "nation" was used during slavery when various African ethnic groups were still aware of their differences and, in some instances, highlighted those differences through cultural performances that were sometimes promoted by slave masters (Warner-Lewis 2003, 115; Allsopp 1996, 399–400). In many African societies, and among the African diaspora, marriage involves not only the bride and groom but also their respective nations.

4. I use the term "captain" to refer to the *kweh-kweh* leader in general. I use "tutor" when referring to individuals such as Lionel Britton who self-identify as such.

5. In the Guyanese community, the word "science" is often used to refer to sex. This is possibly because science connotes knowledge, complexity, and intricacy, which in some ways relates to what many regard as "carnal knowledge" or sex. More importantly, saying "science" instead of "sex" allows the speaker or singer to mask sensitive issues and to save face.

6. Based on an interview with Dr. Rose October-Edun, February 26, 2011.

7. I use the term "primary historical African diasporas" to emphasize that the migration was from the primary (original) homeland to a secondary homeland. I contrast primary diasporas with secondary diasporas, which are created when groups migrate from secondary to tertiary homelands.

8. While historical Africans had for centuries migrated to the New World as free peoples, it was during slavery that they migrated in large enough numbers to constitute a community.

9. Kean Gibson describes *comfa* as "the generic term for the manifestation of spirits. The word has several references to the nonpractitioner. It refers to anyone who becomes spiritually possessed on hearing the beating of drums, or who becomes possessed without apparent reason" (2001, 1).

10. Although historical "black" Africans belong to several distinct ethnic groups and often highlight those differences, they also tend to regard themselves as collectively different from African-Americans and Afro-Caribbean migrants (West Indians) who are members of an earlier Enslavement African Diaspora. Thus, for this discussion, I address them collectively as historical "black" Africans or "new diaspora Africans" (Okpewho and Nzegwu 2009, 5).

11. While many elderly members of the Guyanese community fall into Group 1, youngsters who have migrated from Guyana also fall into this category. It is no surprise, then, that the "migrated diaspora" includes individuals with a diverse knowledge base of and loyalty to Guyana. In fact, in many instances, youngsters of the "migrated diaspora" are more akin to members of Group 2, the "procreated or reproduced diaspora," than to older members of the "migrated diaspora."

Chapter Two

1. See chapter 5 for a more detailed discussion on religion.

2. In Trinidad and Tobago, the term used is *doogla*, even more akin to the original Hindi and Bhojpuri term.

3. Cookup rice is prepared in other parts of the world and is known by various names, including cookup rice (Jamaica) and *pelau* (Trinidad). Additionally, a similar rice-and-peas dish, known as hoppin' John (Singleton 1991; Thurman 2000), is made by the Gullah Geechee and other southerners in the United States.

Chapter Three

1. I use the term "domestication" to refer to matters pertaining to the providence and everyday functioning of the home. This encompasses work (including wage-earning work outside of the home) as well as cooking, cleaning, laundering, and the care of children.

2. Domestic violence is a crucial aspect of gendering in the African-Guyanese community and is referenced in Come to My Kwe-Kwe songs but only addressed minimally here.

3. The view of man as superior and woman as inferior preceded slavery and was observed in most African societies, particularly areas in West Africa from which many enslaved Africans originated. For example, Bolaji Olukemi Olayinka

states that "Yoruba society is 'infected' with the idea that man is superior to woman, ordained by God and nature to dominate the world. A major source of this ideology that subordinates women is incorporated into Yoruba proverbs" (1997, 214).

4. "Suck man" is a derogatory term for a man who engages in oral sex. Some older Guyanese regard oral sex as perverse and demeaning to a man.

5. Many primary and high schools in Guyana teach courses in home economics, which is divided into two branches: clothing and textiles, and food and nutrition.

6. Individual African-Guyanese continue to engage in such practices even today.

7. A scraper is a flat piece of aluminum that is used to scrape off dirt during the cleaning of wet or damp floors.

8. Dry wiping when done by men is not necessarily viewed negatively, as domestication is generally not viewed as a measure of masculinity.

9. Contagious magic is defined as "[r]itual words or performances that achieve efficacy as certain materials that come in contact with one person carry a magical connection that allows power to be transferred from person to person" (Guest 2018, 379).

10. "Cooley" is a derogatory term that is used to refer to East Indian-Guyanese, those originally from India. When East Indians came to Guyana as indentured laborers, they were labeled "bound coolies," a term that has, for many East Indians, maintained its sting (see Seecharan 1999).

11. "Buck" is a colloquial and derogatory term used to refer to Amerindians, the native Guyanese. The term also refers to a novice or an unintelligent person.

12. Proverbs chapter 31 is often used by Guyanese to support their discussions on "the virtuous woman."

13. In Guyana and the Caribbean generally, the game cricket is often used as a euphemism for sex.

14. The term "open sepulcher" is used to refer to promiscuous women. This information was obtained from an interview with members of the Divine Apostolic Mystical Order of Saint Mary in Buxton, Guyana, a branch of the Faithist sect.

15. The word "wine" is a colloquialization of the word "wind." The concept of "wining" is not unique to *kweh-kweh*, as many children's games in the Guyanese community involve wining. Thus, it's the context that determines the message.

16. The word "bembe" is not used in everyday speech, but, in the context of *kweh-kweh*, where it is accompanied by gestures, the meaning is inferred, unveiled, or understood.

17. A calabash is a type of fruit that is cut, degutted, and dried for household use. Dried calabashes are used as kitchen or bathing utensils such as bowls, or they are fashioned into musical instruments.

18. "The word 'obeah' is almost certainly of African derivation, possibly from the Twi word 'obeye,' a minor god ... although it may also be of Ashanti origin, from 'Obboney' or malicious deity" (Bush 1990, 74).

19. Fictive kin are people regarded as family, even though they are not related by blood (consanguineal kin) or marriage (affinal kin).

20. "Madea," "Big Mama," and "Auntie" are some of the terms of reference for othermothers in the larger African diaspora. William Pollitzer also notes that the "adoption of children as a means of enlarging a family is widespread in Africa, and no stigma is attached to the man who 'gives' a child to his sister or other relative" (2005, 133).

21. The *bajirang* might be influenced by both African and East Indian cultures, since East Indians also wore loincloths. In fact, even the word *bajirang* might be derived from an East Indian language.

22. "Contrary to the received truth that polygyny always oppresses women, the polygynous household may offer women a basis for solidarity and task sharing. At the household level, cowives cooperate to organize production, consumption, and child care. Although friction between cowives is widely reported, many studies also stress the economic and political advantages of polygyny, including the autonomy made possible by shared responsibility" (Stamp 1989, 77; see also Mullings 1976, 254; Obbo 1980, 34–35).

Chapter Four

1. Although call-and-response is often executed between the *kweh-kweh* captain and the *kweh-kweh* attendees, frequently, call-and-response is observably between singers and musicians' instruments (Richards-Greaves 2016a).

2. Standard English is Guyana's official language, but Guyanese generally engage in *code switching* (Guest 2018, 105) between Creolese and standard English, depending on the context or setting.

3. I previously referred to the science dance as the "conjugal dance" (Richards-Greaves 2013).

4. *'Nansi 'tory* is a funeral rite based on the concept of "Anansi," which eulogizes the deceased through oral narratives that aggrandize their life and accomplishments.

5. There is a dialectical influence between the instrumentation (and, by extension, the music and dance) and the behavior of attendees at Come to My Kwe-Kwe.

6. More recently, the instrumentation at Come to My Kwe-Kwe has expanded to include an alto saxophonist who plays Guyanese folk songs during intermission, as well as a sound system that plays all types of Guyanese and Caribbean music.

7. Faithists are a syncretic religious group whose practices are informed by indigenous African religions, Christianity, and other religious beliefs.

8. I prefer the term "African continuities" instead of Africanisms or African retentions, because it is a more encompassing term that indicates that the practices in question are continuations of practices of African origin, which might have remained the same, changed, or merged with elements from other cultural elements to produce new or different enactments.

Chapter Five

1. It is important to note that some African-Guyanese non-Christians also oppose African traditions for diverse reasons, but the most vocal opposing group is Christians.

2. *'Nansi 'tory* is an end-of-life ritual in which friends and relatives eulogize the deceased by aggrandizing real and fictional narratives of his or her life.

3. Often depicted with the head and torso of a woman and the tail of a fish, *mami wata* is a water goddess or deity worshipped in many indigenous religions in Africa and the African diaspora as a giver of good fortune (Drewal 2008).

4. Santería is a syncretic religion that emerged among enslaved Africans in Cuba and later spread to various parts of the world. The religious practices of Santería are largely shaped by the Lucumí tradition of the Yoruba people of Nigeria, Catholicism, and other religions. Candomblé is also a syncretic religion, which originated in Brazil and is now practiced in many parts of Central and South America and in other parts of the world. Candomblé is informed by the religious practices of the Yoruba, Fon, and Bantu peoples of Africa and by Roman Catholicism, which was introduced to Brazil by Portuguese enslavers.

Bibliography

Abarca, Meredith E. 2004. "Authentic or Not, It's Original." *Food and Foodways* 12, no. 1: 1–26.

Abímbólá, Wándé. 1994. "Ifá: A West African Cosmological System." In *Religion in Africa*, edited by Thomas D. Blakely, Walter E. A. van Beek, and Dennis L. Thomson, 100–116. Portsmouth, NH: Heinemann.

Abu-Lughod, Lila. 1993. *Writing Women's Worlds: Bedouin Stories*. Berkeley: University of California Press.

Achebe, Nwando. 2011. *The Female King in Colonial Nigeria: Ahebi Ugbabe*. Bloomington: Indiana University Press.

Afolayan, Funso. 2004. *Culture and Customs of South Africa*. Westport, CT: Greenwood Press.

Agawu, Kofi. 2016. *The African Imagination in Music*. Oxford: Oxford University Press.

Ahyoung, Olivia. 2013. "The Cultural Traditions of Guyana: National Musical and Cultural Genres." In *The Garland Encyclopedia of World Music*, vol. 2, *South America, Mexico, Central America, and the Caribbean*, edited by Dale A. Olsen and Daniel E. Sheehy, 441–51. New York: Routledge.

Alajaji, Sylvia Angelique. 2015. *Music and the Armenian Diaspora: Searching for Home in Exile*. Bloomington: Indiana University Press.

Albala, Ken. 2007. *Beans: A History*. Oxford: Berg, 2007.

Aldridge, David, and Jörg Fachner, eds. 2006. *Music and Altered States: Consciousness, Transcendence, Therapy and Addictions*. London: Jessica Kingsley.

Allen, William Francis, Charles Pickard Ware and Lucy McKim Garrison. (1867) 1971. *Slave Songs of the United States*. Freeport, NY: Books for Libraries Press.

Allsopp, Richard, ed. 1996. *Dictionary of Caribbean English Usage*. Mona, Jamaica: University of the West Indies Press.

Alvarez, Luis. 2008. "Reggae Rhythms in Dignity's Diaspora: Globalization, Indigenous Identity, and the Circulation of Cultural Struggle." *Popular Music and Society* 31, no. 5 (December): 575–97.

Anderson, Benedict. (1983) 1991. *Imagined Communities*. London: Verso.

Anthias, Floya. 1998a. "Rethinking Social Divisions: Some Notes towards a Theoretical Framework." *Sociological Review* 46, no. 3 (August): 505–35.

Anthias, Floya. 1998b. "Evaluating 'Diaspora': Beyond Ethnicity?" *Sociology* 32, no. 3 (August): 557–80.

Apter, Andrew. 2002. "On African Origins: Creolization and Connaissance in Haitian Vodou." *American Ethnologist* 29, no. 2 (May): 233–60.

Asantewa, Michelle Yaa. 2016. *Guyanese Komfa: The Ritual Art of Trance*. London: Bogle L'Ouverture; Way Wive Wordz.

Auerbach, Susan. 1989. "From Singing to Lamenting: Women's Musical Role in a Greek Village." In *Women and Music in Cross-Cultural Perspective*, edited by Ellen Koskoff, 25–44. Urbana: University of Illinois Press.

Baily, John. (1994) 1997. "The Role of Music in the Creation of an Afghan National Identity, 1923–1973." In *Ethnicity, Identity, and Music: The Musical Construction of Place*, edited by Martin Stokes, 46–58. Oxford: Berg.

Bakhtin, Mikhail. 1981. "Discourse in the Novel." In *The Dialogic Imagination: Four Essays by M. M. Bakhtin*, edited by Michael Holquist, 259–422. Translated by Caryl Emerson and Michael Holquist. Austin: University of Texas Press.

Baraka, Amiri [LeRoi Jones]. 1966. "Soul Food." In *Home: Social Essays*, 101–4. New York: William Morrow.

Barth, Fredrik. 1969. *Ethnic Groups and Boundaries: The Social Organization of Culture Difference*. Boston: Little, Brown and Company.

Bassir, Olumbe. 1954. "Marriage Rites among the Aku (Yoruba) of Freetown." *Africa* 24, no. 3 (July): 251–56.

Bastide, Roger. 1978. *The African Religions of Brazil: Toward a Sociology of the Interpenetration of Civilizations*. 2nd ed. Translated by Helen Sebba. Baltimore: Johns Hopkins University Press, 1978.

Bauman, Richard. 1971. "Differential Identity and the Social Base of Folklore." *Journal of American Folklore* 84, no. 331 (January–March): 31–41.

Bauman, Richard. (1977) 1984. *Verbal Art as Performance*. Prospect Heights, IL: Waveland Press.

Baumann, Gerd. 1990. "The Re-Invention of Bhangra: Social Change and Aesthetic Shifts in a Punjabi Music in Britain." *World of Music* 32, no. 2: 81–95.

Béhague, Gerard. 1998. "Afro-Brazilian Traditions." In *The Garland Encyclopedia of World Music*, vol. 2, *South America, Mexico, Central America, and the Caribbean*, edited by Dale A. Olsen and Daniel E. Sheehy, 340–55. New York: Routledge.

Behar, Ruth. 1989. "Sexual Witchcraft, Colonialism, and Women's Powers: Views from the Mexican Inquisition." In *Sexuality and Marriage in Colonial Latin America*, edited by Asunción Lavrin, 178–206. Lincoln: University of Nebraska Press.

Benjamin, Jessica. 1988. *The Bonds of Love: Psychoanalysis, Feminism, and the Problem of Domination*. New York: Pantheon.

Berger, Harris M., and Giovanna P. Del Negro. 2004. *Identity and Everyday Life: Essays in the Study of Folklore, Music, and Popular Culture*. Middletown, CT: Wesleyan University Press.

Bhachu, Parminder. 1988. "*Apni Marzi Kardhi*: Home and Work; Sikh Women in Britain." In *Enterprising Women: Ethnicity, Economy, and Gender Relations*, edited by Sallie Westwood and Parminder Bhachu, 61–82. London: Routledge.

Bisnauth, Dale. 1996. *History of Religions in the Caribbean*. Trenton, NJ: Africa World Press.

Bissessar, Ann Marie, and John Gaffar La Guerre. 2015. *Trinidad and Tobago and Guyana: Race and Politics in Two Plural Societies*. Lanham, MD: Lexington Books.

Bledsoe, Caroline H. 1980. "Wealth in People." In *Women and Marriage in Kpelle Society*, 46–80. Stanford, CA: Stanford University Press.

Borde, Percival. 1973. "The Sounds of Trinidad: The Development of Steel-Drum Bands." *Black Perspective in Music* 1, no. 1 (Spring): 45–49.

Bourque, Susan C., and Kay B. Warren. 1987. "Technology, Gender, and Development." *Daedalus* 116, no. 4 (Fall): 173–97.

Bower, Anne, ed. 2007. *African American Foodways: Explorations of History and Culture*. Urbana: University of Illinois Press.

Boyarin, Jonathan, with Daniel Boyarin. 2002. *Powers of Diaspora: Two Essays on the Relevance of Jewish Culture*. Minneapolis: University of Minnesota Press.

Boyes, Georgina. 1993. *The Imagined Village: Culture, Ideology and the English Folk Revival*. Manchester: Manchester University Press.

Brah, Avtar. 1996. *Cartographies of Diaspora: Contesting Identities*. London: Routledge.

Braman, Brian J. 2008. *Meaning and Authenticity: Bernard Lonergan and Charles Taylor on the Drama of Authentic Human Existence*. Toronto: University of Toronto Press.

Brown, Charles Barrington. (1876) 2010. *Canoe and Camp Life in British Guiana*. Georgetown, Guyana: Caribbean Press.

Brown, Ernest D., Jr. 2015. "African American Instrument Construction and Music Making." In *African American Music: An Introduction*, 2nd ed., edited by Mellonee Burnim and Portia Maultsby, 23–33. New York: Routledge.

Brown, Linda Keller, and Kay Mussell. 1984. Introduction to *Ethnic and Regional Foodways in the United States: The Performance of Group Identity*, edited by Linda Keller Brown and Kay Mussell, 3–18. Knoxville: University of Tennessee Press.

Browne, Randy. 2011. "The 'Bad Business' of Obeah: Power, Authority, and the Politics of Slave Culture in the British Caribbean." *William and Mary Quarterly* 68, no. 3 (July): 451–80.

Burnim, Mellonee. 1985a. "The Black Gospel Music Tradition: A Complex of Ideology, Aesthetic, and Behavior." In *More Than Dancing: Essays on Afro-American Music and Musicians*, edited by Irene V. Jackson, 147–68. Westport, CT: Greenwood Press.

Burnim, Mellonee. 1985b. "Culture Bearer and Tradition Bearer: An Ethnomusicologist's Research on Gospel Music." *Ethnomusicology* 29, no. 3 (Autumn): 432–47.

Burnim, Mellonee. 1988. "Functional Dimensions of Gospel Music Performance." *Western Journal of Black Studies* 12, no. 2: 112–21.

Burnim, Mellonee. 2001. "Black Religious Music." In *The Garland Encyclopedia of World Music*, vol. 3, *The United States and Canada*, edited by Ellen Koskoff, 624–35. New York: Routledge.

Burns, James. 2009. "'The West Is Cold': Experiences of Ghanaian Performers in England and the United States." In *The New African Diaspora*, edited by Isidore Okpewho and Nkiru Nzegwu, 127–45. Bloomington: Indiana University Press.

Bush, Barbara. 1990. *Slave Women in Caribbean Society, 1650–1838*. Bloomington: Indiana University Press.

Butler, Judith. 1988. "Performative Acts and Gender Constitution: An Essay in Phenomenology and Feminist Theory." *Theatre Journal* 40, no. 4 (December): 519–31.

Butler, Judith. 1990. *Gender Trouble: Feminism and the Subversion of Identity*. New York: Routledge.

Butler, Kim. 2000. "From Black History to Diasporan History: Brazilian Abolition in Afro-Atlantic Context." *African Studies Review* 43, no. 1 (April): 125–39.

Cambridge, Vibert C. 2015. *Musical Life in Guyana: History and Politics of Controlling Creativity*. Jackson: University Press of Mississippi.

Campbell, Michael. 2012. *Popular Music in America: The Beat Goes On*. Boston: Schirmer Cengage Learning.

Campbell, Susan. 1988. "Carnival, Calypso, and Class Struggle in Nineteenth-Century Trinidad." *History Workshop Journal* 26, no. 1 (Autumn): 1–27.

Carney, Judith A. 2001. *Black Rice: The African Origins of Rice Cultivation in the Americas*. Cambridge, MA: Harvard University Press.

Case, Frederick Ivor. 2001. "Intersemiotics of Obeah and Kali Mai in Guyana." In *Nation Dance: Religion, Identity, and Cultural Difference in the Caribbean*, edited by Patrick Taylor, 40–53. Bloomington: Indiana University Press.

Charry, Eric. 2000. *Mande Music: Traditional and Modern Music of the Maninka and Mandinka of Western Africa*. Chicago: University of Chicago Press.

Clark, Msia Kibona. 2009. "Questions of Identity among African Immigrants in America." In *The New African Diaspora*, edited by Isidore Okpewho and Nkiru Nzegwu, 255–70. Bloomington: Indiana University Press.

Cleary, Theresa. 1986. *Jamaica Run-Dung: Over 100 Recipes*. Rev. ed. Kingston, Jamaica: Brainbuster Publications.

Clifford, James. 1994. "Diasporas." *Cultural Anthropology* 9, no. 3 (August): 302–38.

Clifford, James. 1997. *Routes: Travel and Translation in the Late Twentieth Century*. Cambridge, MA: Harvard University Press.

Cobley, Leslie S. 1976. *An Introduction to the Botany of Tropical Crops.* Upper Saddle River, NJ: Addison Wesley Longman.

Cohen, Robin. 1997. *Global Diasporas: An Introduction.* Seattle: University of Washington Press.

Collins, Patricia Hill. 2003. "Bloodmothers, Othermothers, and Women-Centered Networks." In *Reconstructing Gender: A Multicultural Anthology,* 3rd ed., edited by Estelle Disch, 317–23. Boston: McGraw-Hill.

Collins, Patricia Hill. 2009. *Black Feminist Thought: Knowledge, Consciousness, and the Politics of Empowerment.* New York: Routledge.

Comaroff, Jean, and John Comaroff, eds. 1993. *Modernity and Its Malcontents: Ritual and Power in Postcolonial Africa.* Chicago: University of Chicago Press.

Cone, James H. 1997. *God of the Oppressed.* Maryknoll, NY: Orbis Books.

Cone, James H. (1970) 2010. *A Black Theology of Liberation.* Maryknoll, NY: Orbis Books.

Cone, James H., and Gayraud S. Wilmore. 1993. *Black Theology: A Documentary History.* Vol. 2, *1980–1992.* Maryknoll, NY: Orbis Books.

Costa, Emilia Viotti da. 1994. *Crowns of Glory, Tears of Blood: The Demerara Slave Rebellion of 1823.* Oxford: Oxford University Press.

Counihan, Carole M. 1999. *The Anthropology of Food and Body: Gender, Meaning, and Power.* New York: Routledge.

Counihan, Carole M. 2002. "Introduction: Food and the Nation." In *Food in the USA: A Reader,* edited by Carole M. Counihan, 3–14. New York: Routledge.

Counihan, Carole M. 2004. *Around the Tuscan Table: Food, Family, and Gender in Twentieth-Century Florence.* New York: Routledge.

Counihan, Carole M., and Penny van Esterik. 1997. Introduction to *Food and Culture: A Reader,* edited by Carole M. Counihan and Penny van Esterik, 1–8. New York: Routledge.

Covey, Herbert C., and Dwight Eisnach. 2009. *What the Slaves Ate: Recollections of African American Foods and Foodways from the Slave Narratives.* Santa Barbara, CA: Greenwood Press.

Cowley, John. 1998. *Carnival, Canboulay and Calypso: Traditions in the Making.* Cambridge: Cambridge University Press.

Cunningham, Stuart D., and Tina Nguyen. 2003. "Actually Existing Hybridity: Vietnamese Diasporic Music Video." In *The Media of Diaspora: Mapping the Globe,* edited by Karim H. Karim, 119–32. London: Routledge.

Cutrufelli, Maria Rosa. 1983. *Women of Africa: Roots of Oppression.* London: Zed Books. *Daily Argosy.* 1931. "The History of Music, 1831–1931." October 18.

De La Torre, Miguel A. 2004. *Santería: The Beliefs and Rituals of a Growing Religion in America.* Grand Rapids, MI: William B. Eerdmans.

DeVale, Sue Carole. 1989. "Power and Meaning in Musical Instruments." *Concilium* 202, no. 2: 94–110.

DeVault, Marjorie. 1997. "Conflict and Deference." In *Food and Culture: A Reader,* edited by Carole M. Counihan and Penny van Esterik, 180–200. New York: Routledge.

Diouf, Sylviane Anna. 2003. "Devils or Sorcerers, Muslims or Studs: Manding in the Americas." In *Trans-Atlantic Dimensions of Ethnicity in the African Diaspora*, edited by Paul E. Lovejoy and David V. Trotman, 139–57. London: Bloomsbury Academic.

Dorson, Richard M. 1971. "Is There Folk in the City?" In *The Urban Experience and Folk Tradition*, edited by Américo Paredes and Ellen J. Stekert, 21–52. Austin: University of Texas Press.

Douglas, Mary. 1971. "Deciphering a Meal." In *Myth, Symbol, and Culture*, edited by Clifford Geertz, 61–82. New York: W. W. Norton.

Douglas, Mary. 1982. *In the Active Voice*. London: Routledge.

Douglas, Mary. 1997. "Deciphering a Meal." In *Food and Culture: A Reader*, edited by Carole M. Counihan and Penny van Esterik, 36–54. New York: Routledge.

Downey, Greg. 2005. *Learning Capoeira: Lessons in Cunning from an Afro-Brazilian Art*. Oxford: Oxford University Press.

Drewal, Henry John. 2008. *Mami Wata: Arts for Water Spirits in Africa and Its Diasporas*. Los Angeles: Fowler Museum at the University of California, Los Angeles.

Drewal, Margaret Thompson. 1992. *Yoruba Ritual: Performers, Play, Agency*. Bloomington: Indiana University Press.

Du Bois, W. E. B. [1903] 2009. *The Souls of Black Folk*. New York: Library of America.

Dudley, Shannon. 2002. "The Steelband 'Own Tune': Nationalism, Festivity, and the Musical Strategies in Trinidad's Panorama Competition." *Black Music Research Journal* 22, no. 1 (Spring): 13–36.

Dudley, Shannon. 2004. *Carnival Music in Trinidad: Experiencing Music, Expressing Culture*. New York: Oxford University Press.

Duran, Lucy. 2015. "'Soliyo' (Calling the Horses): Song and Memory in Mande Music." In *Pieces of the Musical World: Sounds and Cultures*, edited by Rachel Harris and Rowan Pease, 27–44. New York: Routledge.

Edwards, Bryan. (1801) 2017. *The History, Civil and Commercial, of the British Colonies in the West Indies*. 5 vols. London: Forgotten Books.

Edwards, Walter F. 1982. "A Description and Interpretation of the Kwe-Kwe Tradition in Guyana." *Folklore* 93, no. 2: 181–92.

Elias, Marianne, Laura Rival, and Doyle McKey. 2000. "Perception and Management of Cassava (*Manihot esculenta*, Crantz) Diversity among Makushi Amerindians of Guyana (South America)." *Journal of Ethnobiology* 20, no. 2 (January): 239–65.

Ellis, Pat, ed. 1986. *Women of the Caribbean*. London: Zed Books.

Ellis, Rhian. 1983. "The Way to a Man's Heart: Food in the Violent Home." In *The Sociology of Food and Eating: Essays on the Sociological Significance of Food*, edited by Anne Murcott, 164–71. Aldershot, Hants., England: Gower.

Epstein, Dena. 1977. *Sinful Tunes and Spirituals: Black Folk Music to the Civil War*. Urbana: University of Illinois Press.

Epstein, Dena. 2015. "Secular Folk Music." In *African American Music: An Introduction*, 2nd ed., edited by Mellonee Burnim and Portia Maultsby, 35–50. New York: Routledge.

Evans-Pritchard, Edward E. (1937) 1976. *Witchcraft, Oracles, and Magic among the Azande*. Oxford: Clarendon Press.

Falzon, Mark-Anthony. 2004. *Cosmopolitan Connections: The Sindhi Diaspora, 1860–2000*. Leiden: Brill.

Fandrich, Ina J. 2007. "Yorùbá Influences on Haitian Vodou and New Orleans Voodoo." *Journal of Black Studies* 37, no. 5 (May): 775–91.

Fernández Olmos, Margarite, and Lizabeth Paravisini-Gebert. 2011. *Creole Religions of the Caribbean: An Introduction from Vodou and Santería to Obeah and Espiritismo*. 2nd ed. New York: New York University Press.

Ferrero, Sylvia. 2002. "Comida Sin Par: Consumption of Mexican Food in Los Angeles; 'Foodscapes' in a Transnational Consumer Society." In *Food Nations: Selling Taste in Consumer Societies*, edited by Warren J. Belasco and Philip Scranton, 194–220. New York: Routledge.

Fischler, Claude. 1988. "Food, Self and Identity." *Social Science Information* 27, no. 2 (June): 275–92.

Flaig, Vera. 2010. "The Politics of Representation and Transmission in the Globalization of Guinea's Djembé." PhD diss., University of Michigan.

Foner, Nancy. 1979. "West Indians in New York City and London: A Comparative Analysis." *International Migration Review* 13, no. 2 (June): 284–97.

Foner, Nancy. 1997. "The Immigrant Family: Cultural Legacies and Cultural Changes." *International Migration Review* 31, no. 4 (February): 961–74.

Foner, Nancy. 1998. "West Indian Identity in the Diaspora: Comparative and Historical Perspectives." *Latin American Perspectives* 25, no. 3 (May): 173–88.

Foner, Nancy, Rubén G. Rumbaut, and Steven J. Gold, eds. 2000. *Immigration Research for a New Century: Multidisciplinary Perspectives*. New York: Russell Sage Foundation.

Fortes, Myer, and Edward E. Evans-Pritchard. (1940) 1987. *African Political Systems*. New York: Routledge.

Friedl, Ernestine. 1975. *Women and Men: An Anthropologist's View*. New York: Harcourt Brace Jovanovich.

Frohne, Andrea E. 2015. *The African Burial Ground in New York City: Memory, Spirituality, and Space*. Syracuse, NY: Syracuse University Press.

Fu-Kiau, Kimbwandende Kia Bunseki. 1994. "Ntangu-Tandu-Kolo: The Bantu-Kongo Concepts of Time." In *Time in the Black Experience*, edited by Joseph Adjaye, 17–34. Westport, CT: Greenwood Press.

Fu-Kiau, Kimbwandende Kia Bunseki. 2001. *African Cosmology of the Bantu-Kongo: Tying the Spiritual Knot; Principles of Life and Living*. Brooklyn: Athelia Henrietta Press.

Gabaccia, Donna R. 1998. *We Are What We Eat: Ethnic Food and the Making of Americans*. Cambridge, MA: Harvard University Press.

Geertz, Clifford. 1966. "Religion as a Cultural System." In *Anthropological Approaches to the Study of Religion*, edited by Michael Banton, 1–46. London: Tavistock.

Geertz, Clifford. 1973. *The Interpretation of Cultures: Selected Essays*. New York: Basic Books.

Geertz, Clifford. 1988. *Works and Lives: The Anthropologist as Author*. Stanford, CA: Stanford University Press.

Gerbner, Katharine. 2018. *Christian Slavery: Conversion and Race in the Protestant Atlantic World*. Philadelphia: University of Pennsylvania Press.

Gibson, Kean. 1996. "Comfa and the Expression of the Guyanese Culture." *Emancipation: The African-Guyanese Achievement* 4: 12–14.

Gibson, Kean. 1998. "A Traditional Analysis of Kwe-Kwe Songs." *Kyk-Over-Al* 48 (April): 163–98.

Gibson, Kean. 2001. *Comfa Religion and Creole Language in a Caribbean Community*. Albany: State University of New York Press.

Gibson, Kean. 2003. "The Social Significance of Kwe-Kwe Songs." In "Writings on Guyanese Music," edited by Vibert Cambridge, special issue, *Black Praxis*.

Gillaspie, Deborah. 2006. "Diddley Bow." In *Encyclopedia of the Blues*, vol. 1, edited by Edward M. Komara, 268–69. New York: Routledge.

Gilroy, Paul. 1987. *There Ain't No Black in the Union Jack: The Cultural Politics of Race and Nation*. London: Hutchinson.

Gilroy, Paul. 1993. *The Black Atlantic: Modernity and Double Consciousness*. London: Verso.

Gioia, Ted. 2006. *Work Songs*. Durham, NC: Duke University Press.

Glasgow, Roy Arthur. 1970. *Guyana: Race and Politics among Africans and East Indians*. The Hague: Martinus Nijhoff.

Glick Schiller, Nina, Linda Basch, and Cristina Szanton Blanc. 1995. "From Immigrant to Transmigrant: Theorizing Transnational Migration." *Anthropological Quarterly* 68, no. 1 (January): 48–63.

Gnuse, Robert Karl. 2016. *Trajectories of Justice: What the Bible Says about Slaves, Women, and Homosexuality*. Cambridge: Lutterworth Press.

Goldenberg, David M. 2003. *The Curse of Ham: Race and Slavery in Early Judaism, Christianity, and Islam*. Princeton, NJ: Princeton University Press.

Gomez, Michael A., ed. 2007. *Diasporic Africa: A Reader*. New York: New York University Press.

Gonzalez, Nancie L., and Carolyn S. McCommon. 1989. *Conflict, Migration, and the Expression of Ethnicity*. Boulder, CO: Westview Press.

Green, Garth, and Philip W. Scher, eds. 2007. *Trinidad Carnival: The Cultural Politics of a Transnational Festival*. Bloomington: Indiana University Press.

Gregory, Steven. 2000. *Santería in New York City: A Study in Cultural Resistance*. New York: Garland.

Guest, Kenneth. 2018. *The Essentials of Cultural Anthropology: A Toolkit for the Global Age*. New York: W. W. Norton.

Guyana Bureau of Statistics. 2012. "Population Composition." Available at http://www.statisticsguyana.gov.gy/census.html, accessed October 28, 2018.

Hall, Gwendolyn Midlo. 2005. *Slavery and African Ethnicities in the Americas: Restoring the Links*. Chapel Hill: University of North Carolina Press.

Handler, Jerome S. 1982. "Slave Revolts and Conspiracies in Seventeenth-Century Barbados." *New West Indian Guide/Nieuwe West-Indische Gids* 56, nos. 1–2: 5–42.

Hanna, Judith Lynne. 1988. *Dance, Sex, and Gender: Signs of Identity, Dominance, Defiance, and Desire*. Chicago: University of Chicago Press.

Hanna, Judith Lynne. 2001. Review of *Dance in the Field: Theory, Methods and Issues in Dance Ethnography*, by Theresa J. Buckland. *Ethnomusicology* 45, no. 1: 177–80.

Harley, George Way. 1941. *Native African Medicine*. Cambridge, MA: Harvard University Press.

Harms, Robert. 1997. "Sustaining the System: Trading Towns along the Middle Zaire." In *Women and Slavery in Africa*, edited by Claire C. Robertson and Martin A. Klein, 95–110. Portsmouth, NH: Heinemann.

Harris, Jessica B. 2003. *Beyond Gumbo: Creole Fusion Food from the Atlantic Rim*. New York: Simon and Schuster.

Harris-Shapiro, Carol. 2006. "Bloody Shankbones and Braided Bread: The Food Voice and the Fashioning of American Jewish Identities." *Food and Foodways* 14, no. 2 (July): 67–90.

Hast, Dorothea E., James R. Cowdery, and Stanley Arnold Scott. 1997. "Timbre: The Color of Music." In *Exploring the World of Music: An Introduction to Music from a World Music Perspective*, edited by Dorothea E. Hast, 139–68. Dubuque, IA: Kendall Hunt.

Haug, Frigga, et al. 1987. *Female Sexualization: A Collective Work of Memory*. London: Verso.

Henderson, Clara E. 2009. "Dance Discourse in the Music and Lives of Presbyterian Mvano Women in Southern Malawi." PhD diss., Indiana University.

Henderson, Laretta. 2007. "*Ebony Jr!* and 'Soul Food': The Construction of Middle-Class African American Identity through the Use of Traditional Southern Foodways." MELUS 32, no. 4 (Winter): 81–97.

Herskovits, Melville. 1930. "The Negro in the New World: The Statement of a Problem." *American Anthropologist* 32, no. 1 (January–March): 145–55.

Herskovits, Melville. (1941) 1990. *The Myth of the Negro Past*. Boston: Beacon Press.

Hill, Jonathan D., ed. 1996. *History, Power, and Identity: Ethnogenesis in the Americas, 1492–1992*. Iowa City: University of Iowa Press.

Hinson, Glenn. 2000. *Fire in My Bones: Transcendence and the Holy Spirit in African American Gospel*. Philadelphia: University of Pennsylvania Press.

Hobsbawm, Eric. 1983. Introduction to *The Invention of Tradition*, edited by Eric Hobsbawm and Terence Ranger, 1–14. Cambridge: Cambridge University Press.

Holtzman, Jon. 2006. "The World Is Dead and Cooking's Killed It: Food and the Gender of Memory in Samburu, Northern Kenya." *Food and Foodways* 14, nos. 3–4 (December): 175–200.

hooks, bell. 2000. *Feminism Is for Everybody: Passionate Politics*. Cambridge, MA: South End Press.

Hughes, Marvalene H. 1997. "Soul, Black Women, and Food." In *Food and Culture: A Reader*, edited by Carole M. Counihan and Penny van Esterik, 272–80. New York: Routledge.

Humphries, Jill M. 2009. "Resisting 'Race': Organizing African Transnational Identities in the United States." In *The New African Diaspora*, edited by Isidore Okpewho and Nkiru Nzegwu, 271–302. Bloomington: Indiana University Press.

Hunter, Margaret L. 2005. *Race, Gender, and the Politics of Skin Tone*. New York: Routledge.

Hurston, Zora Neale. 1981. *The Sanctified Church*. New York: Marlowe and Company.

Hyles, Joshua R. 2013. *Guiana and the Shadows of Empire: Colonial and Cultural Negotiations at the Edge of the World*. Lanham, MD: Lexington Books.

Ibrahim, Azeem. 2016. *The Rohingyas: Inside Myanmar's Hidden Genocide*. London: C. Hurst.

Ikwuagwu, Onwumere. 2007. *Initiation in African Traditional Religion*. Würzburg, Germany: Echter Verlag.

Iliffe, John. 1995. *Africans: The History of a Continent*. Cambridge: Cambridge University Press.

Ishmael, Odeen. 2013. *The Guyana Story: From Earliest Times to Independence*. Bloomington, IN: Xlibris.

Isichei, Elizabeth. 1997. "West Africa: From the Savanna to the Sea." In *A History of African Societies to 1870*, 239–60. Cambridge: Cambridge University Press.

Jackson, Jennifer V., and Mary E. Cothran. 2003. "Black versus Black: The Relationships among African, African American, and African Caribbean Persons." *Journal of Black Studies* 33, no. 5 (May): 576–604.

James, George G. M. 1976. *Stolen Legacy: The Greeks Were Not the Authors of Greek Philosophy, but the People of North Africa, Commonly Called Egyptians*. San Francisco: Julian Richardson Associates.

James, Wendy. 2000. "Reforming the Circle: Fragments of the Social History of a Vernacular African Dance Form." *Journal of African Cultural Studies* 13, no. 1 (June): 140–52.

Johnson, Kim. 1998. "Notes on Pans." *Drama Review* 42, no. 3 (Autumn): 61–73.

Johnson, Sylvester A. 2004. *The Myth of Ham in Nineteenth-Century American Christianity: Race, Heathens, and the People of God*. New York: Palgrave Macmillan.

Jones, Jacqueline. 1985. *Labor of Love, Labor of Sorrow: Black Women, Work, and Family from Slavery to the Present*. New York: Basic Books.

Kaeppler, Adrienne L. 2000. "Dance Ethnology and the Anthropology of Dance." *Dance Research Journal* 32, no. 1 (Summer):116–225.

Kalčik, Susan. 1984. "Ethnic Foodways in America: Symbol and the Performance of Identity." In *Ethnic and Regional Foodways in the United States: The Performance of Group Identity*, edited by Linda Keller Brown and Kay Mussell, 37–65. Knoxville: University of Tennessee Press.

Kanu, Ikechukwu. 2013. "The Dimensions of African Cosmology." *Filosofia Theoretica: Journal of African Philosophy, Culture and Religions* 2, no. 2 (July): 533–55.

Kasinitz, Philip. 1992. *Caribbean New York: Black Immigrants and the Politics of Race*. Ithaca, NY: Cornell University Press.

Kisliuk, Michelle. 1998. *Seize the Dance! BaAka Musical Life and the Ethnography of Performance*. New York: Oxford University Press.

Klein, Herbert S. 2010. *The Atlantic Slave Trade: New Approaches to the Americas*. 2nd ed. Cambridge: Cambridge University Press.

Kliger, Hannah. 1988. "A Home away from Home: Participation in Jewish Immigrant Associations in America." In *Persistence and Flexibility: Anthropological Perspectives on the American Jewish Experience*, edited by Walter P. Zenner, 143–64. Albany: State University of New York Press.

Koskoff, Ellen. 1989. Introduction to *Women and Music in Cross-Cultural Perspective*, edited by Ellen Koskoff, 1–24. Champaign: University of Illinois Press.

Koskoff, Ellen. 2000. Foreword to *Music and Gender*, edited by Beverley Diamond and Pirkko Moisala, 1–24. Urbana: University of Illinois Press.

Koster-Oyekan, Winny. 1999. "Infertility among Yoruba Women: Perceptions on Causes, Treatments and Consequences." *African Journal of Reproductive Health* 3, no. 1 (May): 13–26.

Kottak, Conrad Phillip. 2014. *Anthropology: Appreciating Human Diversity*. New York: McGraw-Hill Education.

Kottak, Conrad Phillip. 2015. *Cultural Anthropology: Appreciating Cultural Diversity*. 16th ed. New York: McGraw-Hill Education.

Landrine, Hope, and Elizabeth Klonoff. 1996. *African American Acculturation: Deconstructing Race and Reviving Culture*. Thousand Oaks, CA: SAGE.

Leante, Laura. 2004. "Shaping Diasporic Sounds: Identity as Meaning in Bhangra." *World of Music* 46, no. 1: 109–32.

Lesser, Jeffrey. 1999. *Negotiating National Identity: Immigrants, Minorities, and the Struggle for Ethnicity in Brazil*. Durham, NC: Duke University Press.

Lesser, Jeffrey. 2003. "Japanese, Brazilians, Nikkei: A Short History of Identity Building and Home Making." In *Searching for Home Abroad: Japanese Brazilians and Transnationalism*, edited by Jeffrey Lesser, 5–20. Durham, NC: Duke University Press.

Levy, André, and Alex Weingrod, eds. 2005. *Homelands and Diasporas: Holy Lands and Other Places*. Stanford, CA: Stanford University Press.

Lim, Tiong Kiong. 2012. *Edible Medicinal and Non-Medicinal Plants*. Vol. 1, *Fruits*. New York: Springer.

Littlefield, Daniel C. 1981. *Rice and Slaves: Ethnicity and the Slave Trade in Colonial South Carolina*. Baton Rouge: Louisiana State University Press.

Liverpool, Hollis Urban. 1994. "Researching Steelband and Calypso Music in the British Caribbean and the U.S. Virgin Islands." *Black Music Research Journal* 14, no. 2 (Autumn): 179–201.

Lomax, Alan, director. 1979. *The Land Where the Blues Began*. Mississippi Authority for Educational Television; Media Generation.

Long, Edward. (1774) 2010. *The History of Jamaica; or, General Survey of the Antient and Modern State of That Island*. Cambridge: Cambridge University Press.

Lorber, Judith. 2003. "The Social Construction of Gender." In *Reconstructing Gender: A Multicultural Anthology*, 3rd ed., edited by Estelle Disch, 96–102. Boston: McGraw-Hill.

Lourenço, Inês, and Rita Cachado. 2012. "Hindu Transnational Families: Transformation and Continuity in Diaspora Families." *Journal of Comparative Family Studies* 43, no. 1 (January): 53–70.

Manekar, Purnima. 2002. "'India Shopping': Indian Grocery Stores and Transnational Configurations of Belonging." *Ethnos* 67, no. 1: 75–97.

Manoukian, Madeline. 1964. *Akan and Ga-Adangme Peoples: Western Africa, part 1*. New York: Routledge.

Manuel, Peter. 2015. *Tales, Tunes, and Tassa Drums: Retention and Invention in Indo-Caribbean Music*. Urbana: University of Illinois Press.

Margolis, Maxine. 2000. *Her True Nature: Changing Advice to American Women*. Prospect Heights, IL: Waveland Press.

Marina, Peter. 2016. *Chasing Religion in the Caribbean: Ethnographic Journeys from Antigua to Trinidad*. New York: Springer.

Marks, Christine. 2015. "Creole Cuisine as Culinary Border Culture: Reading Recipes as Testimonies of Hybrid Identity and Cultural Heritage." In *Dethroning the Deceitful Pork Chop: Rethinking African American Foodways from Slavery to Obama*, edited by Jennifer Jensen Wallach, 79–92. Fayetteville: University of Arkansas Press.

Mars, Perry. 2009. "The Guyana Diaspora and Homeland Conflict Resolution." In *The New African Diaspora*, edited by Isidore Okpewho and Nkiru Nzegwu, 483–99. Bloomington: Indiana University Press.

Martin, Dale B. 1990. *Slavery as Salvation: The Metaphor of Slavery in Pauline Christianity*. New Haven, CT: Yale University Press.

Maultsby, Portia. 1990. "Africanisms in African American Music." In *Africanisms in American Culture*, edited by Joseph Holloway, 185–210. Bloomington: Indiana University Press.

Mbiti, John S. 1970. *Concepts of God in Africa*. London: Society for Promoting Christian Knowledge.

Mbiti, John S. 1999. *African Religions and Philosophy*. Nairobi: East African Educational Publishers.

McCall, John. 2000. *Portrait of a Brave Woman in Dancing Histories: Heuristic Ethnography with the Ohafia Igbo*. Ann Arbor: University of Michigan Press.

McGavin, Kirsten. 2017. "(Be)Longings: Diasporic Pacific Islanders and the Meaning of Home." In *Mobilities of Return: Pacific Perspectives*, edited by John Taylor and Helen Lee, 123–46. Acton, ACT, Australia: Australian National University Press, 2017.

McGowan, Winston, James G. Rose, and David A. Granger, eds. 2009. *Themes in African-Guyanese History*. Hertford, Herts., England: Hansib Publications.

Mehta, Brinda J. 2004. "Kali, Gangamai, and Dougla Consciousness in Moses Nagamootoo's *Hendree's Cure*." *Callaloo* 27, no. 2 (Spring): 542–60.

Meigs, Anna. 1997. "Food as a Cultural Construction." In *Food and Culture: A Reader*, edited by Carole M. Counihan and Penny van Esterik, 95–106. New York: Routledge.

Melville, Caspar. 2015. "Strange Routes: 'Dancing Girl'; Flows, Formats, and Fortune in Music." In *Pieces of the Musical World: Sounds and Cultures*, edited by Rachel Harris and Rowan Pease, 209–26. New York: Routledge.

Messner, Michael A. 2003. "Boyhood, Organized Sports, and the Construction of Masculinities." In *Reconstructing Gender: A Multicultural Anthology*, 3rd ed., edited by Estelle Disch, 119–35. Boston: McGraw-Hill.

Middleton, Richard. 1990. *Studying Popular Music*. Milton Keyes, Bucks., England: Open University Press.

Milbrandt, Jay. 2017. *They Came for Freedom: The Forgotten, Epic Adventure of the Pilgrims*. Nashville: Nelson Books.

Miller, Adrian. 2013. *Soul Food: The Surprising Story of an American Cuisine, One Plate at a Time*. Chapel Hill: University of North Carolina Press.

Mintz, Sidney. 1989. *Sweetness and Power: The Place of Sugar in Modern History*. New York: Penguin.

Mintz, Sidney. 1996. *Tasting Food, Tasting Freedom: Excursions into Eating, Power, and the Past*. Boston: Beacon Press.

Mintz, Sidney. 1998. "The Localization of Anthropological Practice from Area Studies to Transnationalism." *Critique of Anthropology* 18, no. 2 (June): 117–33.

Mintz, Sidney. 2003. Review of *Remembrance of Repasts: An Anthropology of Food and Memory*, by David E. Sutton. *American Ethnologist* 30, no. 3: 474–75.

Mintz, Sidney, and Richard Price. 1976. *The Birth of African-American Culture: An Anthropological Perspective*. Boston: Beacon Press.

Moore, Allan. 2002. "Authenticity as Authentication." *Popular Music* 21, no. 2 (May): 209–23.

Moore, Brian L. 1995. *Cultural Power, Resistance, and Pluralism: Colonial Guyana, 1838–1900*. Ottawa: Carleton University Press.

Mori, Koichi. 2003. "Identity Transformations among Okinawans and Their Descendants in Brazil." In *Searching for Home Abroad: Japanese Brazilians and Transnationalism*, edited by Jeffrey Lesser, 47–66. Durham, NC: Duke University Press.

Morier-Genoud, Eric, and Michel Cahen, eds. 2012. *Imperial Migrations: Colonial Communities and Diaspora in the Portuguese World*. New York: Springer.

Morley, David. 2001. "Belongings: Place, Space, and Identity in a Mediated World." *European Journal of Cultural Studies* 4, no. 4 (November): 425–48.

Morris, Brian. 2006. *Religion and Anthropology: A Critical Introduction*. Cambridge: Cambridge University Press.

Morse, Edwin Wilson. 1912. *Causes and Effects in American History: The Story of the Origin and Development of the Nation*. New York: Charles Scribner's Sons.

Morton, Julia F. 2013. "Passionfruit." In *Fruits of Warm Climates*, 320–28. Brattleboro, VT: Echo Books.

Mullings, Leith. 1976. "Women and Economic Change in Africa." In *Women in Africa: Studies in Social and Economic Change*, edited by Nancy J. Hafkin and Edna G. Bay, 239–64. Stanford, CA: Stanford University Press.

Munasinghe, Viranjini. 2006. "Theorizing World Culture through the New World: East Indians and Creolization." *American Ethnologist* 33, no. 4 (November): 549–62.

Murcott, Anne. 1983. Introduction to *The Sociology of Food and Eating: Essays on the Sociological Significance of Food*, edited by Anne Murcott. Aldershot, Hants., England: Gower.

Murphy, Joseph M. 1993. *Santería: African Spirits in America*. Boston: Beacon Press.

Murrell, Nathaniel Samuel. 2010. *Afro-Caribbean Religions: An Introduction to Their Historical, Cultural, and Sacred Traditions*. Philadelphia: Temple University Press.

Naff, Alixa. 1985. *Becoming American: The Early Arab Immigrant Experience*. Carbondale: Southern Illinois University Press.

Nauta, Doede. 1972. *The Meaning of Information*. The Hague: Mouton.

Needham, Rodney. 1975. "Polythetic Classification: Convergence and Classification." *Man* 10: 349–69.

Nehusi, Kimani S. K. 2015. *Libation: An Afrikan Ritual of Heritage in the Circle of Life*. Lanham, MD: University Press of America.

Nguyen, Phong T. 1995. *Searching for a Niche: Vietnamese Music at Home in America*. Kent, OH: Viet Music Publications.

Nketia, Joseph H. K. 1981. "African Roots of Music in the Americas: An African View." Report of the 12th Congress of the American Musicological Society, London.

Nketia, Joseph H. K. 2005. *Ethnomusicology and African Music: Collected Papers*. Vol. 1, *Modes of Inquiry and Interpretation*. Accra: Afram Publications.

Norfleet, Dawn. 2015. "Hip-Hop and Rap." In *African American Music: An Introduction*, 2nd ed., edited by Mellonee Burnim and Portia Maultsby, 354–90. New York: Routledge.

Norwood, Kimberly Jade, ed. 2014. *Color Matters: Skin Tone Bias and the Myth of a Post-Racial America*. New York: Routledge.

Oakdale, Suzanne. 2004. "The Culture-Conscious Brazilian Indian: Representing and Reworking Indianness in Kayabi Political Discourse." *American Ethnologist* 31, no. 1 (February): 60–75.

Obbo, Christine. 1980. *African Women: Their Struggle for Economic Independence*. London: Zed Books.

Ogbu, John U. 1978. "African Bridewealth and Women's Status." *American Ethnologist* 5, no. 2 (May): 241–62.

Okpewho, Isidore. 2009. Introduction to *The New African Diaspora*, edited by Isidore Okpewho and Nkiru Nzegwu, 3–30. Bloomington: Indiana University Press.

Okpewho, Isidore, and Nkiru Nzegwu, eds. 2009. *The New African Diaspora*. Bloomington: Indiana University Press.

Oladeji, Niyi. 1988. "Proverbs as Language Signposts in Yoruba Pragmatic Ethics." *Second Order: An African Journal of Philosophy*, n.s., 1, no. 2: 45–55.

Olayinka, Bolaji Olukemi. 1997. "Proverbs: Issues of Yoruba Femininity from a Feminist Hermeneutical Perspective." In *Embracing the Baobab Tree: The African Proverb in the 21st Century*, edited by Willem Saayman. Pretoria: University of South Africa Press.

Opokuwaa, Nana Akua Kyerewaa. 2005. *The Quest for Spiritual Transformation: Introduction to Traditional Akan Religion, Rituals and Practices*. New York: iUniverse.

Ortner, Sherry B., and Harriet Whitehead. 1981. Introduction to *Sexual Meanings: The Cultural Construction of Gender and Sexuality*, edited by Sherry B. Ortner and Harriet Whitehead, 1–28. Cambridge: Cambridge University Press.

Osumare, Halify. 2010. "Sacred Dance-Drumming: Reciprocation and Contention within African Belief Systems in the San Francisco–Oakland Bay Area." In *Women and New and Africana Religions*, edited by Lillian Ashcraft-Eason, Darnise C. Martin, and Oyeronke Olademo, 123–44. Santa Barbara, CA: ABC-CLIO.

Ottenberg, Simon. 1988. "The Bride Comes to the Groom: Ritual and Drama in Limba Weddings." *Drama Review* 32, no. 2: 42–62.

Palmié, Stephan, ed. 1995. *Slave Cultures and the Cultures of Slavery*. Knoxville: University of Tennessee Press.

Paton, Diana. 2009. "Obeah Acts: Producing and Policing the Boundaries of Religion in the Caribbean." *Small Axe: A Caribbean Journal of Criticism* 13, no. 1 (February): 1–18.

Paton, Diana. 2012. "Witchcraft, Poison, Law, and Atlantic Slavery." *William and Mary Quarterly* 69, no. 2 (April): 235–64.

Paton, Diana. 2015. *The Cultural Politics of Obeah: Religion, Colonialism and Modernity in the Caribbean World*. Cambridge: Cambridge University Press.

Patton, Venetria K. 2013. *The Grasp That Reaches beyond the Grave: The Ancestral Call in Black Women's Texts*. Albany: State University of New York Press.

Payne, Daniel Alexander. (1891) 2018. *A History of the African Methodist Episcopal Church*. London: Forgotten Books.

Pérez y Mena, Andrés I. 1998. "Cuban Santería, Haitian Vodun, Puerto Rican Spiritualism: A Multiculturalist Inquiry into Syncretism." *Journal for the Scientific Study of Religion* 37, no. 1 (March): 15–27.

Pitts, Walter. 1989. "West African Poetics in the Black Preaching Style." *American Speech* 64, no. 2 (Summer): 137–49.

Polak, Rainer. 2005. "A Musical Instrument Travels around the World: *Jenbe* Playing in Bamako, West Africa, and Beyond." In *Ethnomusicology: A Contemporary Reader*, edited by Jennifer C. Post, 161–86. New York: Routledge.

Pollitzer, William. 2005. *Gullah People and Their African Heritage*. Athens: University of Georgia Press.

Portes, Alejandro, and Rubén G. Rumbaut. 1996. *Immigrant America: A Portrait*. 2nd ed. Berkeley: University of California Press.

Price, Sally. 1983. "Sexism and the Construction of Reality: An Afro-American Example." *American Ethnologist* 10, no. 3: 460–76.

Price, Sally. 1984. *Co-Wives and Calabashes*. Ann Arbor: University of Michigan Press.

Prosterman, Leslie. 1984. "Food and Celebration: A Kosher Caterer as Mediator of Communal Traditions." In *Ethnic and Regional Foodways in the United States: The Performance of Group Identity*, edited by Linda Keller Brown and Kay Mussell, 127–44. Knoxville: University of Tennessee Press.

Purseglove, John William. 1972. *Tropical Crops: Monocotyledons*. 2 vols. London: Longman.

Rabe, Stephen G. 2005. *U.S. Intervention in British Guiana: A Cold War Story*. Chapel Hill: University of Carolina Press.

Rahier, Jean Muteba, Percy C. Hintzen, and Felipe Smith, eds. 2010. *Global Circuits of Blackness: Interrogating the African Diaspora*. Urbana: University of Illinois Press.

Ray, Krishnendu. 2004. *The Migrant Table: Meals and Memories in Bengali-American Households*. Philadelphia: Temple University Press.

Redfield, Robert, Ralph Linton, and Melville Herskovits. 1936. "Memorandum on the Study of Acculturation." *American Anthropologist* 38, no. 1 (January–March): 149–52.

Reed, Daniel B. 2003. *Dan Ge Performance: Masks and Music in Contemporary Côte d'Ivoire*. Bloomington: Indiana University Press.

Reed, Daniel B. 2016. *Abidjan USA: Music, Dance, and Mobility in the Lives of Four Ivorian Immigrants*. Bloomington: Indiana University Press.

Richards-Greaves, Gillian. 2012. "Cookup Rice: Guyana's Culinary Dougla and the Performance of Guyanese Identities." In *Rice and Beans: A Unique Dish in a Hundred Places*, edited by Richard Wilk and Livia Barbosa, 137–60. London: Berg.

Richards-Greaves, Gillian. 2013. "The Intersections of 'Guyanese Food' and Constructions of Gender, Race and Nationhood." In *Food and Identity in the Caribbean*, edited by Hanna Garth, 75–94. Oxford: Berg.

Richards-Greaves, Gillian. 2015. "'Come to My Kwe-Kwe': African Guyanese Ritual Music and the Construction of a Secondary Diaspora in New York City." *World of Music*, n.s., 4, no. 2: 83–98.

Richards-Greaves, Gillian. 2016a. "'Say Hallelujah, Somebody' and 'I Will Call upon the Lord': An Examination of Call-and-Response in the Black Church." *Western Journal of Black Studies* 40, no. 3 (Fall): 192–204.

Richards-Greaves, Gillian. 2016b. "'Taalk Half, Lef Half': Negotiating Transnational Identities through Proverbial Speech in African Guyanese *Kweh-Kweh* Rituals." *Journal of American Folklore* 129, no. 514 (Fall): 413–35.

Richards-Greaves, Gillian. Forthcoming. "'When the War Comes, We Will Have Food': The Intersections of Politics and Food Security in a South Carolina Town." In *Black Food Matters*, edited by Hanna Garth and Ashanté Reese. Minneapolis: University of Minnesota Press.

Richardson, Alan. 1997. "Romantic Voodoo: Obeah and British Culture, 1797–1807." In *Sacred Possessions: Voudou, Santería, Obeah, and the Caribbean*, edited by Margarite Fernández Olmos and Lizabeth Paravisini-Gebert, 171–94. New Brunswick, NJ: Rutgers University Press.

Roback, Judith, 1974. "The White-Robed Army: An Afro-Guyanese Religious Movement." *Anthropologica*, n.s., 16, no. 2 (January): 233–68.

Robertson, Claire C. 1997. "Post-Proclamation Slavery in Accra: A Female Affair?" In *Women and Slavery in Africa*, edited by Claire C. Robertson and Martin A. Klein, 220–45. Portsmouth, NH: Heinemann.

Robinson, John C., and Víctor Galán Saúco. 2010. *Bananas and Plantains*. 2nd ed. Wallingford, Oxon., England: CAB International.

Rosenbaum, Art. 1998. *Shout Because You're Free: The African American Ring Shout Tradition in Coastal Georgia*. Athens: University of Georgia Press.

Roy, Parama. 2002. "Reading Communities and Culinary Communities: The Gastropoetics of the South Asian Diaspora." *Positions: East Asia Cultures Critique* 10, no. 2 (September): 471–502.

Royce, Anya Peterson. 1982. *Ethnic Identity: Strategies of Diversity*. Bloomington: Indiana University Press.

Royce, Anya Peterson. (1977) 2002. *The Anthropology of Dance*. Bloomington: Indiana University Press.

Royce, Anya Peterson. 2011. *Becoming an Ancestor: The Isthmus Zapotec Way of Death*. Albany: State University of New York Press.

Rugemer, Edward B. 2018. *Slave Law and the Politics of Resistance in the Early Atlantic World*. Cambridge, MA: Harvard University Press.

Safran, William. 1991. "Diasporas in Modern Societies: Myths of Homeland and Return." *Diaspora* 1, no. 1 (Spring): 83–99.

Sandoval, Mercedes Cros. 2008. "Santería in the Twenty-First Century." In *Òrìṣà Devotion as World Religion: The Globalization of Yorùbá Religious Culture*, edited by Jacob K. Olupona and Terry Rey, 355–71. Madison: University of Wisconsin Press.

Schacht, Ryan N. 2013. "Cassava and the Makushi: A Shared History of Resiliency and Transformation." In *Food and Identity in the Caribbean*, edited by Hanna Garth, 15–30. Oxford: Berg.

Schramm, Adelaida Reyes. 1999. *Songs of the Caged, Songs of the Free: Music and the Vietnamese Refugee Experience*. Philadelphia: Temple University Press.

Schuler, Monica. 1980. *"Alas, Alas, Kongo": A Social History of Indentured African Immigration into Jamaica, 1841–1865.* Baltimore: Johns Hopkins University Press.

Seamone, Donna Lynne. 2013. "Pentecostalism: Rejecting Ritual Formalism and Ritualizing Every Encounter." *Journal of Ritual Studies* 27, no. 1: 73–84.

Seecharan, Clem. 1999. *Bechu: "Bound Coolie" Radical in British Guiana, 1894–1901.* Mona, Jamaica: University of the West Indies Press.

Seeger, Peter. 1958. "The Steel Drum: A New Folk Instrument." *Journal of American Folklore* 71, no. 279 (January–March): 52–57.

Shelemay, Kay Kaufman. 1998. *Let Jasmine Rain Down: Song and Remembrance among Syrian Jews.* Chicago: University Chicago Press.

Shelemay, Kay Kaufman. 2015. *Soundscapes: Exploring Music in a Changing World.* 3rd ed. New York: W. W. Norton.

Shepperson, George. 1993. "African Diaspora: Concept and Context." In *Global Dimensions of the African Diaspora*, 2nd ed., edited by Joseph E. Harris, 41–49. Washington, DC: Howard University Press.

Shuval, Judith T. 2000. "Diaspora Migration: Definitional Ambiguities and a Theoretical Paradigm." *International Migration* 38, no. 5 (December): 41–56.

Singleton, Theresa A. 1991. "The Archaeology of Slave Life." In *Before Freedom Came: African American Life in the Antebellum South*, edited by Edward D. C. Campbell Jr. and Kym S. Rice, 155–75. Charlottesville: University Press of Virginia.

Sinn, Elizabeth. 2012. *Pacific Crossing: California Gold, Chinese Migration, and the Making of Hong Kong.* Hong Kong: Hong Kong University Press.

Slobin, Mark. 1994. "Music in Diaspora: The View from Euro-America." *Diaspora* 3, no. 3 (Winter): 243–51.

Smith, Daniel Jordan. 2001. "Romance, Parenthood, and Gender in a Modern African Society." *Ethnology* 40, no. 2 (March): 129–51.

Smith, M. G. [Michael Garfield]. (1953) 2017. *Corporations and Society: The Social Anthropology of Collective Action.* New York: Routledge.

Smith, Raymond T. 1956. *The Negro Family in British Guiana: Family Structure and Social Status in the Villages.* New York: Routledge.

Smith, Raymond T. (1962) 1980. *British Guiana.* Westport, CT: Greenwood Press.

Sonneborn, Liz. 2006. *Vietnamese Americans: New Immigrants.* New York: Chelsea House.

Speirs, James. 1902. *The Proverbs of British Guiana, with an Index of Principal Words, an Index of Subjects, and a Glossary.* Demerara, Guyana: Argosy Company.

Stagg, Frank. 1962. *New Testament Theology.* Nashville: Broadman Press.

Stamp, Patricia. 1989. *Technology, Gender, and Power in Africa.* Ottawa: International Development Research Centre.

Stanonis, Anthony. 2015. "Feast of the Mau Mau: Christianity, Conjure, and the Origins of Soul Food." In *Dethroning the Deceitful Pork Chop: Rethinking African American Foodways from Slavery to Obama*, edited by Jennifer Jensen Wallach, 93–106. Fayetteville: University of Arkansas Press.

Stavans, Ilan. (1995) 2001. *The Hispanic Condition: The Power of a People*. New York: HarperCollins.

Stephanides, Stephanos, and Karna Singh. 2000. *Translating Kali's Feast: The Goddess in Indo-Caribbean Ritual and Fiction*. Amsterdam: Brill-Rodopi.

Stokes, Martin, ed. (1994) 1997. *Ethnicity, Identity, and Music: The Musical Construction of Place*. Oxford: Berg.

Stoler, Ann. 1977. "Class Structure and Female Autonomy in Rural Java." *Signs* 3, no. 1 (Autumn): 74–89.

Stone, Ruth M. 2008. *Theory for Ethnomusicology*. Upper Saddle River, NJ: Prentice Hall.

Stone, Ruth M., and Verlon L. Stone. 1981. "Event, Feedback, and Analysis: Research Media in the Study of Music Events." *Ethnomusicology* 25, no. 2 (May): 215–25.

Strobel, Margaret. 1997. "Slavery and Reproductive Labor in Mombasa." In *Women and Slavery in Africa*, edited by Claire C. Robertson and Martin A. Klein, 111–29. Portsmouth, NH: Heinemann.

Stuckey, Sterling. 1988. *Slave Culture: Nationalist Theory and the Foundations of Black America*. New York: Oxford University Press.

Stuckey, Sterling. 2002. "Christian Conversion and the Challenge of Dance." In *Dancing Many Drums: Excavations in African American Dance*, edited by Thomas F. DeFrantz, 39–58. Madison: University of Wisconsin Press.

Sublette, Ned. 2004. *Cuba and Its Music: From the First Drums to the Mambo*. Chicago: Chicago Review Press.

Sugarman, Jane. 1997. *Engendering Song: Singing and Subjectivity at Prespa Albanian Weddings*. Chicago: University of Chicago Press.

Summit, Jeffrey A. 2000. *The Lord's Song in a Strange Land: Music and Identity in Contemporary Jewish Worship*. Oxford: Oxford University Press.

Sundquist, Eric J. 2005. *Strangers in the Land: Blacks, Jews, Post-Holocaust America*. Cambridge, MA: Belknap Press of Harvard University Press.

Sutton, David E. 2001. *Remembrance of Repasts: An Anthropology of Food and Memory*. Oxford: Berg.

Takyi, Baffour K. 2002. "The Making of the Second Diaspora: On the Recent African Immigrant Community in the United States of America." *Western Journal of Black Studies* 26, no. 1 (Spring): 32–43.

Theodossopoulos, Dimitrios. 2013. "Laying Claim to Authenticity: Five Anthropological Dilemmas." *Anthropological Quarterly* 86, no. 2 (March): 337–60.

Thomas, Helen, ed. 1993. *Dance, Gender, and Culture*. Basingstoke, Hants., England: Macmillan.

Thomas, R. Murray. 2014. *Roots of Haiti's Vodou-Christian Faith: African and Catholic Origins*. Santa Barbara, CA: ABC-CLIO.

Thompson, Alvin O. 2003. *Unprofitable Servants: Crown Slaves in Berbice, Guyana, 1803–1831*. Mona, Jamaica: University of the West Indies Press.

Thurman, Sue Bailey. 2000. *The Historical Cookbook of the American Negro*. Boston: Beacon Press.

Tölölyan, Khachig. 1991. "The Nation-State and Its Others: In Lieu of a Preface." *Diaspora* 1, no. 1 (Spring): 3–7.

Trowbridge, Ada Wilson. 1896. "Negro Customs and Folk-Stories of Jamaica." *Journal of American Folklore* 9, no. 35 (October–December): 279–87.

Tsuda, Takeyuki (Gaku). 2003. "Homeland-less Abroad: Transnational Liminality, Social Alienation, and Personal Malaise." In *Searching for Home Abroad: Japanese Brazilians and Transnationalism*, edited by Jeffrey Lesser, 121–62. Durham, NC: Duke University Press.

Turner, Victor W. 1952. *The Lozi Peoples of Northwestern Rhodesia*. London: International African Institute.

Turner, Victor W. 1969. *The Ritual Process: Structure and Anti-Structure*. Chicago: Aldine.

Van Gennep, Arnold. 1960. *The Rites of Passage*. Chicago: University of Chicago Press.

Van Sertima, Ivan. 1976. *The African Presence in Ancient America: They Came before Columbus*. New York: Random House.

Warner-Lewis, Maureen. 2003. *Central Africa in the Caribbean: Transcending Time, Transforming Cultures*. Mona, Jamaica: University of the West Indies Press.

Washington, Margaret. 2005. "Gullah Attitudes toward Life and Death." In *Africanisms in American Culture*, 2nd ed., edited by Joseph Holloway, 152–86. Bloomington: Indiana University Press.

Waterman, Richard A. 1971. "African Influence on the Music of the Americas." In *Anthropology and Art: Readings in Cross-Cultural Aesthetics*, edited by Charlotte M. Otten, 227–44. Garden City, NJ: Natural History Press.

Waters, Mary C. 1994. "Ethnic and Racial Identities of Second-Generation Black Immigrants in New York City." *International Migration Review* 28, no. 4 (Winter): 795–820.

Waters, Mary C. 1999. *Black Identities: West Indian Immigrant Dreams and American Realities*. Cambridge, MA: Harvard University Press.

Watson, James L., and Melissa L. Caldwell. 2005. Introduction to *The Cultural Politics of Food and Eating: A Reader*, edited by James L. Watson and Melissa L. Caldwell, 1–11. Malden, MA: Blackwell.

Weaver, Michael S. 1991. "Makers and Redeemers: The Theatricality of the Black Church." *Black American Literature Forum* 25, no. 1 (Spring): 53–61.

Weismantel, Mary J. 1988. *Food, Gender, and Poverty in the Ecuadorian Andes*. Philadelphia: University of Pennsylvania Press, 1988.

Weiss, Allen S. 2011. "Authenticity." *Gastronomica* 11, no. 4 (Winter): 74–77.

White, Deborah Gray. 1985. *Ar'n't I a Woman? Female Slaves in the Plantation South*. New York: W. W. Norton.

Wilk, Richard. 1999. "'Real Belizean Food': Building Identity in the Transnational Caribbean." *American Anthropologist*, n.s., 101, no. 2 (June): 244–55.

Williams, Joseph John. 1932. "Origin of Obeah." In *Voodoos and Obeahs: Phases of West India Witchcraft*. New York: Dial Press.

Williams-Forson, Psyche. 2012. "Other Women Cooked for My Husband: Negotiating Gender, Food, and Identities in an African American/Ghanaian Household." In *Taking Food Public: Redefining Foodways in a Changing World*, edited by Psyche Williams-Forson and Carole Counihan, 138–54. New York: Routledge.

Wilson, Silvius E. 2008. *Nationalism in the Era of Globalization: Issues from Guyana and the Bahamas; Working People's Contribution to Civil Society, Good Governance, and Sustainable Development*. Bloomington, IN: Xlibris.

Witt, Doris. 1999. *Black Hunger: Food and the Politics of U.S. Identity*. New York: Oxford University Press.

Work, John Wesley. 1998. *American Negro Songs: 230 Folk Songs and Spirituals, Religious and Secular*. Mineola, NY: Dover Publications.

Wrazen, Louise. 2012. "Marysia's Voice: Defining Home through Song in Poland and Canada." In *Women Singers in Global Contexts: Music, Biography, Identity*, edited by Ruth Hellier, 146–60. Urbana: University of Illinois Press.

Yelvington, Kevin A. 2001. "The Anthropology of Afro-Latin America and the Caribbean: Diasporic Dimensions." *Annual Review of Anthropology* 30: 227–60.

Zeleza, Paul Tiyambe. 2008. "The Challenges of Studying the African Diasporas." *African Sociological Review/Revue Africaine de Sociologie* 12, no. 2: 4–21.

Zeleza, Paul Tiyambe. 2009. "Diaspora Dialogues: Engagements between Africa and Its Diasporas." In *The New African Diaspora*, edited by Isidore Okpewho and Nkiru Nzegwu, 31–58. Bloomington: Indiana University Press.

Zheng, Su. 2010. *Claiming Diaspora: Music, Transnationalism, and Cultural Politics in Asian/Chinese America*. Oxford: Oxford University Press.

Index

Illustrations are in **bold**.

About the Author

Photo by Dr. Gillian Richards-Greaves

Dr. Gillian Richards-Greaves is an assistant professor of anthropology in the Department of Anthropology and Geography at Coastal Carolina University. She earned dual PhDs in ethnomusicology and cultural anthropology from Indiana University, Bloomington, and a BA-MA in music education with a minor in mathematics from Hunter College of the City University of New York (CUNY). Her research encompasses the musical, cultural, linguistic, and ritual expressions of the African diaspora, with emphasis on the connections between Africa, the Caribbean, and the United States (Gullah Geechee).